ESSENTIALS OF PSYCHOLOGY

By Walter Bower

CHAPTER I

INTRODUCTION

Psychology the Science of Behaviour. Psychology is defined traditionally as the science of mind. This is the translation of the two Greek words from which ' psychology ' is compounded. The definition is now open to many objections. The most important of these is that the word ' mind ' has in the course of long use taken on many meanings and implications which do not concern psychology as a science. Various terms have been suggested to avoid these objections. Psychology has been denned as the ' science of consciousness/ or as the ' science of experience subjectively regarded.' Each definition has advantages, but no one so far suggested is free from objection. It is most satisfactory to give up the attempt to find a single word that will designate the facts covered by psychology, and to indicate the actual phenomena that it studies, the evidences of mind. First of these is behaviour. We distinguish a man in the full possession of his senses from an imbecile by the character of his acts. We measure the intelligence of an animal by its accomplishments. Mind is known from the activities of the organism. Psychology may be most satisfactorily defined as the science of behaviour. We shall discuss human behaviour.

This definition makes it possible to treat man as objectively as any physical phenomenon. It considers only what he does. Viewed in this way the end of our science is to understand human action. The practical end is to determine upon what human capacity depends and, in the light of this knowledge, to discover means of increasing man's efficiency. In many fields of industry it is becoming more and more evident that an understanding of the laws of human efficiency is quite as important as a knowledge of mechanical laws, that it is quite as important to know what a man can do in a given time and how he should work to obtain the best results as to know the laws for the production of energy in boiler and engine. In fact, it is appreciated in many industries that further progress must wait upon increased knowledge of the human instrument. Psychology is concerned only indirectly with these practical problems. Science always endeavours to understand the laws of nature for themselves and is indifferent to the applications that may be made of them. Psychology is interested in the conditions of learning and forgetting, of imagining and reasoning, and in the methods of acquiring skill in various activities without any thought of the use that may be made of the knowledge. It is probable, however, that all suggestions for improving the efficiency of individuals must be based upon these laws. Indeed, many rules have already been developed from psychological experiments and more are foreshadowed in the general principles now established.

If psychology is to be defined as the science of human behaviour, the term ' behaviour ' must be used in the very widest sense. It must include everything from the simplest movements of walking or of fingering the pen to the activities involved in swaying an audience by speech or in carrying to completion some great engineering work. Certain of the very simplest acts, such as winking and other reflexes, are fairly within the range of physiology. But even these must be taken into consideration by psychology, because the most complicated act can be understood only when analysed into its components which are reflexes or closely related to reflexes. Even the simplest forms of behaviour must be studied by the psychologist if he is to know the laws that govern the more complicated forms. No form of human behaviour, from the simplest to the most complex, falls outside of the province of psychology. As a science our knowledge of human behaviour must be organised and referred to a system of general principles. A science of human behaviour cannot be limited to a series of aphorisms or chance observations about man. ' Perseverance wins success ' is related to the psychology of conduct in very much the same way that ' an east wind brings rain ' is related to the science of meteorology. Each statement embodies the results of numerous observations, but it has no close connection with other facts or general laws. In a science these observations must be related to other bits of knowledge and the whole organised into a consistent system that shall harmonise with the results of other sciences. Scientific laws are based on carefully chosen data and in consequence possess wide validity and are not likely to be vitiated by popular prejudice or ill-founded tradition. They give each particular fact a perspective and make it easy to recall and to use each new observation. Study of Behaviour Involves Consciousness. To define psychology as the study of behaviour does not imply, as has been asserted at times, that we can neglect consciousness. For most individuals, consciousness is as much a fact as the existence of any external object. When a man acts he is aware that he is acting and also aware of the stimuli that produce the act. This awareness is what we mean by consciousness. While the reader might at this moment be observed by a friend to hold the book and move the eyes by jerks across the page with an occasional frown as a difficult sentence is met, the reader himself is aware of the sense of the material, and thinks in some part the ideas intended by the writer. The observer appreciates the behaviour, the reader, consciousness. In this case behaviour is the immediate outcome of consciousness and can only be understood through it. The frown is explained by the hesitation in getting the meaning of a sentence, and that is most evident to the reader. While many kinds of activity are best known from the inside, others may be as well known from the outside. Thus the capacity of an individual for assimilating the material of this chapter may be determined better by the instructor who assigns it and quizzes on it than by the student. This is particularly true if the reading is done under the observation of the teacher. The differences in capacity to learn and repeat can be explained only through long study of the individual in the light of earlier training and habits of work.

Consciousness an End. Psychology, then, must study consciousness as well as behaviour. This is necessary first because much of behaviour is known only from the report of the actor and many of the conditions of behaviour can be studied only through consciousness. This holds particularly of the more complicated acts, of the lines of conduct determined by remote events in the life of the individual. In the second place, consciousness is worth understanding for itself. For the individual man, be he naive or erudite, nothing is so interesting as the working of his own mind. Much of the consciousness of an individual is followed by relatively slight movements, while the consciousness itself is a matter of great moment. Had it no other value, to understand consciousness would be sufficient to warrant the existence of the science. Consciousness is at once an important means of understanding behaviour and an interesting object of investigation for itself. Consciousness and behaviour are closely related ; consciousness in others is known only through behaviour, behaviour in ourselves and ultimately in others is known only through consciousness. If one is made the end, the other must be the means ; if either is understood in its completeness, the other will also be known. They are the inside and outside of the same organism. Even if in the present stage of development of the science it seems best to subordinate consciousness to behaviour in the definition of psychology, for the sake of escaping ambiguity, we cannot eliminate consciousness from description and explanation. Psychology is the science of behaviour, but behaviour must be studied both through the consciousness of the actor and by observation of the acts of others.

Mind, Consciousness, and Mental Process. Before attempting any discussion of mental states it is necessary to define certain of the terms that are to be used. Viewed from within, psychology seeks to explain the experiences of the individual as they run their course, to understand the various perceptions, memories, imaginings, and so on which together constitute the mental life. Any one of the states that may be regarded as detached from the mass for separate consideration is designated a mental process. Your idea of this book as you read it is a mental process, your memory of reading the book yesterday or of the assignment for study is a mental process, as is the flitting thought that you would much rather be out for a walk than reading. Consciousness is the term technically used to designate the sum total of mental processes at any moment. Thus, the perception of the book, the background of tactual and organic sensations that are receiving no particular attention at the moment, the vague emotional dissatisfaction that you are kept indoors on a pleasant day, and many other more or less definite mental processes combine to constitute your consciousness at this moment. Mind is the word that designates the entire series of conscious states of an individual from birth to death. It is the most inclusive of the series of terms and covers all processes, active and passive. Experience includes practically the same mass of states, but it is a little more passive in its implications. All of these terms apply to the description of behaviour as observed from within, the mental antecedents and accompaniments of behaviour. The description of behaviour as it presents itself to the outside observer needs only the vocabulary of popular speech and requires no preliminary comment or definition.

The Methods of Psychology. As has been said, behaviour can be studied in two ways : by observation of another's acts and by observation of one's own conscious states. Observation of another, or what in psychology is known as observation, requires no special comment as a method. In all essential respects it follows the rules of observation common to all of the sciences. Self-observation, known technically as introspection, seems at first sight to offer more difficulties and to require more safeguards. The question has been raised whether introspection is possible at all. The doubt arises from the assumption that the very observation of a mental state changes that state. One does not have the same mental state when questioning how one knows that the approaching footsteps are Smith's, as when one interprets the sounds to mean that Smith is coming. One cannot at the same moment wonder what one is doing and do it to the best advantage. This objection proves to be less serious in practice than in theory. All mental states persist for a little time unchanged and it is possible to observe them during this persistence. One does not observe the mental state at the time it is happening, but examines it a moment later in memory. Observation in memory is accurate and does not alter the process investigated. Observation in any natural science requires the same reliance on momentary memory. One cannot at the same time make an observation and record it. If one tried, mistakes would be made. A thermometer reading, e.g. is taken and held in memory until recorded, and then still later it is interpreted or used in the explanation of related facts. Introspection is no more difficult or uncertain than is observation of external phenomena. '

Experiment. Within the last generation methods have been developed by which both introspection and observation can be carried on under experimental conditions and with the aid of instruments of precision. Experiment makes it possible to control accurately the conditions and antecedents of mental operations. It is possible now to remove from distracting stimuli the individual who is introspecting or being observed, to measure accurately the stimuli that are permitted to affect him, and to record his responses. It is a commonplace that a man who is embarrassed will blush. Delicate physiological instruments used in the psychological laboratory show that the blush is only a heightened effect of the changes in circulation that take place in all parts of the body in connection with almost all mental processes. Similarly it was first observed with the unaided eye that the eyes move by jumps during reading. Later it was found possible to photograph the movements of the eyes, and these results brought out important laws that could not have been known otherwise. Introspection has been aided principally by recording the times that elapse between different parts of a mental operation. The times required have been combined and the results emphasised relations that were unnoticed in introspection. While experiment is only a means of increasing the accuracy of observation and introspection, it has through its wide application made possible important advances in nearly every field of psychology. To its great benefit psychology has become an experimental science.

But momentary introspection and observation combined; even with all the help that may be had from experiment, do not exhaustively explain behaviour or consciousness. The observer sees the occasion for action and notes the response ; the actor sees the object and feels the response, but neither knows what happens in between nor appreciates fully the conditions of the act. For example, a wasp approaches, the man draws back or strikes. The observer notes the occasion for the movement and the movement itself, but nothing more. The man attacked sees the wasp and knows that he is moving or has moved, but nothing more. Neither can know why the movement takes place. One sees the stimulus vanish into the physical organism and movement result ; the other sees the insect, moves, and all the time is perturbed by an emotion, but neither can absolutely foresee the act, neither knows why it comes. These more fundamental explanations may be supplied in part on the basis of present knowledge. Two elements must be taken into consideration in the interpretation, the character and nature of the action of the nervous system, and the past life and native endowment of the individual. One can understand what intervenes between the excitation and the movement only if one can trace the course of the impulse through the nervous system. The earlier history of the individual and of the race also plays a very large part in the determination of all sorts of behaviour. The man's responses will differ according to the amount and nature of his experience with wasps. The influence of earlier experiences can be traced in many more subtle ways in the interpretation of any mental phenomenon. Both the nervous system and the effects of earlier life upon the acts of the individual can be known only through observation and introspection, controlled and recorded, together with much experiment and reflection upon the connections of present with past activities. Human behaviour, then, can be understood by careful, long-continued observation of man in action from the inside and from the outside, and by relating the results of these observa-tions to the earlier experiences of the individual and to the facts concerning the nature and action of the nervous system established by the anatomist and the physiologist. Relation of Psychology to Other Sciences. The relations of psychology to the other sciences are particularly close and important. The biological sciences shade over into psychology so gradually that it is not always possible to decide whether a problem belongs to psychology or to one of the biological sciences. The sciences that explain the nature and action of the human body, the sciences of anatomy and physiology, merge gradually into psychology. One can understand behaviour only if one knows something of the living organism, of the sense organs that receive the impression from without, of the muscles that produce the actions, and of the nervous system that connects them. From the outside one can understand man's behaviour most fully and easily by comparing it with the behaviour of animals and tracing the gradual development of man's action in connection with th*; simpler forms of animal behaviour. Experimental biology gradually shades over into experimental psychology. The biologist has recently been devoting himself very largely to the problems of animal behaviour. The light cast upon human conduct by these experiments is only less important than that cast upon the actions of animals themselves. Still more general results of biological science have been profoundly important for the explanation of human consciousness. The very general acceptance in recent times of the doctrine of evolution has forced us to read the story of mind in the light of the development of the human organism from the lower forms of life. The result is a very much fuller understanding of many of the more fundamental phases of human activity. All of the physical sciences furnish some material for the psychologist, since the sense processes can be understood only in connection with the physical forces that act upon the organism.

The Social Sciences. In addition to the sciences from which it receives material and methods, psychology has come into a position where it may offer help to many sciences. If psychology can give information concerning human behaviour, it is evident that all the human and social sciences may look to it for aid in the solution of their problems. Sociology, or the study of man in the group, evidently must found its results upon a study of the individual. In less degree, history, when it seeks to trace connections between its observed facts, must look to psychology for its fundamental principles. Economics, too, works with psychological materials. Its fundamental problems are essentially psychological. Values and human needs are largely mental. It must be said, however, that psychology is least well developed in the fields where it would be most helpful to the historian and to the economist. Last of all, the relations of psychology to philosophy are very numerous and are those of mutual helpfulness. Psychology was the last of the sciences to separate from philosophy, the parent of all of the sciences, and the bond is still very close. The history of psychology is still very largely a part of the history of philosophy. The results of psychology constitute much of the foundation of philosophy, and on the other hand philosophy supplies the psychologist with general principles and sets very many of his problems for him.

Practical Applications. Of the immediately practical subjects, education has probably made the largest demands upon the results of our science. Learning and teaching are both psychological operations. When any real attempt to understand either is made, education becomes an application of psychology. This is more and more appreciated in the modern schools, and in them psychology and education are coming closer and closer together. The psychologist is paying more attention to the problems of the educator, and the modern educational theorists are making more use of the results of psychological investigations. But the applications of psychology need not be confined to education. With the advance of knowledge all who have to deal with man will look to the psychologist to increase the knowledge that may be put at his disposal. The physician and the lawyer, the advertiser and the clergyman, are all dealing in one way or another with psychological problems. To the physician and the advertiser psychology has already given appreciable aid and it should be in a position at no distant day to offer help to the others. Too much of practical value is not to be expected from the science, however. In all of these fields there is a great difference between principles and practice. Often the rules that grow from daily practice are in advance of scientific principles. Science serves but to explain the truth of the practical precept. Theory does not always lag behind, and one can already see places in which psychological results point the way to improvement in practice. As a rule, however, all of the arts are more grateful for confirmation of the established custom than for the suggestion of improvements. This incomplete list of the relations of psychology may suffice to indicate how closely psychology is bound up with other fields of human knowledge. Any science that tells us any thing of the nature of the physical universe or of the nature of the living organism will throw some light upon the problems of psychology. On the other hand, any science that deals in any way with human conduct, or that is dependent in any way upon human capacity (and what science is not?), can draw with profit upon the results of psychology. Either as creditors or debtors, all the sciences stand in some relation to psychology, the science of human behaviour.

Divisions of Psychology. Each of the sciences that furnish material for psychology has given rise to a different sort of psychology, or at least to a different name for a psychological work. Psychophysics grew out of an attempt by Fechner to determine the quantitative relations between the physical stimulus and the intensity of the mental state. Physiological psychology is the name Wundt gives to his work, that has for its primary object the explanation of the relation between mental states and the bodily organism. Each of these treatments has grown beyond its original scope to cover the entire field of psychology. The name now indicates nothing more than the attitude that is taken toward the subject. Other branches of the subject are named from the phase of behaviour that is discussed. Genetic psychology treats of the development of behaviour. The behaviour of animals has given rise to a flourishing science and in the last few years has made much progress. Child study has made numerous contributions to the more theoretical problems. Each has thrown some light upon the nature of adult human behaviour, as well as collected many facts in its own field. Abnormal psychology, the study of abnormal and imperfect individuals, has also been a rich field for the psychologist and has given many important results. Each of these partial sciences may be considered by us only so far as it throws light on the behaviour of the adult normal man. A few years ago it was customary to classify psychological systems according to the methods of investigation. There was a rational psychology, an empirical psychology, an introspective psychology, and an experimental psychology. Now it is seen that no science can be developed by one of these methods alone, and all are used by any psychologist worthy of the name. At the most it can now be said that there is an empirical and a rational method in psychology, a method of introspection and a method of observation, both aided by experiment. The results of each method should be the same if the methods are adequate. And as a matter of fact the results are the same although one method may be adequate for one problem, another for another. All the so-called branches of psychology, then, are closely related to the central science and at the most designate merely different fields for observation, or the preference of writers for different methods.

Summary. Our problem is to understand behaviour, and to investigate consciousness as the immediate antecedent and condition of behaviour. To understand either consciousness or behaviour it is necessary to know something of the character and action of the nervous system. As has been said, all knowledge of the world comes to consciousness through the nervous system and all expressions of consciousness in actiop are rendered possible by the nervous system. This i? not psychology but is a necessary prerequisite for psy chology. The psychological inquiry proper begins with an analysis of the elements of behaviour and of consciousness, both structural and functional; it involves a study of how these elements interact and unite in the constitution and control of the more complicated activities. The various partial problems will be taken up in the order named : first, a brief statement of the facts of nervous physiology that have a bearing upon psychology ; second, an analysis of the facts of consciousness and behaviour to discover the elementary components, and third, a study of the more complicated activities in the light of these simplest forms.

QUESTIONS

1. What are the evidences of mind (a) in an animal, (6) in another man, (c) in yourself?

2. How far does knowledge of behaviour involve consciousness ?

3. What is a science ? Is it possible to have a science of mind ? of behaviour?

4. What is the method of introspecting? What question of its accuracy has been raised ? How can the objection be met ?

5. What is a psychological experiment ? Illustrate its application to observation and to introspection.

6. What sciences aid most in the solution of psychological problems ?

7. Enumerate some of the divisions of psychology. What is the basis of division in each case ?

CHAPTER II

THE NERVOUS SYSTEM

BEHAVIOUR must be explained in large part by the action of the nervous system. It does not follow that the operation of the brain or of the nervous system is open to observation. On the contrary, one knows nothing directly of the nerves or of nerve-cells. Only consciousness and behaviour are known. The parts that act are altogether hidden, the effects alone are known. So completely is this true that even Aristotle, the most acute observer of antiquity, had no suspicion that the brain had much to do with mental processes. He held that the brain was merely a gland for the secretion of tears and that its only function in thinking was to cool the animal spirits that originated hi the heart and circulated through the brain.

Dependence of Consciousness on the Nervous System. If one cannot observe the workings of the nervous system directly, one may ask what right we have to assert that consciousness is related to it. Two facts bear most strongly in proof of the relation. The first is that behaviour increases in complexity with increase in the complexity of the nervous system. In the rudimentary organisms no nervous system can be distinguished. The same protoplasm that cares for the nutrition of the body also receives the stimulus and contracts. All parts are alike and each does all things necessary to its own welfare. The movements are correspondingly simple and the organism poorly adjusted to its surroundings. As we go higher, nerve-cells are present, but they are few and the connections are relatively scant. Behaviour is more complicated as the nervous system is better developed. In the lower vertebrates, a reptile for example, the nervous system is larger, the parts are more highly developed, and the connections between the elements are more numerous. The movements are also more numerous, and they are more closely adapted to the environment. The animal is better equipped to live and to act. The climax of evolution, both in behaviour and in the structure and connections of the nervous system, is found in man. In short, mind or behaviour develops in the same degree as the nervous system, whether we measure the development of the nervous system by the character of the nerve unit, by the nature of the connection between nerve units, or, with few exceptions, by the ratio of nervous tissue to body weight.

Defects of Brain and Mental Defects. The evidence from pathology for the close relation of mind and body is even more striking. A slight injury to the head may destroy consciousness. Injury to certain small portions of the brain gives rise to paralyses of small groups of muscles, to other portions causes the loss of some sense. Injury to almost any portion of the nervous system impairs some capacity in some degree. Conversely if behaviour or consciousness is affected, some change in the nervous system is usually found. These two facts taken in connection with what we know of physiology, and what can be seen directly of the action of nerve in connection with muscle in the lower organisms, suffice to make indisputable the very intimate relation between mind and brain.

Development of the Nervous System. It is perhaps easiest to understand the nervous system if we consider it in connection with the development of the animal organism from the lowest forms. All higher organisms can be regarded as developed from the simplest of unicellular forms. The amoeba may be regarded as the type of the original simplest animal. The amoeba is a single cell. This cell is at once nervous system and muscle, mouth and stomach. When it moves, the cell contracts or expands or changes its form as a whole. When it is stimulated, the impression is received by part of the cell and the result is to call out a contraction in the same and in neighbouring parts. When the stimulus is a food particle, it induces a movement of the cell or part of it toward the particle and about it until the particle is entirely surrounded. Then the same protoplasm that received the stimulus apparently acts as a digestive organ to assimilate the morsel. The original cell is thus possessed in some degree of the capacities of all parts of the human or higher organism. The development of the higher organisms may be regarded as due -to the coming together of many of these simplest cells to form a single whole or colony. Whether or not separate cells ever did combine in this way is a matter of indifference. It at least illustrates the nature of the relation of simple cells to the more complicated organism. The different cells take on different functions and, in many cases, different forms. No matter how changed, each cell of the body is regarded as a separate organism that has lost something of its individuality, but is nevertheless descended directly from the independent amceba-like prototype. The bone cells perhaps are most removed from the original ; the white corpuscles of the blood have changed hardly at all. Next to the white blood corpuscles the nerve-cells probably have been least changed from the original type. Except for its dependence upon the other members of the colony for its food, and for the fact that the other cells serve to give it form, a nerve-cell is still independent. The function of the nerve-cells in the colony is to make possible the coordination of the activities of the cells. When one cell is stimulated, a group of cells at a distance, constituting a muscle, may respond. The nerve-cells compel the parts to act 'together and make the organism a unit for action rather than a mere mass of separate entities. ,

The Divisions of the Nervous System. As one looks at the central nervous system of man, one can observe three fairly distinct structures, (i) The largest is the cerebrum, enclosed by the skull. This is a mass roughly like a sphere much corrugated on its surface by irregular folds. The folds are known as convolutions; the depressions between, as fissures. Two of the fissures are most prominent. One, the median fissure, serves to divide the cerebrum into two parts throughout more than half its height. It is in the approximate centre of the mass. This division makes it customary to regard the halves as distinct, and hence we speak of the two hemispheres. The other, on the outer side of each hemisphere, is not so deep, and is known as the fissure of Sylvius. Slanting upward from the lower front part of the brain, it will be seen from the diagram to constitute a prominent landmark. (2) Below the cerebrum at the back are large masses of nerve-cells and connecting masses of white fibre. These together constitute what is called the brain stem. Among them are the cerebellum at the back, the pons in front, and the medulla below. Each can be made out in Figure 2. The other structures in this region are too numerous to mention, and the action is too complicated to discuss within the limits of our brief sketch. (3) Lowest is the cord. The whole mass is contained in a bony box. The cerebrum, the cerebellum, and the brain stem are within the skull; the cord, within the spinal column. From the central nervous system nerves extend to the sense organs and muscles. The sense organs in the head send their nerves to the brain stem. The sensory nerves entering the cord have enlargements near the cord, the spinal ganglia, which contain cell bodies. In addition to the central nervous system which alone we shall consider, there are masses of cells in many parts of the trunk and head with relatively few connections with the central system. These are the ganglia of the sympathetic system.

White Matter and Grey Matter. Each of these large masses when cut across shows some tissue of a reddish grey colour, the grey matter, and other tissues of glistening white, the white matter. Isolated masses of grey matter are called ganglia (singular, ganglion). The grey matter is made up of cell bodies, the white matter of nerve fibres. In the cord the grey matter is in the centre, where it constitutes a butterfly-shaped central core. The butterfly shape is well marked in the sections, as can be seen in Figure 7. In the cerebrum and the cerebellum the cell bodies are for the most part upon the cortex (bark), the outermost layer; the white connecting parts are within and below. In the medulla and brain stem, no law for the distribution of white and grey matter can be stated in a few words. Strands of fibres are interspersed with masses of cell bodies, here one, there the other, is on the surface. The Growth of the Nervous System. The architecture of the different parts can be understood most clearly from a study of the development of the system. In the early stages of the embryo the central nervous system is but a groove in the outer layer of the mass. This groove gradually becomes deeper, and the tops of the sides approach until they grow together to form a tube. The different parts of the entire nervous system grow from different parts of the wall of the tube. The original hollow persists to the adult stage and is modified by the changes in the shape of the wall. The brain develops from the anterior, the cord from the posterior part of the tube. The anterior portion of the tube is first constricted in two places to form three vesicles ; later the anterior and posterior again divide to make five vesicles in all. See Figure 3. The hemispheres of the cerebrum grow out at the sides of the anterior or head end and grow up and back until they cover the structures that develop from the other vesicles. The structures of the brain stem develop by the thickening of the walls of the four lower vesicles, or swellings of the tube, and the cord from the posterior part of the tube. The connections of the parts retain in the adult many traces of the earlier stages of development. The relation of the parts was not well understood until the development of the system was known.

The Elements of the Nervous System. We may represent the nervous system most clearly as a colony of some eleven thousand million amceba-like organisms crowded together for the most part within the bony wall of the skull and spinal column with prolongations extending to all parts of the organism. The unit of the nervous system is the neurone. Each is connected with numerous other units, and also at innumerable points stands in close functional relations to the other cells of the body. To understand the action of the nervous system we must learn to know (i) the character of the single unit and (2) the connections the units make with each other and with other parts of the body. The neurone consists of a cell body and two sorts of prolongations or processes, the axone or axis cylinder, and the dendrites. The axone is a long, hairlike extension that may reach more than half the length of the body. Most nerves are bundles of axones. The axone ordinarily terminates by splitting into branches, the end-brush. The dendrites are similar to the end-brush. They are made up of a number of branches of the cell protoplasm and are usually relatively short. The function of the dendrite is to carry impulses to the cell bodies; the function of the axone is to carry them away from the cell bodies. The end-brush of one cell is ordinarily in contact with, or very near, the dendrites of other cells. The points of contact are called the synapses. The form of the neurone varies greatly. In some cases the cell body is approximately round and relatively smooth. In other cases it is more spindleshaped, in others again the surface is much broken by the processes. In certain parts of the cortex the cells are almost pyramidal in their general shape, with processes at each of the angles. In the spinal ganglia the cells that receive and transmit the impressions from the skin and muscles have dendrites and axones combined in a single process. The division is only recognizable some little distance from the cell body. All of these forms are to be regarded as departures from the type. But the character of the cell has no demonstrable relation to the function. The number of dendrites and the number of branches of the axone determine the number of connections that the cell may make ; the form of the cell depends upon the number and position of the processes, but so far as is known that is the only relation that holds between form and function.

The Parts of the Neurone. The neurone is a vital unit. The processes receive nourishment only from the cell body, and when cut off from the cell body, they die. The substance or protoplasm of the cell body is continuous with the protoplasm of the processes. The central protoplasm of the neurone shows no important differences in the character of its parts. The only points worthy of mention are : (i) the sheaths of the axone, and (2) the nucleus of the cell body. Two sheaths may be distinguished, an inner or myelin sheath, and an outer, the neurilemma. The inner sheath is found in all except a few fibres in the higher centres, the second is present outside of the central nervous system. In the sympathetic system the outer sheath is usually the immediate covering of the protoplasm. The myelin sheath seems to have some importance for the function of the neurone, but just what has not been made out. The nucleus of the cell stands in some vital relation to the action of the cell. In fatigue the nucleus has been shown to become smaller and irregular in outline. Its exact function, however, has not been determined. Recently small fibrils have been traced within the substance of the nerve-cell, but their function also is not agreed upon.

The Transmission of the Impulse within the Neurone. What goes on in the neurone when it acts has not been definitely determined. Theories have varied at different periods from assuming that some fluid was transmitted through the nerves or that some wave was propagated along the substance of the nerve, to the assumption that the action was electrical in character. To-day a generally accepted theory is that the impulse is due to some form of chemical change which spreads through the neurone. This hypothesis is supported by several facts, (i) The rate of propagation, about one to two hundred metres a second, is altogether too slow for electrical transmission, but is within the limits of chemical action. (2) The action of the nerve-cell is accompanied by electrical phenomena. Whenever a nerve is stimulated, an electric current passes from the cut end of the nerve to the uninjured sheath. If a frog's nerve be dissected out and one end be connected to a point on the neurilemma through a delicate galvanometer, the galvanometer will indicate the passage of an electric current when the nerve is stimulated in any way. Similar electric currents are induced, as is well known, by the chemical action in a battery. (3) The action of nerve-cells frees certain chemical substances, products of decomposition, that are removed by the blood. These three facts point to the assumption that action of the nerves is due to some chemical change. This assumption fits in with most of our detailed knowledge of the action of the nervous system. Our picture of the propagation of an excitation through a neurone is that it corresponds to the spread of chemical processes through its substance in very much the same way that a spark runs along a train of gunpowder. In the nerve the burning is but partial, and the materials used up are constantly replenished from the blood, but both processes are oxidations, in each the destruction spreads from part to part within the mass.

An alternative theory that is coming into favor regards the local electrical effects, excited by the chemical changes, as more closely connected with the nervous conduction. In the normal living organism the change is transmitted only in one direction. The stimulus is always received by the dendrite and is transmitted along the axone to the end-brush. It never runs in the reverse direction. One apparent exception may be noted. The cells in the spinal ganglia receive the impressions from the skin by a long process that extends to the surface of the body and is in its structure similar to an axone. We may either call this a peculiar form of dendrite or regard it as an exception to the law that the axis cylinder does not receive, but always transmits, the impulse. Which of the alternatives for disposing of the exception is to be adopted is not as yet a matter of common agreement.

Our picture of the nervous system is of a mass of ten thousand millions or so of these minute organisms enclosed within a bony case, the skull and the spinal column. Each cell is structurally independent, but the terminals are in contact. In the mass we ordinarily distinguish three sorts of neurones, the sensory, the motor, and the associating. The difference is one of connection and function rather than of structure. The sensory are receiving neurones; the motor send impressions out to the muscles, while the associating neurones serve to bring sensory and motor neurones into connection. As the sensory neurones always lead towards the centre, they are sometimes called centripetal or afferent, and for a similar reason the motor neurones are the centrifugal or efferent elements. There is no constant difference in structure between sensory and motor neurones. The difference in function is probably largely dependent upon the connections. In terms of neurones the white matter is made up largely of axones, the prolongations of cell bodies; the grey matter is a mass of cell bodies. Neither can be understood apart from the other. The white matter is merely a bundle of transmitting fibres, the grey matter nothing more than a mass of central cells, but every fibre of the white matter is a prolongation of some cell body and cannot live without it.

The Connections of Neurones. The action of the neurone is dependent upon its connections. A cell never acts alone. It is always a link in a reflex arc. All action of animal or man is excited by some stimulus in the external world, and every sensory excitation ends in some movement. The reflex arc in the nervous system always has its origin in a sense-organ and ends in a muscle. In between there may be any number of associatory cells, but these beginning and end structures must always be present. The problem of action from the side of nerve physiology is one of determining the paths of connection between the sensory and motor neurones. The course of transmission from neurone to neurone is determined by the openness of the paths. These connections are in part fully formed in the organism at birth, in part they are acquired through the activities of the animal during life. Of these paths of connection we may recognise three levels: first, the direct connections of the cord; second, the paths through the brain stem, the medulla, and general midbrain region; and third, the more indirect and complicated lines of connection in the cerebral cortex. Each is to be looked upon as a path between sense-organ and muscle. They are different ways by which the sensory impression may be transmitted to the muscle: they are different primarily in the directness with which the transfer is made; the higher paths permit more connections and make possible the cooperation of a greater number of sensory impulses in the control of movement.

The Action of the Cord. In the cord impressions from the skin and from internal structures are carried across to the muscles of limbs and trunk. Through it appropriate responses are made to stimuli of various sorts on the skin. Drawing back the hand when burned is primarily due to the nervous connections in the cord. The simplest reflexes of the cord involve two neurones only. The end organ in the skin is connected with the dendrite of the T-shaped cell in the spinal ganglion, the axone of that cell extends into the butterfly-like section of grey matter in the cord, and the end-brush comes in contact with the dendrite of a cell on the anterior side of the cord. This motor cell in its turn sends out an axiscylinder to a muscle. The chemical change induced by the physical stimulus travels to the cell body, thence to the end-brush or synapse, where it excites an impulse in the efferent neurone that travels down to the muscle. The chemical change is transferred at that point from nerve to muscle and excites the chemical change involved in the muscular contraction. The diagram shows that the spinal cord consists of a mass of white fibres which surround a core of

grey matter. In the latter are the cell bodies of the motor nerves, and the associating or connecting neurones. The surrounding white matter is divided by the extensions or horns of the grey matter into four parts or columns. Of these the posterior is made up of axones from the cells in the spinal ganglia, is sensory in function, while the others are both sensory and motor, outgrowths of cell bodies in the central grey or from cell bodies in the cortex or brain stem.

The Paths in the Cord. If the central grey may be regarded as the transferring station, the surrounding white constitutes the transmitting paths by which the cortex and higher centres in general are connected with the world outside. The sensory tracts bring impressions in from the periphery and transmit them to the cerebrum. The motor tracts serve, on the other hand, to connect the upper centres with motor cells in the cord, and thus with the muscles of the lower parts of the body. Not only do these outer fibre layers connect the upper portion of the nervous system with senseorgan and muscle, but they also connect the different levels of the cord with each other. A sensory impulse excites not only muscles that have their cells at the same level in the cord, but also groups of muscles at different levels above and below. If we return to consider the simple reflexes, we find that the sensory stimulus may spread not merely to the single motor neurone or group of motor neurones at the same level, but it may make connections with neurones that lie higher and lower in the cord, or more frequently, it extends to neurones lying in the opposite side of the cord and produces movements of members on the other side of the body. If one destroy the brain of a frog or, by pithing, cut the cord off from the upper nervous system, it will be seen that all of these reflexes may still be called out by stimuli. If a bit of paper moistened with acid be placed upon the left foot of a frog, the foot will be drawn up. If now the foot be held so that it cannot be moved, it will be found that the other is brought over to remove the stimulus. If this is not successful, the muscles of the forelegs and trunk will contract and the contractions will continue until the stimulus is removed or the neurones exhausted. The first movement (of the left leg) is due to the transfer of the stimulus to the motor cell, or cells, on the same side of the cord. When the foot is held and the stimulus grows strong enough, the impulse is transmitted to the group of neurones on the opposite side of the cord, and muscles of the right leg are contracted. When the excitation becomes still stronger, the discharge spreads to neurones higher up, and the muscles of the trunk and forelegs are made to contract.

Action of the Synapse. Since there are evidently many possible lines of transmission, the question naturally arises, what decides which of the many paths shall be followed? The answer is found in a recent theory that the course of the impulse is determined at the point of connection between neurone and neurone, the synapse. The end-brush of the receiving neurone is in contact with the dendrites of several motor neurones. Each of these points of contact or synapses has a different resistance. The path to muscles of the same leg is most permeable ; next in degree of permeability are the synapses to dendrites of the motor neurones that control the muscles of the other leg, while the synapses that connect with the muscles of the upper trunk open with still greater difficulty. The lines of discharge depend primarily upon the openness of the synapses. In these lowest reflexes the ease of transmission depends upon the character of the synapses as they are determined in the individual at birth, and thus the responses are prepared in advance of any experience. When the sensory excitation is weak, only the easiest paths are followed. As the impulse becomes stronger, more and more difficult synapses will be crossed, and the motor discharge will become more and more diffuse.

Reflexes of the Second Level. At the second level of reflexes the same general laws hold. The possibilities of connection are, however, very much more numerous. Many senses contribute impressions and the muscles over which the discharge may take place now include all of the muscles of the body instead of the muscles of trunk and limbs only. The synapses for the reflexes of this level lie in the region of the central nervous system between the top of the cord and the cortex. The anatomy of this region is too complicated to be described within our limits, but the connections are made in the numerous accumulations of cell bodies found in the structures of the medulla, midbrain, and on up to the lower ganglia of the cerebrum. Wherever the synapses may be located, we may distinguish two general groups of connections.

First each stimulus tends to excite certain movements immediately and directly. Thus in the eye, when a ray of light falls upon the retina, the pupil at once contracts. This movement is called out by the sensory stimulus transmitted to one of the lower centres for vision. There the motor neurone connected with the muscles is excited and the pupil contracts. The visual impressions, too, excite and control the movements of the trunk and limbs through the midbrain centres and their connections with the motor tracts in the cord. A frog, for example, that has had its hemispheres removed will avoid obstacles in swimming or hopping and will give other evidences that its movements are guided by sight. In man the neurones of the brain stem are not so independent of the cortex, and it is difficult to demonstrate that they can act alone. The functions of these structures at the second level are : (i) to serve as reflex centres by which the senses at this level may be connected with muscles of the head ; (2) to connect the special sense-organs of the head with the motor neurones of the cord, and so with the muscles of trunk and limbs ; and (3) to connect the cortex with the sense-organs and with the muscles. It is probable that all the senseorgans are represented in the brain stem by neurones, and that in every case the impulse from a sense-organ is transferred from one neurone to another in some ganglion in this region. The mechanism of the reflexes is the same as in the cord. The only difference is that the sources of excitation are more numerous and the possibilities of connection are greater. Action of Cortex. By far the most important division of the nervous system is the cerebrum. In man the cerebrum is the largest of the nervous structures, constituting rather more than half of the total nervous system. It is also the part of the nervous system most closely related to consciousness. In fact, it is very doubtful if any consciousness at all accompanies the action of any other portion of the nervous system. Its structure and functions are very complex, but our guiding principles still suffice to explain its action. It, too, is made up of neurones in various connections, and the neurones act to transfer sensory impressions to motor neurones, and so to excite muscles. The only region is just below the fissure of Sylvius, above (H). (FA) designates the frontal, (PA) parietal, and (TA) the temporal association centres. There is some evidence that the dotted regions about the sensory and motor areas are areas in which particular associations are formed with them. The diagram embodies the results of A. W. Campbell, but has been modified in one or two respects to agree with the results of Flechsig and Gushing.

differences between it and the structures considered above are : (i) that it offers vastly greater possibilities of connection, and (2) that impressions received at an earlier period in the life of the individual play a large part in controlling the course of the movements. In consequence the processes that intervene between stimulus and response may be regarded as much more important here than they are in any of the reflexes already considered.

Localization of Cortical Functions. Cell bodies are found for the most part only in the cortex or bark, a superficial layer of the cerebrum only a few millimetres thick. The inner mass consists of fibres, axones of cell bodies in the cortex or in the brain stem, which serve to connect different parts of the cortex, and the cortex with the muscles and sense-organs. We must distinguish three sorts of areas or regions in the cortex. Certain areas receive the impressions from the outside world and are known as the sensory regions. Others send out impulses to the muscles and are known in consequence as the motor regions. The remaining areas serve to connect the sensory and motor and constitute what are known as the association areas. The first two are often grouped together as the projection areas, since they represent regions of the body in very much the same way that parts of the screen may be said to represent the slide when a picture is thrown upon it by the projection lantern. The relation between these areas and the senseorgan and muscle is very close.

Localization of Motor Areas. The position of the motor region is more easily demonstrated. If the brain of a man be exposed for an operation and the motor area be stimulated electrically, some muscle of the body will respond and the same muscle or group of muscles will always respond provided the same region be stimulated in the same degree. The areas that correspond to the different muscles are sufficiently well known to permit the physician to decide what part of the brain is defective in case some group of muscles be paralysed. The motor area of the brain is shown in the diagram. It lies just in front of the central fissure, the fissure of Rolando, and extends upward from near the fissure of Sylvius to the median fissure and over to the mesial surface of the hemisphere, the wall of the median fissure. As is generally the case in the upper part of the nervous system, the right brain contains the motor centres for the left half of the body and vice versa.

Sensory Areas. The sensory regions are scattered and their positions are less certain than the motor regions. The part of the cortex connected with the eye is in the back of the brain, the occipital region. The area to which vision may certainly be ascribed is in the cuneus, a wedge-shaped convolution on the mesial surface. It is marked in the diagram. The auditory region is in the temporal lobe, just below the fissure of Sylvius near its junction with the central fissure. The impulses from skin and muscle are received in the region just behind the central fissure. Smell is less certainly localized, but is probably on the mesial surface, as indicated in the diagram. Taste may be near it, but the localization is hardly more than conjecture at the present stage of knowledge.

Association Areas. It will be noticed that after all the regions with known relations to sensation and movement are enumerated, the greater part of the cortex is left without assigned function. It is the contention of Flechsig, now generally accepted, that the remaining portions of the brain have as their function to make cross connections between the sensory and the motor regions, to unite sensory with motor, and sensory with sensory areas. For example, the axone from a cell body hi the optic region extends to the intervening association region and there comes into contact with the dendrites of numerous association neurones, each of which in its turn will connect with other sensory or motor neurones, or with other association neurones. Each intervening association neurone will increase the connections that a sensory neurone may make, and so increase the possible responses that the same stimulus may call out.

Action of the Cortex during Speech. If we turn from structure to function, we find that the nervous excitation transmitted from the sense-organ to the sensory cells in the cortex must sooner or later find its way to a motor neurone. In some cases the motor cell affected is in the same region of the brain. Thus movements of the eye may be excited by stimulating the occipital lobes, and it is probable that movements of the eyes evoked by visual stimuli may have a path in the cortex that does not extend beyond the wider limits of the optic region. More characteristic, however, are the interconnections that control the movements involved in speech. These are of interest because the disturbances of speech were among the earliest to receive an explanation. In ordinary repetition of spoken words, the excitation is transmitted from the ear by way of a lower centre to the auditory region, thence along the axones of sensory neurones to association neurones in the Island of Reil (the bottom and sides of the fissure of Sylvius) and from there to the motor area for speech in the lower Rolandic region. Here the end-brushes of the association neurones come into functional union with the dendrites of motor neurones. The axones of the motor neurones end through the mediation of other neurones in the muscles of the vocal organs and the sound is repeated. That this is the approximate course of the nervous impulse we know from a comparison of the defects of speech with the injuries in different parts of the brain. If the auditory cells are destroyed in any way, the patient cannot repeat the words. The effect is the same as if the ear were destroyed. Again, if there is an injury to the association region in the Island of Reil, the ability to repeat words heard is impaired. Finally, if the motor centre for speech is injured, speaking of any kind will be impossible. The condition is known as aphasia, sensory aphasia is due to disturbance of the auditory region, motor aphasia to disturbance of the motor region. The existence of sensory aphasia is of particular importance as an evidence that the action of the cortex is dependent, like the action of the lower centres, upon the excitations of sense, that all action is sensori-motor. There is no response unless an impulse is received from some sensory region.

The relations of vision to speech, and of vision and audition to writing, follow the same general rules. When one reads aloud, the impulse is transferred from the visual area to the motor speech region through an association centre. Injury to the visual area or to the sight-speech association region may interfere with the process. The resulting disease is known as alexia. Writing on dictation ordinarily disappears with speech in the sensory forms of aphasia. Each of these paths has been developed through long practice and is relatively firmly established. Any other simple response to stimulation would take a corresponding course and would involve sensory, associatory, and motor regions. When the paths are less well established and the response is less completely prepared, as when one answers a question and several replies are possible, the association regions probably play a larger part. There are more possible connections and more open association paths, or at least the open paths in the association regions are more nearly on a par. In consequence there is smaller chance of prophesying in advance what course the response will take. The necessity for the cooperation of sensory, associatory, and motor neurones is none the less certain.

In addition to the connections between sensory and motor regions there are a number of cases in which two sensory regions must be connected. Thus when one touches a pencil in the dark, the picture of the object will present itself before the movement is made, or simultaneously with the movement. In this case the tactual neurones excite a visual neurone or group of neurones. In the perception processes such associatory transfers are the rule rather than the exception, as will be seen in a later chapter. Ordinarily the association leads finally to action of some sort, but so far as important action is concerned, that may be very long delayed. This fact of arousing other sensory processes raises the uestion as to the cortical seat of memory processes and imaginings. The most generally accepted answer at present is that the memories have the same cortical regions, in fact the same cortical cells, as the sensations, and that in remembering the same cells are excited as in seeing or hearing. Visual memories are in the visual region, auditory memories are in the auditory region, and so on. The process of arousing memories is one of retracing old paths, very much as habit depends upon the renewed action of a group of motor neurones. The details of the process must occupy us in the later chapters.

Nerve Elements do not Act in Isolation. One word needs to be added in this connection, and that is that the single parts of the nervous system probably do not act alone. When we speak of the action of a single group of cells it is probable that the group is merely the centre of excitation in a very wide region. The excitation that arouses that group spreads to very remote parts of the brain. Action is always of large masses of nervecells, but of the mass certain parts are emphasised, the others respond in very much slighter degree. There is a complicated interplay of part and part throughout a very large portion of the mass of neurones, although only relatively few are in great activity. The interactions which themselves do not directly affect action serve to guide the course of the other responses. Each contributes its share to the total action, although one alone stands out prominently.

The action of the nervous system, then, is always dependent upon a transfer of some sort of energy from neurone to neurone. The original excitation is received from the external world and has its final outcome in some sort of movement. At least two sets of neurones are involved in every action. As the act becomes more complicated, a larger and larger number of neurones intervene, and a larger and larger number of stimuli contribute to the excitation and control of the movement. At the lowest level the stimulus is ordinarily single or at least of one sort, and the paths of motor discharge are relatively few. At the second level the neurones involved are still relatively few, but the stimuli are numerous and varied and the paths of discharge are more numerous. On the highest level in the cortex very many of the sensory and motor paths are concerned, and in addition the effects of the stimuli that were earlier received and are stored in the nervous system contribute their share to the control of action.

Interaction between Cord and Cortex. The different levels ordinarily interact in any response. Thus, when the hand is burned or pricked it will usually be drawn back reflexly. This means that the sensory impulse is transmitted to a spinal ganglion and thence to the anterior grey cells of the cord, and so down to the muscle. But suppose that the man is working in a bit of machinery with the hand in front of a knife, and the finger is burned. The reflex, if it is not too strong or if the stimulus is not unexpected, will be checked by the knowledge of the danger from the knife. This means that the visual impression of the knife has been carried to the visual area in the cortex by way of the eye and midbrain centres. The effect of the arousal of the visual area is transferred to the motor region, and serves to inhibit the activity of the motor cells in the cord that would otherwise be involved in the reflex, or it may contract the muscles that oppose the reflex. In this way the impressions from the eye or the memories derived from the eye oppose and may overcome the effects of the excitation from the skin. The movement is controlled, not by the tactual sensations alone, but by tactual sensations together with any visual sensations and memories that bear upon the situation. At each level in the nervous system as we go upward from the cord, there are more neurones involved. The action is in the light of a constantly increasing number of sensations, and many more forms of response are possible. But the difference is one of complexity alone. The beginning and the end of the process may be identical. The impulse is propagated in the same way and the laws that govern the selection of the path are the same. Our first picture of the simple reflex explains the fundamentals of the most complicated voluntary act. It is only necessary to add new stimuli and new possibilities of response, to recognise that many currents of nervous activity are adding their quota to the control of action.

QUESTIONS

1. What is the sheath of the axone? (a) neurilemma ? (b) medullary sheath ?

2. Distinguish afferent nerves, efferent nerves, ganglia, white and grey matter in terms of the parts of neurones or relations of neurones that compose them.

3. Describe the functions of the nervous system in the simplest and most general terms.

4. What passes along the nerve as an impulse is transmitted? How is the action of the neurone like that of an amoeba ? like that of a battery?

5. How are the acts controlled by the three levels of the nervous system similar? how different ?

6. What level is involved in each of the following acts?

Drawing up the foot when the sole is tickled.

Sneezing as you breathe in dust.

Winking as the eye is threatened.

Turning a corner when thinking of something else.

7. What difference is there between the function of the anterior and posterior association centres?

8. Why does injury to the left side of the cerebrum produce a paralysis on the right side of the body?

EXERCISES

1. Draw neurones of three different types. Designate axones, dendrites, and end-brush of each. How many axones has a neurone? how many dendrites ? how many end-brushes ?

2. Draw a diagram to illustrate the course followed by an impulse when you burn your finger.

3. Draw a cross section of the cord. Show the path followed by a simple reflex.

4. Draw the cerebrum in lateral and mesial view and indicate the sensory, motor, and associatory areas.

5. Trace on the diagram the path followed by an impulse as you copy a sentence from a book.

6. If possible examine neurones and their connections in a section of a cord under a microscope.

7. If opportunity offers procure the brain of an animal, sheep or cat, dissect it, and compare the structures with the diagrams.

CHAPTER III

NEURAL ACTION IN RELATION TO CONSCIOUSNESS AND BEHAVIOUR

AFTER a discussion of the structure and action of the nervous system the question of the relation between these physical processes and the mental processes or behaviour naturally arises. Popularly there is a tendency to confuse mind with brain. A man is said to have a good brain when it is meant merely that he is effective or unusually intelligent. This identification is altogether without warrant. On the contrary, there is little if any similarity between nejvous activity and the mental state. If one could bring the processes that go on in the brain when one looked at a landscape side by side with the landscape itself and compare them, the two would not be at all alike. Where the landscape shows various forms and masses of colour, the nervous activity would show chemical reactions running here and there in the visual area at the back of the brain and in the nerves leading to and away from it. We have every reason to believe that the chemical changes stand in some essential relation to the mental processes, but it is obviously impossible to assert that the two are identical or even that they are similar in character. One of the problems most discussed in psychology and in philosophy is what is the exact relation between these constantly shifting chemical changes in the nervous system as the landscape affects it and the mental image of the landscape ; or, in general, between brain action and consciousness. While the answer makes little practical difference for the treatment of psychological problems, it is well before going farther to have a statement of opposing theories and a provisional working hypothesis.

Relation of Mind and Body. A large part of the difficulty in understanding the relation of body and mind grows out of the different ways in which one must approach the explanation of behaviour. The observer sees only the stimulus or occasion for the action, the actor appreciates the mental states that follow the stimulus and precede the action, but neither can see both sides at once. Even if the observer calls anatomy and physiology to his aid and goes as far as he can by analogy from experiments on animals in the attempt to find an explanation of behaviour, he gets only nerves and thenconnections ; he can never have a view of the consciousness of the actor. The actor from his side can never pass beyond consciousness; he does not become aware directly of nerve or nervous activity, no matter how he may seek to penetrate beneath his immediate consciousness. The outside observer sees excitations vanish into the nervous system and sees actions result ; the actor sees the occasion for his act approach, is conscious of the resulting sensation, and knows that he has acted, but knows nothing of the nervous system that intervenes. So far no one has been able to bring the two aspects of behaviour together in a single system of explanations, either by direct observation or in theory. At present it is universally accepted that mental state and bodily or nervous activity are always found together, but care is taken not to assert that one is the cause of the other. The implication is that they are related in some essential and fundamental way, but what that relation is, is not stated. It is customary to explain any mental process in terms of other mental processes, and to explain all nervous action by other nervous activities, but no attempt is made to explain one in terms of the other, further than to say that the two series are always found together and run on side by side. For our purposes it is not necessary to discuss the theories that have been developed to explain the connection. We may leave the whole problem open, as the facts of psychology are the same whatever theory may ultimately prevail. For convenience we shall often seem to imply that activity in sensory neurones produces changes in consciousness and that ideas start the motor discharges which lead to action. This is not to be regarded as committing the author to any theory of the real connection between body and mind, but as a lapse into popular speech.

The Connections of Neurones. While it is assured that consciousness is dependent upon the activity of the nervous system, and that certain conscious processes are connected with the activity of certain nervous structures, it is also important to know what change there is in the elements of the nervous system as a result of action. Upon their changed character as a result of earlier action depends most of the possibility of education and of improvement in behaviour. Formation of habits and the acquirement of memories are the most striking of the mental and physical capacities directly referred to the nervous system.

At present the tendency is to explain all learning as due to a change at the point where two neurones come together, where the end-brush of one comes into contact with the dendrites of anothei. This point, as was said, has been called the synapse. As was seen in the preceding chapter, the synapse governs the course of the impulse. Each sensory path makes connections with several motor and associating paths or neurones and any impulse will take the path that offers least resistance. The ease with which the synapses may be crossed determines the path, and this in turn is determined first by inheritance, second by use. The reflexes of the cord run their course through synapses already prepared at birth. The course of an impulse through the cortex is largely controlled by synapses whose degree of resistance depends upon the frequency with which they have been used. Evidently, then, the most important question of nervous physiology for the psychologist is what is the nature of the synapse and of its action.

The Amoeba Theory of the Synapse. The details of the mechanism of the synapse are still altogether lacking, although numerous theories have been developed to explain it. All agree that whenever two neurones are active at the same time some change is induced in the synapse that makes it act more readily later. The two neurones become more nearly a single unit for action. Two suggestions as to what the change is may be mentioned as typical. The older, and in many ways the simpler, regards the neurones as living organisms that still possess at their extremities the power of motion inherent in the amceba-like prototype. When both cells are active, the processes extend and come into contact, and the chemical action of the one in some way excites a similar activity in the other. The action of the processes, particularly of the dendrite, leaves behind it a disposition to act again more easily in the same way. As a result of this disposition, the same extension is repeated on suitable occasion and the connection between the cells and their simultaneous action is renewed.

What the nature of the change may be is not made very clear. It may be an actual physical bond that persists when the end-brush of one neurone has once been brought into contact with the dendrite of another, or it may be that one or the other of the processes takes on a habit of extending in the way that brought it into contact with the other. The original obstruction to the transfer of the action from one neurone to another is spatial, and this original gap is bridged by the movement of processes, a movement, which when once made, leaves a permanent tendency to the union of the neurones.

Sherrington's Theory of the Synapse. The more recent theory, proposed by Sherrington, the English physiologist, is that the synapse opposes the passage of an excitation in much the same way that a membrane opposes the transfer of fluids. At first this resistance is very great, but it is lessened with each act. On this theory the change in the synapse is chemical in character. Here again the exact nature of the change is not asserted. On either theory the synapse is the point where action leaves its impress upon the nervous system, it is here that learning has its effect. The change that comes with action is a lessened resistance at the synapse, whether it be due to the coming closer of the processes or to a chemical change that makes more permeable the relatively impermeable membrane that at first separates the neurones. On either theory it is possible to picture the synapse as a valve that controls the interaction of nerve elements, that governs the passage of the nervous impulse from unit to unit. At first the valves are stiff and open only to strong currents ; with use they work more easily until those most difficult at birth may become as delicate in action as those that were at birth most permeable. It should be emphasized to avoid giving a wrong impression that there is no real valve ; it is only that the action is like what might be expected were there a valve at the synapse. As the outcome of our discussion, we have a picture of the nervous system as a mass of relatively independent amceba-like cells that are held in a definite position and relation to one another by a cage of bone. At the beginning certain of the neurones constitute a path for an impulse from senseorgans to muscles. These original paths are few and make possible only the activities most essential to the continuance of the life of the individual. Additional paths of connection are formed by each activity, physical and mental. Whenever any two neurones chance to act together a connection is formed between them, the original gap is bridged, and they come to form part of a new pathway from sense-organ to muscle. This holds also for the action of the neurones within the cortex, when the learning that results is primarily of ideas rather than of movements. Learning, whether of new movements or of new ideas, is a process of making easier the passage of an impulse from neurone to neurone and is fundamentally the same everywhere.

Reflexes Determined by the Synapse. When the connections in the nervous system have once been formed, the course of a nervous impulse is determined by the intensity of the stimulus and the openness of the synapse. The course of a reflex through the nervous system depends upon the innate connections of the synapses. In the cord, for example, a slight stimulus on the hand arouses the muscles of that arm ; a stronger one excites the corresponding member of the opposite side ; still stronger impressions cause contractions in the legs, and finally contractions will spread to all of the muscles of the trunk. Translated into terms of neurones and synapses, this indicates that the synapse which opens most readily is the one between the sensory neurone and the motor neurone at the same level and on the same side of the cord. Slight stimuli are strong enough to force their way across this gap. As the stimulus becomes stronger, the synapses which lead to the opposite side of the body open, then those that lie at the higher and lower levels. The course of the impulse and the selection of the movement depend altogether upon the ease with which synapses open and the strength of the stimulus. Habit a Change in the Synapse. The same factors determine the selection hi the more complicated reactions of the higher brain centres. In man the action that will be called out by a situation depends upon the habits he has formed, and these in turn are due to connections between neurones in different parts of the brain. In a soldier trained to answer to the word of command the readiest response is to obey, however that action may conflict with his instincts. The synapses have opened so frequently between the centres for hearing and the movements evoked by the order that the stimulus leads to action at once, however unfavourable the other circumstances. In these responses, too, stronger stimuli arouse more diffuse responses. Where a single command when in ranks meets with immediate response, the sudden charge of an enemy when the ranks are broken and the men are in disorder may cause sudden diffuse responses that will overcome the effects of the long drill. Similarly, in a game of baseball the habitual response will be made immediately and accurately when the stimulus is slight and the circumstances normal, but when some strong stimulus or some emotionally disturbing event takes place at the moment, the suitable habitual response is frequently lost in the general overflow to neighbouring muscles. The ball is often thrown over the first baseman's head at a critical moment. While in the higher habitual responses more complicated factors must be taken into consideration, the character of the response still depends upon the openness of the synapses at the moment and the intensity of the stimulus or its appeal to the individual. In essentials, the response of the higher neurones and paths of connection follow the same laws as the lower.

The Formation of Habits. One of the most important facts that can be referred to the action of the nervous system is the formation of habits. This, as has been said, is due primarily to the opening of synapses by use. Habit, whether for good or ill, is one of the most striking elements in any explanation of behaviour. As it is fundamental for many of the psychological explanations, we may begin our discussion with a brief summary of its laws and applications. In popular speech habit, for some reason, implies bad habit, but this restriction of the term is altogether unjustifiable. Absence of habit would mean complete loss of efficiency. Most of eating, walking, talking, and all of the frequent and important actions of everyday life are habits in whole or in part. Dressing is a habit. You do not think as you put on your garments. Your hands find their way to the buttons without thought and without your being conscious that they are moving. The tie is adjusted with no knowledge of the separate movements. Were you asked to describe the movements made in tying a cravat, you probably could not do so, although the operation is run through daily without mistake. If we turn from a discussion of the omnipresence of habit to the question of what goes on in the nervous system when a habit is acquired, we get back to our problem of the synapse and its relations. Each time an act is performed, it matters not how, there is some change in the synapses between neurones. The effect of the act persists and becomes stronger with each repetition. After several repetitions the connection between the cells becomes so close that whenever the particular sensory cell is excited, the impulse spreads to the motor cells active with it before, and the neurones grow more and more to constitute what is practically a single structure. The formation of habits is thus a process of decreasing the resistance of the synapses in the different possible paths of transmission. Ultimately it is due to a change of some kind in the synapse. When a sensory neurone is excited, one of the synapses is more open than the others. This is traversed by the impulse and the corresponding muscle responds. The opening of the synapse has in every case been brought about by the simultaneous action of the two neurones. The Omnipresence of Habit. The process of forming a habit is relatively simple, but the effect of habit formation has the most far-reaching importance. Every act of any kind is the forerunner of other acts of the same kind. At first the habit is easily changed; but if fre.quently persisted in, the time comes when that movement must be made whenever the particular occasion presents itself, without reference to the other circumstances of the moment. Obviously when the movements are repeated until they are so completely fixed, it is essential that the movements chosen for fixation shall be helpful or harmless. The useful man is for the greater part marked off from the useless and the vicious by the nature of his habits. Industry or indolence, good temper or bad temper, even virtue or vice, are in the last analysis largely matters of habit. One forms the habit of working at certain times of the day, and soon if one is not busy at that time one experiences a lively sense of discomfort. Or, on the contrary, one forms the habit of loafing all day. Work then becomes distasteful and indolent irresponsibility is established. Losing .one's temper is largely a habit, as is self-control. Each time one is provoked by a trifle, it becomes the more difficult to look calmly at an unpleasant episode ; while each time one remains calm under difficult circumstances, strength is gained for later difficulties. Similarly, whenever temptation is resisted, virtue gains a victory; when temptation is yielded to, new weaknesses develop. Frequent yielding makes resistance practically impossible. A bank president of established morals could no more step out and pick a pocket that was temptingly unprotected than he could fly. The habitual drunkard can no more resist the invitation to have a glass than he can resist the action of gravitation while falling freely through space. Frequent giving in has entirely destroyed his original freedom of choice.

We are all constantly forging chains of action in our. nervous system that we shall never be able to break. Fortunate is the man whose chains are all suited to the life he is compelled to live. He was once free in the sense of our present problem, but after a few experiences he becomes bound to his past by chains that only the strongest impulses can break. Habits are not restricted to action, but show themselves even in the features. Much has been said, particularly in semi-popular writing, of the ability to determine character from the face. Each movement of the muscles of the face has left its impress upon the muscles and the skin, just as each action has left its impress upon the nerve-cells. One can tell at a glance at the face, even in repose, what its most characteristic responses have been and can form some idea of the character of the man, of the effects that have been left by the same actions upon the nerve-cells which show themselves when the man is called upon to act. A weak man, a strong man, even more truly a jovial man or a crabbed man, carries the marks upon his face. These marks are but evidence of the changes that the same set of acts has left upon the synapses of the nervous system everywhere along the paths of action.

Habits Essential to Action. Habit not only limits choice but through early training makes choice possible. The adult ordinarily chooses one habit rather than another ; he does not choose between some habitual action and something never done before. What has never been done is ordinarily not within the power of the individual. For example, you cannot speak the Russian word for prince and could not if some one should first pronounce the word for you. You cannot because you have never developed the habit. When you do choose to speak an English word, you do it because you have that habit fully developed. Had you never formed habits of speaking you would be as powerless in English as in Russian. As all of our intellectual operations are expressed in language, habit is in the highest sense a powerful, an indispensable tool of thinking. But that is not all. If you eliminate from the various intellectual activities all that belongs to habit, most of the higher mental operations become impossible. Habit, like fire, is a cruel master but an invaluable servant. Without it all action would cease or at the best become but a painful process of feeling one's way through even the simplest act.

Association of Ideas a Form of Habit. The association of ideas, fundamental for thinking, is similar to habit. The recall of any memory necessitates the stimulus of some earlier connected event. An old experience returns only in connection with some other event now revived in consciousness. On the nervous side this means that the cells in the cortex corresponding to the two ideas have been active together and that the resistance of the common synapse has been reduced by the simultaneous action of the two neurones. When one presents itself, the impulse spreads through the synapse of least resistance to the related cell and the old idea is recalled

All recall is dependent upon the connection of ideas, and ideas are connected only as the neurones are united through the reduced resistance of the synapses. The association processes are thus hi every particular similar to habits. They might be called habits of neurones in the cortex. The only difference worth emphasising is that in this case there is no movement of muscles accompanying the activity of the cortical cells. Even this difference is not always present; for the cortical cells, whenever active, tend to call out movements, often very slight, sometimes nothing more than the tendency to movement. If we include association among the habits, we may say with complete assurance that no intellectual activity of any kind goes on except on the basis of habit. Habit and association are the two fundamental facts upon which all of our activity, mental or physical, depends. That either should be lacking is inconceivable. Were they lacking, man, either as a mental or as a physical being, would not be what he is.

QUESTIONS

1. Describe the nervous processes that accompany seeing a landscape. How are they different from the perception?

2. When the idea initiates the act of writing a description, can you say that the idea causes the movement ?

3. Discuss the two theories of changes in the synapse.

4. Give acts that are determined (a) by heredity, (b) by use.

5. What elements of character may depend upon habit?

EXERCISES

1. List ten acts of the day that you may be sure are habits.

2. Trace the different steps in forming the habit of adjusting some new article of attire, e.g. adjusting a new tie. 3. Try to break some undesirable habit and keep a daily record of progress.

CHAPTER IV

SENSATION

SINCE all acts and all conscious processes are initiated by sensory stimulation, it is necessary to have a full knowledge of the different stimuli which affect man and of the sensations they produce. We might determine without the use of introspection what stimuli are effective by studying the responses of the organism. In man, however, it is much simpler to study the direct effects in consciousness. This has the added advantage of revealing the qualities of sensations. Knowledge of behaviour is dependent upon a knowledge of the stimuli, and sensations are interesting and important in themselves. We may turn then to our first task, a study of the character of consciousness.

Components of Consciousness. We may follow tradition and begin our study of consciousness by attempting to discover its elementary components. At this moment the consciousness of the reader is made up of a number of processes. Experiences are received through the eyes that constitute or suggest the book with its physical appearance. At the same time you acquire certain elements of knowledge from the words on its page. Your mind wanders now and again to the thought of the game you would like to be having or of the recitation that you would like to make on the morrow, or to the entertainment of the evening, or to some other topic. Accompanying each of these processes are feelings of pleasure or displeasure, and in many cases emotions of greater or less intensity. Obviously even the simplest consciousness is a very complex affair. To attempt to describe or to classify the different sorts of consciousness taken in this concrete way would evidently be an endless task. In practice the undertaking is made easier by the fact that the memory processes and the immediate sensation processes have approximately the same qualities. A remembered or imagined red is of the same quality, approximately, as the red that is seen directly. Leaving aside the feeling processes for the moment, we may say that the qualities of consciousness are the qualities of sense. Since Locke it has been an axiom of psychology that there is nothing in mind that was not previously in sense. It is true undoubtedly that one cannot think of a colour that has never been seen. Try to picture to yourself what the ultra-violet waves would be like to an eye that had developed a capacity to see them, and you will find that each colour you call up is compounded out of those already familiar. All -attempts to produce an imaginary quality that has not been received through some sense-organ are fruitless. Every quality of memory and imagination is received through the senses. New things may be compounded out of these qualities, but the number of qualities is fixed by these elementary sensations. Evidently, then, the first task that confronts us as we undertake a description of the nature of consciousness or of its components is to determine the number of simple sensations. We approach this task confident that its solution will determine, not merely the number of sensory qualities, but the number of qualities that may be remembered or imagined as well.

Doctrine of Specific Energies of Sensory Ends. The enumeration of sensory qualities is not so simple and easy as might at first appear. Whether one shall call each distinguishable colour in the spectrum a single sensation or shall regard them all as compounded of a few simple qualities, is a question that cannot be decided by direct observation. A theory that was first suggested by Johannes Müller, the pioneer m modern physiology, offers perhaps the most convenient principle to guide us in our task. Briefly, this law asserts that any senseorgan must always give its own quality of sensation, no matter how it may be excited. Simplest evidence of this may be offered by pressing the eyeball with the finger. You will notice about the circle of pressure a ring of light of a quality that might have been induced by a ray of light. An electric current passed through the eye will also produce a visual sensation, as will jarring the optical apparatus by falling (' seeing stars'). Conversely, it may be said that there can be no more qualities of sensation than there are different kinds of sensory end organs. If the quality of the sensation depends upon the character of the sense-organ that receives it, and not upon the nature of the stimulus, the number of sense qualities must be as great as, and no greater than, the number of sensory ends. Since the same stimulus often gives different results upon several different senseorgans, the difference must be due to the organ, not to the stimulus. Many instances may be cited. A vibration of ether excites the sensation red upon the retina of the eye, a sensation of warmth upon the skin. The electric current gives a different sense quality for each sense-organ, pain on the skin, taste on the tongue, and so on. If we accept this law, it follows that we can determine the number of different kinds of sensation if we can discover the number of distinct sensory end organs.

The Development of Sensations. The development of the sense qualities depends upon and goes hand in hand with the development of the sensory endings. In the simplest organisms there is no differentiation of sensory tissue, and consciousness perhaps shows no differences whatever. All stimuli give rise to exactly the same effect. Taste is not different from touch, sight from hearing, if hearing be present at all. All forms of stimuli excite the same organ and in consequence must give the same effect. As differentiation takes place in the animal series, new organs are developed and new sense qualities make their appearance. At the level of insects most of the senses found in man are pretty well differentiated. Even in man, however, not all of the physical stimuli have corresponding sensations. The electric and magnetic forces have no sense-organs and are not recognised as separate qualities. For that reason, too, knowledge of electrical and magnetic phenomena developed relatively late. Indirect evidence obtained through the other senses alone gives knowledge of their existence. Our problem in this chapter is to determine the number of different kinds of sensory ends that the human organism presents to the external world, confident that this will also give the number of distinct conscious qualities.

Sensations of Temperature. We may begin with the sensations derived from the skin, since the skin is probably the simplest of the sense-organs, although far more complex than one is inclined to believe. The ordinary assumption seems to be that the skin is a comparatively homogeneous surface with but one sense quality. Recent investigation, beginning in the early eighties of the last century, has shown that the skin has four senses and that each is distinct in quality and in sensory ending. Two of these respond primarily to mechanical stimulation, two to temperature. The mechanical senses are pressure and pain, the temperature senses are warmth and cold. Evidence for the two temperature senses is most readily obtained by the beginner. If one will but run over the skin with the point of a rod heated above the body temperature, one will notice that the rod feels warm only here and there at points well separated. These spots were found by von Frey to average about one and one-half to the square centimetre. If the rod be cooled below the temperature of the skin, cold is noticed at many more spots, about thirteen to the square centimetre, but still wide areas without temperature sensations intervene. While, then, the physicist assures us that cold is nothing but the absence of heat so far as energy is concerned, it is undoubted that, physiologically and psychologically, cold is just as truly a distinct sensation as warmth. Not only is it proved by mapping the spots that the temperature senses are distinct, but the result is confirmed by a number of related facts, (i) Stimulation of a well-marked cold spot always gives cold only, no matter what the source. Pressure, the electric current, even the warmth obtained by concentrating the sun's rays upon the spot by a small lens, all give the same sensation of cold. Warm spots may also be aroused by inadequate stimuli but they require greater intensity than the cold spots. (2) Certain parts of the body, the cornea of the eye, e.g., lack warm spots altogether, and there are relatively large areas where cold spots are lacking. (3) Certain chemicals, e.g. menthol for cold, carbon dioxide for warm, will excite one sort of spot, but not the other. All these facts go to show that cold and warmth are independent senses with independent nerve ends in the skin. Physiological Temperature Scale. The response of the nerve ends to the different changes in temperature is indicated in the accompanying diagram. The physiological zero point lies somewhere in the neighbourhood of 30 C. The variation is from 28 or below to 34 or above, according to the temperature to which the body has been adjusted. At any one time the limit will be only a fraction of a degree. Below this point all temperatures excite the cold organ ; above, all excite the organ of warmth. Very low temperatures, from 12 downward, also excite the nerves of pain which give the sensation of burning or biting cold. Above the neutral point, at about 45 C., warm becomes hot. In consciousness it is marked off from warm by a very sharp line. Physiologically, the difference is due to the presence of the sensation of cold. Hot is a compound of warm and cold. This excitation of cold spots by heat has been called the paradoxical cold sensation. Beyond this, at some 50 C., pain is also aroused and gives burning heat. All the temperature effects are produced by combinations of the excitations of the three sense endings of cold, warmth, and pain.

Cutaneous Sensations from Mechanical Stimuli. Two sense qualities may be excited mechanically, pressure and pain. Somewhat the same differentiation must be made between them as between the temperature senses. Gentle pressure upon the skin with a sharply pointed wooden rod or a short hair is felt only here and there. These points are known as the pressure spots. They are found closer together on the average than either class of temperature spots. They vary from about nine to some three hundred to the centimetre.

These pressure spots are relatively easy to excite, they are affected by hairs that exert a pressure of little more than a milligram. The pain spots are much closer together and require greater pressure for their stimulation. They are most easily found by pressing upon the different points on the skin with a well-sharpened horsehair. It has been shown that 200 or more points to the centimetre give rise to the pain sensations. That pain is not merely a more intense pressure, as was thought for a long time, is proved (i) by the fact that a pressure spot always responds more quickly than a pain spot, and (2) that certain parts of the body are sensitive to pressure but not to pain, e.g. the inner membrane of the cheek, while the cornea of the eye always responds with pain, never with pressure, no matter how slight the excitation. Again, (3) certain drugs destroy one sense quality and leave the other unaffected, e.g. cocaine when first applied destroys the sensitiveness to pain but not to pressure; a rare drug, saponin, destroys sensitiveness to pressure but not to pain. It is now generally held that pain and pressure are distinct senses with distinct kinds of sensory endings in the skin.

The Organs of Cutaneous Sensation. Pressure and pain may with some certainty be referred to particular sense-organs. The nerves of pressure for the greater part of the body are the nerves at the roots of the hairs, as illustrated in the accompanying diagram. On the palms of the hands and the soles of the feet where hairs are lacking, the organ of pressure is the touch corpuscle of Meissner found in the papillae of the skin. (Figure 14.) The nerves of pain are the free nerve ends that extend into the outer skin. They too may be seen in Figure 13. That pain has a very superficial organ is evident from the fact that an acid will give rise to pain before it affects any other of the sense ends. It needs only to eat into the most superficial layer of the skin, and the sensation of pain is aroused. The organs of warmth and cold have not been made out with any certainty. The skin, then, is not a single sense-organ, but a mosaic in which four separate senses may be distinguished, each with a special end-organ. These are pressure, pain, warmth, and cold. With their combinations they give rise to all knowledge of the outer world obtained through the skin.

The Gustatory Sensations. The principles established for touch can be readily transferred to taste. As every one knows, the chief organ of taste is the tongue. More particularly the sense endings of taste are to be found on the sides of the foliate, the fungiform, and the circumvallate papillae on the tongue. Essentially the papillae are folds of skin on the surface of the tongue. The sense endings proper are the taste beakers which are arranged along the sides of the depressions formed by the papillae. The beaker itself, as may be seen from the diagram, is a group of nerve ends interspersed with supporting cells. The whole looks not unlike a flower bud. The papillae are scattered fairly thickly over the tip, sides, and back of the tongue. They can be seen on the tip of the tongue as little bright red depressions. Four separate taste qualities are distinguished, sweet, salt, sour, and bitter. The different qualities cannot be so easily connected with different spots on the tongue as can the touch qualities with spots on the skin.

The taste-buds are well concealed in the papillae and a single papilla often possesses more than one quality. It is assumed, however, that each taste beaker responds to but one quality, although several beakers of different kinds may be present in the same papilla. In general, sweet is perceived on the tip, sour on the sides of the tongue, bitter on the back, while salt is pretty evenly distributed. At the most this arrangement is only partly carried out, and there are many exceptions. The best evidence for the doctrine of specific energies is the fact that different drugs dull or destroy the capacity to discriminate different tastes in different degrees. Cocaine, for example, first destroys the sensitiveness to bitter and affects the other tastes more slowly. Gymnemic acid first destroys the sensitiveness to sweet. The time required for the nerves to respond is also different for each taste. These facts together seem sufficient to justify the statement that the four taste qualities have each a special sort of taste beaker, although several different sorts of beakers are usually found in a single papilla.

Combination of Taste with Other Sensations. One may be inclined to question the statement that only four taste qualities can be distinguished, for certainly ordinary experience seems to show a large number. This objection must be admitted. The other qualities are, however, not tastes but additions from other senses. The most evident are the ordinary cutaneous sensations. Temperature seems to modify taste, as is seen in the peculiar effect of the cold of ice cream or the heat of coffee. Melted cream seems to have a different taste from the frozen; cold or lukewarm coffee, from hot. Roughness or smoothness adds a quality not easily distinguished from taste. Witness the difference between granulated and pulverised sugar. Other instances will be recalled by the practical housewife. By far the most important additions are those that are made by smell. Most of what we seem to taste we really smell. All of the delicate tastes, so called, are largely odours that reach the sensory region in the nose by way of the inner air passages. That much of the taste of food is really received through the nose is evident from the fact that a cold destroys nearly all taste. Moreover, if the nostrils be closed, substances will be confused that ordinarily are easily distinguished. Cinnamon is said not to be distinguishable from flour under these circumstances. In short, in what is ordinarily called taste we have a mixture of the four simple tastes with the qualities of cutaneous sensation and with odour. The stimulus for taste is some chemical dissolved in a liquid and brought into contact with the taste-buds by being caught in the papillae. A substance to be tasted must be dissolved either before it is taken into the mouth or by the saliva.

Sensations of Smell. Of the sense of smell we know practically nothing. All that can be determined is that the organ of smell is the olfactory membrane in the upper nasal cavity. The sense nerves are simple cells with hairlike projections that come to the surface of the membrane between supporting cells. In their structure they are the simplest of the sense-organs. The stimulus for odours is some chemical substance carried to the olfactory membrane in particles. It produces some chemical change in the sense ending and this starts the nervous impulse toward the brain.

No definite answer can be given to the question of the number of different organs and the number of different olfactory qualities. Zwaardemaker has suggested that there are nine, but his results cannot be accepted as conclusive. Certain facts connected with pathology and with fatigue indicate that there are different organs for the different odours. In diseased conditions a patient may lack one class of odours alone. Also the nose may be fatigued for one odour and remain sensitive to others. After one has smelled camphor for some time, alcohol will not be noticed, but iodine will still have its usual effect. While these experiments are suggestive of the presence of distinct sense-organs for different odours, they have not been carried far enough to determine the number of qualities. The uncertainties of science are reflected in the popular speech. There are no names for odours other than those of the objects that give rise to them. The difficulty is increased by the fact that tactual and taste qualities mix with the olfactory. The sweet odour of chloroform is really a taste. The odour of ammonia is largely pain, and the resulting holding of the breath adds a feeling of suffocation. Zwaardemaker classes as nauseating certain odours that receive their peculiar quality from the incipient retching reflexes excited in the throat. Of smell we know only that the organ is simple and has its seat in the upper nasal passages, that there are distinguishable qualities, but that their number is uncertain, and that smell combines with taste and tactual impressions to produce very complex fusions.

Hearing. The first of the so-called higher senses is hearing. It is higher in its importance for the mental life, in the degree of complexity of the organ, and in the richness of its qualities. In each of the higher senses we must consider the sense excitation at three different stages: (a) the physical stimulus, (b) the change excited in the sense-organ, and (c) the resulting conscious qualities. The stimulus for hearing, physics teaches, is vibration in the air. The wave-lengths vary in three ways: in the rate of their vibration, in the distance through which the particles vibrate or the amplitude of vibration, and in the form or complexity of the wave. The rate of vibration corresponds to the pitch of the tone, the amplitude corresponds to the intensity of the tone, and the form to the timbre or tone colour. The form of the wave gives the tone of each instrument its character, e.g. [the C of the violin differs from the C of the piano only in its wave form.

Structure of the Ear. The organ of hearing is the ear. The ear is for convenience of description divided into three parts, the external ear, the middle ear or drum, and the inner ear or labyrinth. The outer ear is the trumpet of cartilage, popularly called the ear, together with the tube that extends into the skull. Its only function is to gather the sound-waves and bring them to the drum. The middle ear extends from the membrane of the drum backward to the bony inner ear. In essentials the middle ear is an irregularly shaped hollow in the skull separated from the outer world by the drum membrane, and connected with the throat by the Eustachian tube. So far as it concerns us, it is a cavity across which extends a chain of three bones, the hammer, anvil, and stirrup, from the membrane of the drum to the oval window of the labyrinth. The drum head is a membrane stretched obliquely across the opening of the ear. On its inner surface is the handle of the hammer. The head of the hammer fits into the anvil, and this is attached to the head of the stirrup. Each bone receives its name from its shape. When a sound-wave strikes against the membrane of the drum, the membrane is forced inward slightly, and this inward motion carries the handle of the hammer with it. The hammer and the other bones revolve about a ligament attached to the top of the middle ear. The pressure of the air wave upon the drum membrane turns the bones about this as a pivot, and the stirrup communicates the motion to the liquid of the inner ear. When the pressure of the air is relaxed, the membrane of the drum returns to its original position or a little beyond and carries with it the chain of bones and the foot of the stirrup. The foot of the stirrup fits closely into the oval window of the inner ear, and the joint is closed by a delicate membrane that makes the whole water-tight. While this is the ordinary course of stimulation, high tones apparently pass through the bones of the head. In some cases, too, hearing is normal when the bones have been destroyed by disease.

The Mechanics of the Cochlear Vibration. The movement of the stirrup transmits the excitation to the inner ear, the point where hearing as a nervous process begins. The auditory portion of the ear is the cochlea. The cochlea, as its name implies, is a tube coiled up like a snaii shell for two and a half turns. It is divided down the middle by a ridge of bone and a thin membrane known as the basilar membrane. Figure 18 shows a cross section of the tube of the cochlea. One of the first questions in connection with the action of the ear is how it is possible for the vibrations of the stirrup and of the oval window to have any effect upon the liquid that fills the cochlea and the inner ear. The vibration of the liquid is rendered possible by the round window, an opening in the bony wall, closed by a delicate membrane. It is below the oval window, at the point marked Pt in Figure 17. Pressure upon the stirrup at the oval window is transmitted through the entire length of the cochlear fluid to the round window. The membrane gives and thus makes possible the vibration of the fluid. The vibrations of the outer air push the membrane of the drum in and out. The drum head starts an oscillation of the chain of bones, the stirrup presses against the liquid of the inner ear, and this is permitted to vibrate by the delicate membrane of the round window. The Helmholtz Theory of Hearing. All of this is only preparation for the excitation of the nerve of hearing. The nerve of hearing ends in connection with the fibres of the basilar membrane. The exact connection between the nerve fibres and the fibres of the basilar membrane has not been altogether made out, but nerve fibres come through the spiral of bone and end in connection with hairs upon the basilar membrane. These hairs are excited in some way by the vibrations of the basilar membrane and they, in turn, excite the auditory nerve. The most generally accepted theory of hearing was suggested by Helmholtz, who regarded the basilar membrane as a series of strings like the strings of a piano. Each string is tuned to some one of the audible tones. Whenever the tone to which a string is tuned is represented in the vibrations of the liquid of the inner ear, that string is thrown into sympathetic vibration. The vibration of the fibre starts a nervous impulse in the nerve connected with it, and this impulse is transmitted to the brain through a series of neurones. The sensation of sound makes its appearance upon the excitation of cells in the temporal lobes of the cortex. The process of exciting a vibration in the fibre is very similar to that which accompanies speaking into a piano when the keys are held down. When you speak, the strings tuned to your voice are excited sympathetically and can be heard after you finish speaking. In the basilar membrane the fibres are said to number between eighteen and twenty thousand, while the tones that can be distinguished by the ordinary ear have been computed at approximately eleven thousand. The number of strings is then sufficient for the tones that may be heard. The case for the Helmholtz theory is strengthened by the limited number of tones that may be appreciated. The upper and lower limit of hearing may be explained by the limited number of fibres. The lowest tone that may be heard has approximately sixteen vibrations per second; the highest varies from about thirty thousand to forty-five thousand per second. Another strong bit of evidence for the theory is that after death there have been found in individuals, who were deaf to certain notes of the scale only, regions of the basilar membrane in which disease had destroyed the fibres. The objections to the Helmholtz theory are to be found primarily in the physical improbability that fibres as short as those of the basilar membrane from 0.48 to 0.04 mm. in length, should be able to vibrate in sympathy with the lower tones that are heard. Several authorities have asserted that the fibres are too rigid to vibrate to faint tones. Whatever the objections, the Helmholtz theory is the one at present generally accepted.

Complex Tones and Noises. If we may assume that the simple tone corresponds to the excitation of a single fibre of the basilar membrane, it seems probable that the complex tones are due to the excitation of several fibres. A complex tone like a note of the piano would be made up of one tone, the fundamental, and of others of a rate two, three, four, and other even multiples of that rate. The timbre of the tone varies with the number and character of the overtones. In the violin tone the high overtones predominate; in the piano tone the overtones decrease in strength as they increase in pitch. In the ear each of these overtones is taken up by a different fibre and is carried to the cortex separately. In consciousness they ordinarily fuse to form a single quality, although by close attention the elements may be distinguished. What then in the air is fused into a single wave of characteristic form is analysed by the basilar membrane into its separate elements and reunited in consciousness to form a complex tone. Noises of the continuous kind may be regarded as very complex tones made up of many vibration rates that have no simple arithmetical relation to each other. Each is received by a separate fibre and transmitted to the cortex, where the result is a jumble of sensations. The single crash or crack, the second form of noise, arises from a twitch of the fibre of the membrane that does not persist long enough to give a full tone. Any tone will give a single puff of noise if it is permitted to affect the ear during but two full vibrations. In either case the noise is heard by the same part of the ear that perceives the tone, the fibres of the basilar membrane in the cochlea.

Summary. In short, vibration in the air is received by the membrane of the drum and is transmitted to the oval window through the chain of small bones. At the oval window the oscillations of the bones produce vibrations in the liquid of the inner ear. The several tones are received by the different fibres of the basilar membrane attuned to them. The vibration of the fibres excites a change in the auditory nerve, and the nervous impulse is carried to the cortex where sensation arises. It is still a question whether we are to assume that each fibre has its own quality of sensation and that there are therefore eleven thousand distinct sensations and eleven thousand distinct sorts of nerve fibre, or whether the different fibres are grouped in some way in larger classes. The objection to the assumption of so many distinct nerve processes and sensations is that it gives hearing a disproportionate number of qualities when compared with the other senses. More cogent is the argument that notes an octave apart seem more alike than notes within the octave. Two C's are more likely to be confused than C and G, or C and B. But if we assume that there are fewer simple primary qualities than there are distinguishable tones, there is as yet no agreement as to what these primary qualities are, or how many there are of them.

Visual Sensations. By far the most important sense is sight. We trust vision above the other senses in perception, and most people think in images. When we recall an object, we remember how it looks rather than any other of its sensory qualities. In discussing sight we have again to consider the three phases of the visual process, external stimulus, sense-organ, and sensation. There is in vision rather greater dissimilarity between the different phases than in hearing. k The physical stimulus is a vibration in the hypothetical ether. The physicist tells us that the ether vibration varies in the same three ways as the sound vibration. Changes in rate or in length of the wave give quality ; changes in the amplitude of vibration give intensity ; while changes in complexity give greys and colours of different degrees of saturation, varying mixtures of greys with colours. The rate or length corresponds to colour. Red has a wave-length of some 800-833 n n (thousandths of thousandths of a millimetre), violet a wave-length of less than half, or 380-400 ^ /*. The colours between have intermediate wave-lengths. Change in amplitude produces varying brightnesses, from black through the colours (what colour depends upon the wave-length of the light) to white. Mixtures of certain light-waves give white or grey, and of others give different spectral colours according to the wave-lengths that are mixed. In any case it is evident that the qualities of the things as we see them are not at all like the vibrations which cause them. There is nothing in the colours to indicate that violet is a more rapid vibration than red. There are many disparities even in relations. Red and violet are more unlike physically, but the sensations are more alike than those of red and yellow, or of red and any intermediate colour nearer red in vibration rate.

The Structure of the Eye. The key to the difference between the physical stimulus and the qualities of colour must lie in the eye. That vibrations of different lengths give similar sensations must be due to the similarity of the physiological processes which they arouse in the retina. The eye can be best understood if it is compared to a camera. Three parts are essential to a camera: the box or container, the lens, and the sensitive plate. The box or frame of the eye is to be found in the sclerotic coat, the tough membrane that holds the parts together, and is kept distended into a sphere by the pressure of the liquid within. The organ is mounted in its socket, a conical hollow in the skull. It is held in its socket by threads of connective tissue and is turned by three pairs of muscles. Within the sclerotic coat is first the choroid coat which nourishes the eye and has some nerves and muscular fibres ; within that is the retina which corresponds to the sensitive plate. The lens system of the eye is made up of two parts, the cornea and the crystalline lens. The cornea is really only a part of the sclerotic coat which projects slightly and forms in consequence a stronger lens. It is transparent instead of white and opaque as is the sclerotic coat. The lens is just back of the iris, the membrane which by its pigment gives the characteristic colour to the eye. It is attached to the choroid coat by a ligament, the suspensory ligament. That in turn is connected with the ciliary muscle which forms part of the choroid coat. In front of the lens lies the anterior chamber filled with a liquid much like water, as its name, aqueous humour, implies. Back of the lens is a large chamber, filled with the jellylike vitreous humour.

The Eye as an Optical Instrument. The rays of light are bent at the front surface of the cornea, and at the two surfaces of the lens. The whole system has the same effect as if the light came through a single pinhole 15 mm. in front of the retina or 7 mm. back of the cornea. The size of the image of any object thrown upon the retina will be found by drawing a line from the sides of the object to the retina through this nodal point where the pinhole might be. One extremely important function of the lens is the accommodation or focussing of the eye. A camera that cannot be adjusted for different distances is of little value since pictures could be taken at one distance only. An eye with a fixed system of lenses could see objects at but one distance. The eye is accommodated for different distances by changing the shape of the lens. The lens is relatively flat when one is looking at a distant object, but becomes thick and well rounded when one looks at a near object. This thickening of the lens may be seen if one will look across another's eye as he looks at objects at different distances. When the eye is adjusted for distance, the iris is flat; when it is focussed on a finger held close, the iris is pushed forward by the lens. The shape of the lens is changed by the contraction of the ciliary muscle. When looking at a near object the muscle contracts and permits the lens to take on its normal, rather round shape. When the muscle is relaxed, the lens is tightly stretched by the suspensory ligament and so becomes flatter and thinner. (See diagram.) Another adjustment of the eye that may be mentioned is the change in the size of the pupil. The iris is really a part of the choroid coat that might have been drawn away from the attachment to the cornea. The pupil is the hole in the iris. When the eye is in the dark, the muscles that hold the pupil open are contracted ; when the light is bright, the sphincter of the iris contracts, the other muscles relax, and the pupil becomes small. The dilation permits a larger amount of light to enter the eye, the contraction protects the eye against too bright light.

The real seeing portion of the eye is the retina. The retina is a part of the brain that has come to the surface in the course of development. It is made up of three layers of neurones. The structures that receive the light are the rods and cones. These are farthest away from the light, nearest the .choroid coat. There is an intermediate and an inner neurone layer. The axones of the inner layer of so-called large ganglion cells combine to form the optic nerve. In exciting the eye a ray of light traverses the outer neurones as a physical impulse (vibration in the ether), strikes upon the rods and cones, is there transformed into a nervous impulse and transferred, first to the intermediate bipolar cells, then to the outermost large ganglion cells, and finally is carried back to the brain. Thus the nervous impulse goes back over part of the course that was traversed originally by the light-wave.

Fovea and Blind Spot. At the centre of the retina is a small depression or pit known as the fovea. In and about this the retina has a yellow pigment which gives the name, yellow spot, to the general region. Owing to the pit the light suffers less absorption than at other portions of the retina in reaching the sensitive structures. In the fovea there are only cones, and they are more closely set than elsewhere. The lack of absorption and the slight distance that separates the cones make the fovea the point of clearest vision. From the fovea outward the cones decrease in number until on the periphery they practically disappear. The entrance of the optic nerve is not provided with rods and cones and in consequence is not sensitive to light. It is what is known as the blind spot. We know, then, that the vibrations in the ether come to the rods and cones in the deepest coat of the retina. There in some way they are transformed into nerve impulses, pass from one to another of the three neurones in the eye, and then to the basal ganglia and cortex.

Vision a Photo-chemical Process. The first question of function is how ether vibrations are changed to nerve impulses. An analogy for this is found in the action of light in producing chemical changes in the photographic plate. It is possible to observe directly changes of this kind in the visual purple found in the outer portions of the rods. This bleaches when exposed to light and becomes purple when the eye is kept in the dark. The bleaching of the visual purple has, however, only an indirect relation to seeing. The increased sensitiveness that comes after a long period in the dark is due to the effect of the visual purple, but ordinary daylight vision is practically unaffected by it.

Primary Colours and Their Combinations. For an explanation of the action of the retina we are compelled to rely upon indirect evidence obtained by experiment and observation. We may be guided again by the doctrine of specific energies. There are apparently six specific qualities from which all visual processes must be derived. These are the two brightnesses, white and black, and four colours, red, yellow, green, and blue. The spectral qualities and purple are obtained from the four primary colours. Orange is a combination of red and yellow and may be produced by combining red and yellow lights in the right proportions. When a spectrally pure ray of orange light falls upon the retina, it excites the two responses red and yellow in different degrees, and the results of the two physiological processes combine in the brain or in consciousness to produce the single sensation of orange. Similarly, yellow and green combine to produce canary yellow, green and blue to give robin's egg blue and other shades. Finally the circle is completed by the fact that red combines with blue to give first indigo, then violet and the whole series of purples that fill the gap between the ends of the spectrum. It is interesting to note that, while all the other mixed colours may be produced either by having a single pure light-wave fall upon the retina or by combining two lights in proper proportions, the purples can be induced only by combining -lights. There is no single ether-wave that gives a purple colour. Nevertheless, purple is quite as unitary in sensation as any of the colours due to a single wave-length.

The relation of the spectral colours to the simple colours may be illustrated by a square. (See diagram, Fig. 21.) The corners represent the simple colours, the sides the combinations that may be produced from them. With each of these colours a brightness is combined. These series of brightnesses extend from black to white. All wave-lengths excite the brightnesses, and the quality of the brightness depends

. ,., PI

upon the amplitude of the wave, not at all upon the length. Each of the waves at a certain moderate intensity excites brightness in very slight degree, colour in larger amount. This is the pure spectral colour. A faint red light appears black because it affects the brightness organ only ; as it grows brighter it becomes first dark brown, then dark red, then red, then bright red and pink, and with very great intensities approaches white. Where the colour is present in greatest propertion, it is said to be saturated. As the grey becomes more and more prominent, the colour is said to be less and less saturated. These degrees of saturation are represented by the radiating lines on the square of the colour pyramid.

Complementary Colours. One result of mixing colours, the phenomenon of complementary colours, is particularly important for theory. When colours at opposite corners of our colour square are mixed in suitable proportions, they give, not an intermediate colour, but brightness. Apparently the complementary colours produce exactly opposite effects upon the substance sensitive to them: each destroys the effect of the other. When they thus neutralise each other, the only effect is to excite the organ of brightness, and the result is white, grey, or black, according to the intensity of the colours. When any two colours are mixed, there is always partial cancellation, and the resulting colours are always less saturated than the components would be. If all the colours of the sun's rays are mixed, the components all cancel each other and the result is the white or slightly yellowish daylight. We may represent the greys upon our diagram by a line BW through the centre of the square extending above and below. The fact that each light ray at a slight intensity excites only grey or black may be indicated by connecting each corner of the square with the ends of the line. It seems probable, too, that the lights in maximum intensity excite only the brightness organ. This is represented by connecting each corner of the square with the top of the brightness line as well. Thus drawn, every point on the pyramid inside and out represents some colour or shade, and all visual qualities are represented.

After-images. The fact of complementariness makes it probable that the colour qualities of each pair have their seat in a single organ. This assumption is furthered by other facts of vision. Thus if one looks at any colour or any brightness for a few seconds and then looks at another surface, the complementary colour will be seen. Red gives an after-image of green, yellow an after-image of blue, and vice versa. It is assumed that the after-image is due to the fact that when the organ is excited in one way, recovery from the excitation gives the complementary colour.

Colour-Blindness. Even stronger evidence for assigning each pair to a single organ is derived from the phenomenon of colour-blindness and the distribution of the colours upon the retina. Individuals are found who lack altogether the red and green components of colour, but none who can be shown to be altogether lacking in one alone. If one is colour-blind, it is either to red and to green or to all colours, never to red or to green alone. Approximately three per cent of the male population is colour-blind in sufficient degree to be uncertain in the discrimination of red from green. Since for some reason the railway and navigation authorities hit upon these two colours for their signals, it is essential that all colour-blind men be excluded from their employ, hence the careful examination to which they subject applicants for work. The phenomena of colour-blindness are present in every normal eye. In a band about the centre red and green cannot be seen. Beyond this band the eye is totally colour-blind; only black and white are appreciated there. This outer colour-blindness may be demonstrated by moving a small bit of paper of some colour out toward the periphery of the field of vision while the eye is kept fixed upon a point. If the colour be primary, it will turn to grey when it changes at all in quality. If it be a composite colour like orange, it will change first to yellow and then, when it gets beyond the blue-yellow zone, to grey.

The Colour Pairs Seen with a Single Organ. These phenomena taken together indicate that colour qualities are connected in pairs with their organs. Red and green have a single organ as have blue and yellow, black and white. The process that gives red is in some way opposed to the process that gives green. Yellow is opposed to blue in the same way. There is less evidence that black and white are opposed, but that is still the usual assumption. When opposed processes are excited, they destroy each other ; when one is excited and the stimulus withdrawn, the other colour makes its appearance. When one colour disappears or is not found, the other also is not present. No altogether satisfactory explanation of what the change is, or of what the nature of the opposition may be, has been found, but that the process is a chemical one, and that the two directions are opposed is generally accepted.

Colour Contrast. One other phenomenon related to complementariness and after-images is contrast. If two complementary colours are placed side by side, each becomes brighter because of the presence of the other. If a colour is seen against a grey background, it will be surrounded by a fringe of the complementary colour. Red will give a green, blue a yellow, and so on. Thecontrast effect may be observed if a small patch of grey paper be placed upon a coloured surface. The effect will be increased if a bit of translucent paper be put overthe colour and the square of grey. Contrast colours are also very clearly seen when a shadow is thrown upon a coloured field, as when two shadows of the same object are cast by different coloured lights. The explanation of contrast is probably to be found in the opposition between the chemical processes excited by complementary colours. When a surface is stimulated by one light, the opposite process is induced in the surrounding areas of the retina.

The Colourless Visual Sensations. Whenever light which does not affect the colour processes stimulates the retina, brightness or black-white sensations result. All light affects the blackwhite organ, but when the colour processes are also stimulated they are appreciated only as they make the colour brighter or darker or reduce its saturation. Brightness alone is appreciated, as has been seen, when complementary colours cancel each other ; in the eyes of the totally colour-blind and on the periphery of the normal eye ; when the lights are too faint to excite the colour processes ;

and when the coloured objects are very small or the stimulus has a very short duration. In the dark all colours become greys of different shades. Very small patches of colour are also grey. A coloured object at a great distance becomes a grey of a brightness that corresponds to the; intensity of the light. It is for this reason that very brilliant colours may be used in the uniforms of troops. When seen from a distance these stimulate a very small patch on the retina, and if they are of the brightness of the surrounding natural objects will not be observed. The light blue of the French uniforms, the khaki of the British and American troops, and the light grey of the German are equally difficult to detect at a distance. When different colours of slight extent are interspersed or larger patches side by side are seen from a great distance, they combine just as they do when mixed by rotation. Thus the small bits in a mosaic, or the different coloured threads in worsted combine to produce uniform shades.

At present all agree that there are two organs for brightness, one for faint and another for bright or moderate lights. The faint lights affect the rods alone, and the brighter lights, the cones. The light that is noticed at night after one has been long in the open excites the rods. The greater sensitiveness of the eye after long adaptation to the dark comes from the increase in the amount of visual purple which sensitises the rods, as sensitive plates may be increased in sensitiveness by the application of proper chemicals.

Summary of the Facts of Vision. In brief we may assume that there are six processes in the retina from which all of the visual qualities are compounded. These six qualities are grouped in pairs, red and green, blue and yellow, and black and white, and each pair finds physiological explanation in opposed processes in the same substance. When the two processes are equally excited simultaneously, there is no effect upon the colour organ, but only the resulting effect upon the brightness organ. When one process has been aroused, its opposite succeeds it after a brief persistence of the first. In colour-blindness the red-green organ is most often lacking. Next most frequently wanting is the yellow-blue organ, while the blackwhite organ is always present unless the eye be totally blind. It is interesting to note that the manifold wave-lengths in ether affect the retina in but six different ways. However, what is lost in complexity in the retina is got back with interest in consciousness. The six processes by their combinations give rise to from thirty to fifty thousand distinguishable qualities. It is interesting to note that the physiologically complex colours are little if any less simple as conscious qualities than the simple physiological colours. So true is this that just what are the simple physiological qualities is still a matter of dispute. Each colour theory has a different set of primary colours and the only hope of agreement depends, not upon introspective analysis, but upon physiological experiment.

Kinaesthetic Sensations. In addition to the traditional five senses of man, many new sense qualities and sense-organs have been discovered relatively recently. Most important of these is the sensation complex that tells us of the movement of the body, of weight, and resistance. When one moves the hand, one knows at once the amount and direction of the movement even with the eyes closed. Pathological cases are found, however, in which the patient is unconscious of movement and of weight. When he moves, he has no idea that he has moved, and he has no idea of the position of his members when they are at rest. These cases emphasise the fact that the normal man must have some special sense-organ for the detection of movements. Investigation has shown that the sensations come from organs in the muscles and tendons. In the tissue of muscles and tendons are sense-organs not unlike some of the organs found in the skin. When the muscle is contracted, the cells of the muscle become shorter and thicker. This change exerts pressure upon and stimulates the sensory ends between the muscle cells. For example, whenever the arm is moved, there is a contraction in one set of muscles and a relaxation in the opposing set. In one set of muscles the sense-organs will be compressed, in the other set the pressure will be relaxed. Each movement and each position has a complex of increasing and decreasing stimulations which is characteristic for that movement in quality and intensity. Strains and weights when the arm is not moved reveal themselves in similar pressure exerted upon the sense-organs of the tendons in addition to that upon the muscle-organs. It is by these organs that we become aware of the fundamental physical properties of the world, of motion, of energy, and of mass.

The Static Sense. One of the most interesting of the recently discovered sense-organs is the organ of the static sense found in the semicircular canals and neighbouring organs of the ear. Hairs project into the liquid of the semicircular canals. When the liquid is disturbed by the motion of the body, the hairs are moved and they in turn excite the nerves connected with them. These impulses are transmitted to the motor neurones that control the movement of the body, and movements are made which adjust the members to the new position or bring the body back to the upright. When the organs of the labyrinth are injured, proper motor adjustments are difficult or impossible. An animal with injured semicircular canals will not be able to stand, or at least to stand steady. When the organs are lacking in man, reflex eye-movements are wanting. It is, perhaps, a question whether the static sense is a real sense, for we become aware of its action only indirectly through the movements it induces or, when the excitation is more intense, by the disturbances of the alimentary tract that give rise to the sensation of giddiness. When still more intense, the stimuli from these organs call out the more active phenomenon of vomiting involved in seasickness. What the immediate quality of the sensation from the static sense may be, is not known.

Organic Sensations. Many other sense-organs and sense qualities are known less definitely. The sensations from them have not been satisfactorily analysed, and their organs are not well known from physiological experiments. We ordinarily group them into a single mass of organic sensation. Of these hunger has been shown recently to be due to the reflex contraction of the walls of the stomach. Thirst has its seat in the upper throat or back of the mouth. It is probable that there are special organs that inform us of circulatory disturbances, of the respiratory processes, and of many others less well distinguished. One is aware of feeling well or feeling ill, and if one will examine the experience more closely, vague sensory qualities may be analysed from the mass. It is to be hoped that these complexes of organic sensation may some day be analysed and their sense-organs determined. Until that time we can merely refer to the mass and say nothing more.

Summary of Sense Qualities. If we sum up the results of this discussion of the qualities of sensation, we find that there are relatively few simple qualities received from sense-organs and, regarded from the physiological side, relatively few sorts of sense endings. A table will show the number of qualities from each sense.

Qualities from the skin 4

Qualities of taste 4

Qualities of smell uncertain (9?)

Qualities of hearing uncertain (11,000?)

Qualities of sight 6

Qualities of kinaesthetic sensations . . . . i or 2

Qualities of organic sensations ioori2(?)

In all there are but forty or fifty different sorts of nerve ends from which all the varieties of our conscious qualities are derived. We might obtain a much larger total if we considered the number of qualities that could be recognised by unaided observation as distinct in consciousness. Then we should have 11,000 tones, some 40,000 colour qualities, unlimited tactual qualities, the different complexes of taste and smell, one for each distinguishable substance, to say nothing of the vast number of organic complexes that change with each of our moods, and with our condition of health. Enumeration on this basis has never been attempted except for sight and sound, but it is probable that the other senses give similar large numbers of sensations or complexes of sensations.

Intensities of Sensation. One other aspect or attribute of sensation important in practice is intensity. The intensity of sensation is dependent upon the intensity of the stimulus. The more energy acts upon the senseorgan, the greater the intensity. While intensities play a very large part in our life, they are not easily described or even thought of in absolute terms. They cannot be easily remembered. We have no accurate names for the degrees of intensity in our non-scientific vocabulary. Pounds and kilograms, ergs and horse-power, are obviously artificial units and correspond to nothing that we can picture easily. For everyday usage slight, moderate, and intense are the only terms available to designate intensities. The difficulty in description and discussion is all the more marked because experiments show that there is no direct relation between the intensity of the physical stimulus and the resulting consciousness. As nearly as one can make out a thousand ounces do not give a thousand times as much weight sensation as one ounce. Sensations seem to increase in amount very much more slowly than stimuli increase in intensity, if one may speak of the amount of sensation at all. Intensities of sensation cannot be described by words as we describe qualities of sensation, and they cannot be measured by measuring the intensity of the physical stimulus and assuming that the sensation will harmonise with that. Both the simple methods of approach fail us.

Weber's Law. The attempt to discover some means of dealing with the intensities of sensation led indirectly to the establishment of a law of relation between stimulus and sensation which is known from the name of the man who first noticed the relation as Weber's law. This asserts that the least noticeable difference between two stimuli is not constant for all intensities, but varies with the intensity of the stimuli compared. Thus in lifting weights one can distinguish between an ounce and an ounce and a fortieth. But if a pound be the standard, one cannot notice the addition of a fortieth of an ounce ; a fortieth of a pound must be added. In any sense-department it has been found that an addition to be just noticed must be some fraction of the stimulus present, rather than an absolute amount. The fraction that must be added is different for each sense. It varies from about one one-hundredth for sight to about one-third or one-fourth for smell. Several different formulae have been used to express the relation. Perhaps the best known and the simplest is that sensations increase in arithmetical ratio, as stimuli increase in geometrical ratio. The stimulus must always be multiplied by some fraction, for passive pressure, e.g. by fourthirds (|) to obtain the next unit of sensation.

Deviations from Weber's Law. The most obvious outcome of the law in everyday life is that only relative differences can be appreciated. One is aware of the relative difference in brightness between the black of the print and the white of the page, but is not aware of the absolute change in the brightness of each between noon and evening. Were the law to hold absolutely, the light might fade and we be unaware of it. The fraction that can be noticed is not absolutely constant, however, but holds only for the middle ranges of intensity. As the light grows dim, the just distinguishable differences must increase, until at twilight white must be more than sixty times as bright as the black of the print to be readily noticed as different from it. Similarly, as the absolute brightness is increased, the fraction increases or, put the other way, the relative sensitivity decreases. Slight differences are not so easily noticed in the full glare of the sun as in diffuse daylight. One cannot read ordinary print at night or with ease in the glare of the noonday sun.

The Sensation Threshold. Not only may differences between intensities be too slight to be noticed, but stimuli may be too faint to give rise to any sensation whatever. As one moves a watch away from the ear, the sound becomes fainter and fainter until it finally disappears. One may touch a pressure spot on the skin with a hair so soft that it gives no sensation. The intensity that can be barely noticed, that first gives rise to a sensation, is called the liminal or threshold stimulus. At the other extreme it is probable that a stimulus may be too intense to be felt. Probably, however, intensities that do not destroy the sense-organ merely tend to be lost in the accompanying pain ; they do not actually disappear. The upper limen is of relatively little importance, and there is little known about it because of the injury which work upon it might do to the sense-organ.

QUESTIONS

1. What is a sensation? Is it a physiological or psychological process?

2. What determines the quality of a sensation? Does it depend more upon the stimulus or upon the organ stimulated? Is there sound when there is no ear to hear?

3. What is the physiological zero point? Is it always the same? Is it the same for the exposed hand and for the elbow which has just been uncovered?

4. What elementary sensations are excited when the hand is put into water at 48 C.? at 10 C.? What is the paradoxical cold sensation?

5. Name the components of the 'taste' of ice cream; of hot coffee; of pepper.

6. Describe the action of the three small bones of the ear during hearing.

7. Is the basilar membrane broader near the oval window or near the apex of the cochlea?

8. What is a noise: (a) physically? (c) physiologically?

9. What is an octave? an overtone? How are the C of the violin and of the piano different?

10. State the Helmholtz theory of hearing. What facts tend to prove it; what to disprove it?

11. Are the ganglion cells or the rods and cones nearer the vitreous humour? nearer the pupil?

12. Why is vision clearest at the fovea?

13. Describe the different forms of colour-blindness. What sensation does the colour-blind man receive from a primary red? from orange?

14. Under what circumstances does the normal eye see grey? What different organs are excited when we see grey?

15. What is the visual purple? Where is it and what is its function?

16. How does seeing the stars at night and not during the day illustrate Weber's law?

17. What is meant by the sensation or absolute limen? the difference limen?

EXERCISES

i. Mark off an area on the skin a centimetre square. Touch each point of the area with a pointed metal rod warmed to about 40 C. Mark the spots where warmth is felt. Repeat with the rod cooled by immersion in ice-water. Mark the points where cold is felt. Compare with the warm spots. Are they the same ? Stimulate a definite cold spot with a rod heated to about 55 C. What stimulus do you receive ? Why?

2. Press gently upon the different regions of the area above with a pointed toothpick or human hair. Mark the points where pressure is felt. Go over the same area with a sharpened horsehair fastened by wax to a handle. Note the points where pain is felt. Compare with pressure and with the temperature spots. Can you make out any law of arrangement?

3. Observe in a glass the red openings of the papillae on the end of the tongue. Mark five papillae on a drawing of the tongue. With a brush stimulate each papilla successively with a solution of salt, sugar, vinegar, and quinine. Are all of the spots sensitive to each substance? How can you explain the results by the doctrine of specific energies?

4. Fatigue the nostril for camphor by smelling a lump of the gum until it is no longer perceived. Try the nose for iodine. Fatigue again for camphor and try for vanilla. Test in the same way for rubber, asafcetida and other substances. What do the results prove of the nature of olfactory qualities ?

5. Draw the ear to demonstrate the relations of the bones of the middle ear to the cochlea and the auditory nerve.

6. Demonstrate the presence of overtones in a note of the piano. Strike the lowest C while the key that gives the octave is held down. As the first key is dropped you will hear the octave still resounding by sympathetic action induced by the first overtone of the fundamental. Proceed in the same way to determine what other overtones are present in the note first struck. How do these overtones affect the ear?

7. Mix blue and yellow in different combinations on a rotating colour-mixer. If this be not at hand, a substitute may be prepared as follows : Place a square of yellow paper and a square of blue paper of the same size a foot apart upon a black cloth on a table. Hold a pane of clear glass vertical midway between them and look through the glass at one, and adjust the second square so that its reflected image covers the first. When the two colours are brought to coincide the apparatus makes a simple colour mixer. The intensities of the colours may be varied by turning the glass plate about the line of contact with the table. What colour does the mixture of blue and yellow give rise to when the apparatus is adjusted to give equal amounts of each? Try mixtures of other primary colours to give the list of spectral colours.

8. Place a bit of green paper over a dot on a sheet of grey paper. Look intently at the green paper for ten seconds. Blow the green bit away and look for three seconds or so at the dot. What colour replaces the green? Repeat with the other colours and record results.

9. Place a centimetre square of grey paper on a large square of red. Cover both with tissue or other translucent paper. Note the colour of the small square as seen through the tissue paper. What gives it a colour? Test on surfaces of other colours. What is the general law?

10. Look steadily at a point on a wall, preferably a grey wall. Have an assistant move centimetre squares of coloured paper away from the fixation point. Note the point where the different colours disappear or change. Measure the distance from the fixation point in different directions. Compare the distances for different colours. Can you interpret the results by the phenomena of colour-blindness mentioned in the text?

1 1 . Draw the eye showing the lens system and its relation to the iris, retina, and various coats. On a larger scale draw a portion of the retina that shall indicate the nervous connections between the rods and cones and the fibres of the optic nerve.

12. Bend the finger at the second joint. Can you detect deeper lying sensations? Can you distinguish them in quality from the pressure sensations? What is the sense-organ that gives rise to them?

CHAPTER V

SELECTION AND CONTROL ATTENTION

Omnipresence of Selection. One of the most striking facts of consciousness is selection or control. A man is not absolutely under the domination of habit, of external stimulation, or of the habitual elements in the thinking processes, but can decide for himself, within limits, what he shall hear or see, what he shall think or what he shall do. He may admit faint stimuli to consciousness while stronger ones are acting upon the sense-organs ; he may repress a strong habit and permit a weaker one to run its course; or he may choose a faint memory when several that are ordinarily more insistent are pressing for return. Evidently, selection is of fundamental importance in perception, in action, and in memory. Since selection affects so many different processes and has so many different phases, it becomes necessary to distinguish between the questions that may be answered in the same way everywhere and those that must be treated differently in each field. Three questions must be answered in connection with each kind of selection : (i) what is the effect of selection upon the process affected? (2) what determines the course of selection ? (3) what are the concomitants of the selective activity? Of these the first takes different forms in each field ; the second and third are gerieral : an answer in one connection will hold with little change for both of the others. The conditions of selection and the means of knowing that selection is being made are the same for perception, for memory, and for will. In this chapter we shall discuss primarily attention or the selection of sensations but we shall also point out the similarities between the attention processes and the control processes in thought and action.

Effects of Attention on Sensation. The general effects of selection are the same for perception, for thought, and for action. We read on a railroad train in spite of the noise and other distractions; we hear the faint sounds of a conversation in a storm or in a boiler shop and are for the moment not aware of the din. When studying attentively, one may be spoken to several times without being disturbed. Similarly, one can continue a train of thought even when other very pleasant memories suggest themselves or in the midst of external disturbances. A stimulus that has given rise on different occasions to a number of different responses and might now be the means of exciting several different movements will arouse but one of these, that one will be selected from the other possible ones. Each of these selections is of the same kind. One process is given free rein ; all others are checked.

More frequently in attention, the processes not selected are not absolutely excluded from consciousness, but are given a subordinate place. As one attends, certain sensations are clearly appreciated ; the others are less clear. One of the much discussed problems of attention concerns the difference between the sensation directly attended to and the others that constitute the background of consciousness. Two conflicting theories have been held : one, that attention increases the intensity of the sensation, the other, that the change is peculiar and must be given a different name, clearness. All agree that the effect of attention is similar to increased intensity. Both make the sensation easier to describe, make all judgments about it more accurate, and give it a more important place in consciousness. But the two effects must be different in some way for one seldom mistakes a change in attention for a change in the intensity of the stimulus. It is not assumed that the violin has increased in intensity when its tones are picked out from the mass of an orchestra, nor is it assumed that the tactual sensations grow weak when they are not attended to. It is certain that attention and intensity are sufficiently different in their effect upon consciousness to prevent them from being mistaken for each other. It is generally asserted that attention increases the clearness of a mental state. The state becomes clearer, its details are more prominent, it can be more easily used and understood. This quality of clearness is, however, different from intensity in spite of the fact that both make a mental state more important.

Analysis and Synthesis. Analysis and synthesis may both be referred to the effect of selecting different states. In analysis some one part of a total process is made prominent, and this makes possible the recognition of its constituents. As one attends to one of the notes of a chord, that note becomes prominent in the complex. Analysis of the chord consists in making each of its components prominent one after another. Synthesis is also a result of increasing the clearness of mental states. It differs from analysis only in that the total effect of the mass is attended to rather than some one component. With the chord one may attend to determine the closeness of fusion of the components or the pleasantness of the compound. This serves to unite the elements into a single whole. The results of attention may be either to analyse or to synthesise, but in either case the primary effect is to increase the prominence of part or of whole. This change in clearness with the resulting analysis or synthesis may affect memory or thought processes as well as sensations. One may analyse either the memory or the sensational elements from a perception, or one may turn from a perception to study mental imagery, or may attend to one part after another of an idea. The effect upon ideas is the same as upon sensations. In action, selection is more likely to be of wholes than of parts, although on occasion one element of a complex act may be emphasised without changing the others.

The Conditions of Attention. Why one selects or attends is not so easy to determine. Usually the conditions are hidden. Attention comes without antecedent desire or warning. One often finds one's self attending without any preliminary intention and even against one's will. When one desires to attend, in advance of attention, it is a problem why one desires, and this usually escapes notice even when the question is raised. Nearly always one is concerned to know only that one desires to attend and does not care to know why. Indirect methods, however, have thrown considerable light upon the conditions of attention. These methods consist in studying the circumstances in the individual and the outside world that precede attention, and in generalising the results of the observation in laws. In the light of these observations two sets of conditions may be distinguished, the subjective and the objective. The one is a series of circumstances in the outside world that precedes attention, the other the earlier experiences of the individual. These conditions may be first determined for attention to external stimuli, although the results hold for all selection.

Objective Conditions of Attention. The circumstances in the outer world that favour the entrance of a sensation are to be found in the amount of energy exerted by the stimulus upon the sense-organ. The amount of energy expended may be due to the intensity of the stimulus, to its duration, or to the area of the sense-organ affected, (i) An intense sound such as an explosion, a bright light, a strong odour, will force themselves upon attention, however much one may desire to attend to something else. (2) Similarly a large object will be seen where a small one might escape notice. (3) Up to a certain point, too, the greater the duration of a stimulus, the more likely it is to enter consciousness. Beyond that, greater duration leads to neglect; one attends and passes on to something else, and the stimulus is no longer appreciated. This is but another way of stating that change is more important than absolute intensity or extent in determining the course of attention. One notices a whistle of changing pitch or intensity where a constant one would escape notice. One even appreciates the ticking of a watch as it stops, although the preceding continuous ticking has not been noticed at all. Similarly, objects that move towards or away from us are noticed, although the same objects would escape notice if stationary, and our only way of knowing that they move away or approach is from the changing size. Change, whether in size or intensity, whether it be increase or decrease, attracts attention. These characteristics of the outside world that tend to compel us to receive a sensation may be said to be opposed to attention. They express, not the selective activity of consciousness, but the forces in the outside world that oppose voluntary selection. If they alone acted, consciousness would be but a plaything of external forces. It is usual to extend the meaning of the term attention to cover all the factors that explain the entrance of sensations, and one cannot understand the subjective factors without a knowledge of these objective conditions, whether one calls them conditions of attention or not. One might add in this connection, in anticipation of the later discussions, that there are similar objective conditions which oppose subjective control, both in memory and in action. In both, these are found in the closeness of connection between sensation or idea and other ideas or movements. The development of the laws must be left to the later chapters.

The Subjective Conditions of Attention. The subjective conditions give the individual spontaneity and self-expression in the selection of sensations. They reflect the earlier life of the individual in very much the same way that the objective conditions reflect the outer world at the moment. It is possible to enumerate five factors of greater or less generality that determine the nature of attention. Enumerated in the order of nearness in time to the particular act of attending, these are : (i) the idea in mind, (2) the purpose or attitude at the moment, (3) the earlier education, (4) duty (as the expression of social or individual ideals), and (5) heredity. The first can be seen either in the influence of an immediately preceding sensation or of an immediately preceding idea. If one has heard or seen or is thinking of some object and that object presents itself, it will be noticed where otherwise it might escape attention. It is easier to hear an overtone if a tone of the same pitch has been heard at full strength just before. Similarly, in listening to an orchestra, recalling the tones of a violin or looking at the violin will be certain to make the tones of that instrument prominent, when otherwise they might not be noticed. If when looking for an object one will hold its picture in mind, one will see it at once. When a bird in a tree has been seen once through a glass, it will continue to be seen easily, although it may have been looked for in vain a long time, before it was first discovered.

Mental Attitude a Condition of Attention. The second of the subjective conditions of attention takes three forms. Each is an expression of a mental attitude and is a little more general than the idea or sensation prominent at the moment. The most usual and most definite way of arousing the attitude is to ask a question. This may be illustrated by a simple experiment. Cut a number of bits of paper of different shapes and colours. Cover them with a piece of cardboard and expose them for an instant as you ask, ' What colours do you see? ' After exposure the observer can tell pretty accurately what colours were shown. If then you ask him what the forms were or how many bits were shown, it will be found that he can give no correct answer. One sees what corresponds to the question; all else is excluded from consciousness. Sometimes the question arises spontaneously or is suggested by a sensation. You wonder if it is raining, and as you look out of the window with this question in mind, you notice a drizzle or see spots upon the roof that would otherwise have escaped you. Very many observations grow in this way out of specific questions, and it is surprising to note how certain the question is to bring to mind any object that may contain the answer to, or correspond to, the question, and how little one sees that does not correspond to some question. Most people cannot say whether the four on the watch is IIII or IV, because they look for the time, not the characters. Purpose as Mental Attitude. Next in order of explicitness of conscious anticipation is the purpose. This differs from the formulated question only in that the end to be attained is less definite or less definitely formulated. Often one first has a vague general problem and this suggests one definite question after another and these in turn control the specific acts of attention. Usually one has some definite purpose in observation as in action, and this serves to control attention even when there is no definite question in mind. In a laboratory one may be seeking for the solution of some problem with no definite question formulated. Under those circumstances one is very likely to notice anything that harmonises with the purpose. Similarly one notices animal life in the field of a microscope more easily in the zoological laboratory, and plant structures more easily in the botanical laboratory. The purpose is not very insistent in these cases but is none the less operative. In everyday life what is appreciated corresponds very closely to the purpose, whether that purpose be serious and permanent or trivial and transitory. On a hunting trip one is set for the perception of game, as in a classroom one is set to understand a lecture or hear a question. This ' set ' constitutes the purpose, and is effective even when not kept in mind. One often has still less definitely conscious ' sets.' In these one is not aware of a purpose and has no definite question. The bias arises from some previous experience and is not preceded by a desire to see one thing or group of things rather than another. Nevertheless any object that corresponds to the attitude will be noticed at the expense of other objects. After one has detected escaping gas, other odours often will be noticed, even after all thought of detecting an odour has vanished. All three of these factors serve to quicken attention for one group of things rather than for another, and together they constitute its most important condition. What does not correspond to the attitude, purpose, or question of the moment is not admitted to consciousness, and all that does correspond to it will be noticed, no matter how unfavourable the circumstances in other respects. Practically the only difference in the three sorts of attitudes is to be found in the degree of anticipation of the object attended to. The question very definitely foreshadows the object to be seen; the purpose gives only a general idea of the class of objects to be expected ; while the attitude is not at all conscious and gives noexpectation. The attitudes change from hour to hour,, and even from moment to moment. They are practically the only occasions for the shifting of attention.

Education as a Condition of Attention. The influence of the earlier life in determining the general character of attention is as marked as the influence of the attitude in the changes of its temporary character. Two influences of education may be distinguished. First it makes certain forms of attention more effective. The skill of tea and wine tasters, the keenness of the savage for following a trail, are due, not to any improvement in the sense-organ through practice, but to training in attention. In every sense department and in every sort of observation one comes with practice to appreciate differences that at first cannot be detected. One important result of any sort of education is the increased capacity for observation. A second influence of education upon attention is the more usual one of determining the stimulus to be effective. What is seen or heard is usually an indication of the character of earlier experiences. If a man enters a strange room, he will notice first some object which his education has prepared him to see. A fisherman will notice the rod on the wall, the athlete, the mask and foil or the lacrosse stick, the scholar will see the books, and the artisan the implements of his trade. It is possible to determine what a man's occupation or training is by studying the objects he observes and the order in which he sees them. Even more generally one will hear one's own name when spoken in a conversation of which nothing else is heard. Sometimes education acts indirectly by preparing questions and purposes; often education acts directly one is not aware of any preliminary purpose. In brief, education gives capacity for discrimination and also determines the order in which presented objects shall enter consciousness, and whether they shall enter at all. Social Determinants of Attention. One effect of education upon attention is important enough for separate mention. This is the effect of social training which serves to hold attention to the momentarily unpleasant for the attainment of future benefits. One is constantly being taught that certain things must be attended to in spite of the fact that others are more in harmony with the momentary mood. It is of course not possible to analyse, in their completeness, the forces that make for this sort of attention, but so far as they can be analysed they may be referred to social influences and be brought together under the term social pressure. One ordinarily works for the object at present less pleasant to gain some greater remote good. The value of the remote good is learned from and usually enforced by society, and enforced as a duty, not as a good. The impulse to work for it is given through ideals, and the ideals can be traced to the society of the individual. The boy of to-day seeks to avoid manual labour and to enter the professions, even when they are relatively unremunerative, because of the small esteem in which working with the hands is held by society. Each ideal demands for its attainment holding attention for a long time to matter that is not pleasant. When you turn from reading a novel to this chapter, you are governed by social pressure. First is the pressure exerted by teacher and class to stand well, and then the desire to attain the end for which this knowledge is a preparation. Both ends are desirable in the last analysis because of the social approval they receive. The punishment of failing to attend is social contempt ; the reward of persistent attention is social approval. Society sets the end, social pressure compels one to attend for its attainment. The attention that comes from social pressure is distinguished from the other forms of attention due to education in that the end and the process are unpleasant, and attending seems the result of effort, while in the others the end and process are pleasant and are interesting.

Heredity and Attention. To understand certain characteristics of attention we must go back of the experience of the individual to his original nature. This is determined first by the evolution of the race and second by the immediate heredity of the individual. The first explains the fact that all are attracted by movement and by individuals of the opposite sex, and that love stories and stories of fighting universally hold us. Under the second fall the differences in taste shown by individuals. Liking for music or art goes back in part to a tendency to observe certain stimuli rather than others. Many similar characteristics and capacities must be explained in large part by innate differences in attention. It is still impossible to say how far any particular act of attention is due to an hereditary influence and how far to education and other acquired tendencies. Certain it is, however, that each plays an important part. The more fundamental ways of attending are hereditary.

The Nervous Basis of Attention. In harmony with our preliminary statement that all mental action has a corresponding activity in the cortical cells, it is necessary to relate the conditions of attention to nervous processes. The nervous basis of attention is undoubtedly the selective preparation of certain cortical cells that makes excitation easy. This preparation is a state of partial activity that needs but to be increased by the stimulus to give full consciousness. In consequence a stimulus too weak to affect cells not thus prepared will arouse these to full activity. Each of the conditions discussed above may be traced to some prepaTation of this sort. The influence of the immediately preceding stimulus is to leave the cells it excites in a state of partial activity ; they are still quivering from the earlier stimulation, and so respond easily to the new stimulus. The influence of the question or purpose is to arouse in some slight degree a whole group of connected cells. When a question is asked, the nervous impulse spreads from the cells excited by the question to others that have previously been excited in the same connection. An object appealing to any one of these cells will "Tnd entrance to consciousness made easy for it.

Part of the work has already been done. The influence of education is, first, to connect the nerve-cells into large groups, and so to prepare for questions and purposes, and secondly, to make possible the spread of preparation from group to group, and thus to determine the course of the spread of preparation. It probably also makes certain paths permanently more permeable, and so more open to excitation than they were in advance of training. The hereditary bias has a similar explanation, except that the selective permeability is present in advance of training. Preliminary preparation in the nervous system is correlated with selection of sensations in consciousness, and each of the conditions of selection induces in the nervous system a state of partial activity which prepares for full activity.

Interest and Non-voluntary Attention. The conditions of attention can be reduced to certain peculiarities in the outside world and to different events in the life of the individual. But if one should ask the average nonscientific individual why he attends, he would answer in practically every case that he attended because he was interested or because he made an effort. If we examine our own consciousness, it is evident that attention from interest and attention from effort are natural divisions. It is desirable to refer this popular explanation and classification to the conditions already discussed. A list of the things that are interesting includes those that are attended to naturally and universally, such as stories of conflict. Attention to these we have seen to be due to heredity, to education, or to passing attitude or purpose. Some interests are general and innate, some are acquired by education, and some are temporary and seem to come and go without cause. To say that attention is due to interest is merely to say that it is due to some one of the subjective conditions other than social pressure. Attention from these conditions is pleasant and spontaneous. It has sometimes been called nonvoluntary attention.

Effort and Voluntary Attention. Attention due to effort falls almost universally under the socially conditioned. When one is said to strive to attend, the incentive is ordinarily some ideal of social origin. The real occasion for attending is the social approval that is expected or the blame that is feared if one fails to attend. The social incentive is generally given the name duty. This sort of attention is also marked off from the others by the accompanying diffuse contractions in different parts of the body that give sensations of strain. These constitute the feeling of effort. Attention induced by ideals of social origin and accompanied by effort is called voluntary attention.

Involuntary Attention. Attention conditioned by the nature of the stimuli from the external world completes the list. This is called involuntary attention, since it may be opposed to the purpose and to the dominant ideals of the moment. It is always effortless, but may or may not be interesting. To exclude these stimuli is the usual object of effort. We may say that there are three sorts of attention : voluntary, non-voluntary, and involuntary. Voluntary attention is conditioned by social pressure and is accompanied by effort ; non-voluntary attention is conditioned by the idea in mind, the mental attitude of the moment, education, or heredity, and is accompanied by interest; involuntary attention is conditioned by the character of the stimuli that are presented, and either is accompanied by interest or is attention to the distraction that should be resisted and so through conflict gives occasion for effort. The different forms cannot always be distinguished, but they serve the practical purposes of classification.

The Motor Phenomena of Attention. Movements are among the most striking characteristics of the attentive consciousness. They serve as the only sign of attention to the onlooker, and are prominent in the experience of the individual attending. As one attends, the various sense-organs are adjusted to receive the impression most effectively. When one attends to an object in the field of vision, the eyes spontaneously turn toward it, the two eyes converge that it may be seen with the fovea in each eye, and the lens is adjusted to give the clearest possible image. The turning and converging of the eyes can be seen by the observer. One knows when talking to a person whether one is being looked at or whether the gaze is directed beyond and infers from that the degree of attention one is receiving. This is the most common indication of the nature of the thing attended to. Not only is there a characteristic position of the eyes for attention hi the field of vision, but for hearing also and even for touch and taste. Attention to objects perceived by the other senses is usually followed by visual attention to the same object. When one hears a sound, one turns the eyes toward it, and when touched, one looks to see what is against the skin. There are definite adjustments of the other senses to give the best condition for observation. In addition to the adjustment of the sense-organs essential to perception, many more general muscular contractions accompany attending. One of the most important is the inhibition of all movement. When one is listening, all movements cease; even those that have started are stopped in mid course. Any sort of strong attention causes an unintentional cessation of activity. At the same time the breath is held momentarily, the heart beats faster, and other changes in circulation may be noticed. Quite as obvious and more important from the conscious side are numerous general contractions hi voluntary muscles. In any attending the muscles everywhere are slightly tense. In marked degrees of voluntary attention the brow is wrinkled, the muscles of the jaws are set, and the fists may be clenched. All of these are to the observer signs of attention, and at the same time they indicate to the man who attends that he is attending. The diffuse contractions give rise to the strain sensations which constitute the feeling of effort in voluntary attention. The motor processes serve to adjust the sense-organs to the most adequate reception of stimuli, holding the breath and inhibiting general movements prevent the interference of distracting sensations, while the circulation is adjusted to the increased demands of the organism. On the other side they indicate to the observer that the man is attending, and to himself they give some idea of the degree of attention or at least of the amount of conflict in attention.

Is Attention or Movement Primary? Much controversy has arisen in the last few years as to whether attention or movement is primary. One theory is that attention is due to the motor response ; the other that attention is first and the response a mere accompaniment or result. The truth seems to lie between them. The essential fact in attention is the selective preparation. Movements of accommodation and clearness of conscious states are both results of this preparation. The preparation, as has been seen, is the outcome of the preceding activities of the individual, near and remote, and of the effects that these activities have had upon the nervous organism. The effect of this preparation as expressed in the attitude toward any stimulus is what we call attention. As seen by the individual, this is marked by selection of stimuli and by clearness of certain conscious states. As seen by another, attention is a series of movements, a visual fixation, a bodily attitude, or general strain. Of the effects of the preparation, we can never be sure whether clearness or movement comes first. In many cases it can be observed that the stimulus presents itself in some vague way and the sense-organs gradually adjust themselves to give greater definiteness of impression. This is the usual order in involuntary attention. When the stimulus is expected, the sense-organs are prepared in advance. In that case preparation is usually determined by some memory process which precedes and initiates movement. This is true of voluntary and of certain forms of nonvoluntary attention.

Attention Means Preparedness. Attention, then, means neither the clearness of consciousness nor the movements that accompany the clearing up of a conscious state, but fundamentally the condition of preparedness of the individual and the organism that gives rise both to the change in consciousness and to the movements. This preparedness makes for selection, not merely of sensations, but of ideas and of movements. These have the same conditions and the same accompanying states of effort and interest. One is interested in mental states and actions as one is interested in objects, and one feels effort in holding to a train of thought or in selecting a course of action as in carrying out a difficult bit of reading or observation. The same characteristics that are prominent in attention are prominent in the selection of thought and action. The fundamental phase of attention is the preparedness that determines selection. It is the same in essence as the factors to be discussed later which control thinking and action. This, not any conscious change in sensation or movement, is what must be emphasised in attention. This preparedness is not, however, itself conscious. One does not know that one is likely to see one thing rather than another until one sees it, and one does not know that certain movements of accommodation are coming until they are made. The only sign of the change that has been wrought by earlier activities is the effect in modifying selection and in inducing the accompanying actions. The Duration of Attention. Two practical questions arise with reference to attention. The first is, how long any single stimulus may occupy the dominant place, the second, how many things may be attended to at once. To the question how long one may attend, various answers have been given. The ordinary opinion is that one may attend indefinitely. One seems to pay attention to the book one is reading for hours at a stretch, and one listens to a lecture for an hour with slight distraction. In all such cases, however, the material is constantly changing, one is not attending to the same stimulus, nor to the same sensation during the whole period. If one attends to any faint stimulus, the ticking of a watch or a faint grey ring on a revolving disk, it will be seen that one does not hear the sound nor see the ring all the time. It will be seen for a second or two, will vanish for four or five seconds, and then appear again. The total length of the cycles will be about six to ten seconds. These alternations are often called attention waves. More recently they have been referred to some periodical change in the sense-organ or in the nervous system, so are not to be regarded as changes in attention in the narrowest sense. We must find some other answer to the question how long one may attend. While watching the faint ring to see when it comes and goes, one is aware of a constant shifting of attention. One drifts away from the ring to wonder whether one is attending or is attracted by some extraneous matter or thing, and often the change in the sensation comes while thus distracted. A record that has been made recently of the maximum time that attention can be held to any single stimulus indicates that the pulsations are very short indeed. If one attempts to keep attention fixed upon a single point in a picture, it will be found that at least once a second something about the point will come in to crowd it out of consciousness. If the stimulus be absolutely simple and one is careful to record each appearance of something else, it seems that one can hold attention strictly to a single thing for less than a second. When in the popular sense attention is given to a thing for an hour at a time, attention is constantly shifting from part to part, or is turning to other objects or thoughts for longer or shorter periods. Attention for more than a second or so to absolutely the same stimulus is either impossible or results in the pathological condition of hypnotism.

The Range of Attention. The question how many things may be attended to at once has also been variously answered at different periods in the history of psychology. The first statement, on purely a priori grounds, was that a unitary mind could have not more than one conscious process at one time. More recently experiments demonstrated that if a number of objects were shown for one-fifth of a second or less, four or five objects might be seen. More recently still, however, careful observation of the process of determining the number of objects shows that even with short exposures the objects are not attended to at once, but are impressed upon consciousness and persist for a time in the memory afterimage, where they may be attended to separately and counted. It is as if one took an instantaneous photograph of a group of objects and counted them on the film after development. The memory after-image persists only a second or two, however, and the number of objects that may be seen with a short exposure depends upon the number that can be attended to and counted before the image disappears. It seems probable from all the experiments that only a single object may be attended to at once.

Very much the same conclusion has been reached about the related problem of the number of things that may be done at once. Often two or more operations are apparently carried on at the same time. Careful investigation, however, shows that two things can be done at once only if one has become so habitual as to require no attention. One may easily carry on a conversation while walking, but in this case walking has become so automatic that it requires no conscious guidance. Should the way become very rough, conversation will cease or will suffer long and frequent interruptions. Experiments have been made to show that one can read a selection and add a series of figures at the same time more quickly than one could do both in succession, but if either task is difficult enough to require full attention, the two will take more time when carried on together than when done successively. When easy and familiar, one task will be carried on automatically while attention is given to the other, but when both require full attention, only one can be carried on at a time to advantage.

Attention and Inattention. A natural question arises as to what the opposite of attention may be, or whether there is ever a time when one does not attend. Complete inattention is noticed only during sleep or periods of unconsciousness. Even in sleep there is apparently some selective adaptation to stimuli. A sleeping man will be aroused by his name even if spoken in a tone so low that he has heard nothing else of the conversation.

In profound slumber a mother is ' set ' for the movements of her child, the nurse for the patient. In the insane, too, attention is present although in a reduced or distorted form. The so-called states of inattention of the normal man are really states of attention, but of attention to something at the moment undesired. They divide into two forms, scattered or diffuse attention, and absent-mindedness. In the one, attention is constantly shifting to a new object, and no one is kept before consciousness long enough to be fully appreciated. In the other, attention is so absorbed in some one thing or course of thought that other sensations have little chance to enter. The first form is more frequent in childhood and in certain pathological states, the other is more usual in maturity and is frequently found in men of more than usual training and ability. Both forms of inattention are desirable if not in excess ; in fact they are extremes of the two desirable characteristics of attention. Attention is most effective when all useful objects are attended to, and attention is kept upon them long enough to appreciate them fully. Dispersed attention insures entrance of all important objects, the abstracted state protects against distraction that might prevent full understanding. It is only excessive instability or too great and inappropriate immersion in anything that should be guarded against.

Attention and Distraction. It is generally thought that any distraction, any stimulus that may present itself at the time one is endeavouring to attend to anything else will diminish the amount of attention and so render observation less accurate. Experiments show that this is not always true. If one is comparing two intensities, e.g. first undisturbed and again when a phonograph is playing near by, it is found that at times the judgment made during the distraction may be more accurate. Certain individuals and all individuals under certain conditions seem to do better work when the room is not too quiet. Much depends upon the strength of the distraction and the health and attitude of the individual. Acts that require a very short time are less affected than those that occupy more time. Recent experiments by Dr. Morgan offer a suggestion that may explain the apparent contradiction. He asked a number of students to press a certain key when one of a number of colours appeared upon a disk and to press another key when another colour appeared, etc. Other complications were introduced which demanded very close attention. The quickness of mental processes was measured by the time required to make the response. Simultaneous records were taken of the pressure exerted upon the key, and of the depth of breathing. The task was performed first without, then with, distraction. In most subjects the distraction at first caused a decrease in the quickness and accuracy of work, but this soon changed to an increase in effectiveness. Study of the records of breathing and of the pressure exerted upon the key showed that while the distraction acted, the key was pressed harder, the breathing was deeper, and that slight vocal movements were used to aid in thinking of the movement to be made. The apparent explanation of the effect of distraction in the light of the results is that the individual exerts himself to overcome the distraction and puts forth more than enough extra effort to overcome it and in consequence does more than before, but at the expense of extra fatigue.

The Genesis of Attention. Attention must be present in the child in some form from the very earliest months ; the change with years is primarily in the conditions that control selection and the constancy with which attention is kept upon one object. At first, selection must be controlled by the external stimuli and heredity. The infant is attracted by intense stimuli of any sort and by moving objects. Very early, experience shows its effect and the child begins to notice, in the chaos of the new and unfamiliar, objects that have been seen frequently. From this time on, each experience prepares the way for a new experience. The effect of these experiences is determined by the closeness of the relation of the experience to inherited tendencies. When they oppose heredity the effect is slighter than when they aid it. At this stage the development of interests begins. These are to grow with all learning and all experience and must change and develop with each new experience. With .the school years or earlier comes the appreciation of duty and other rudimentary social demands. At this stage the child makes a beginning in keeping attention fixed upon the more unpleasant thing which is approved by society in the face of the more pleasant. Training in attention of this sort comes at first through seeing the advantages of attending in harmony with social ideals as enforced through discipline. Later, obedience to the calls of duty becomes more or less habitual and the habit constantly grows and changes through application in new fields. In terms of our classification, attention begins with the involuntary and the hereditary sort of non-voluntary attention ; soon the other non-voluntary forms develop ; and last of all the voluntary.

Summary. As sensations constitute the primary structures of consciousness, so attention or selection is the primary function. It is possible to select sensations, memories, and actions. The conditions that lead to the selection are the same in each case. They are to be found in the intensity of the stimuli, the strength of the memory or the habit on the one side, and in the momentary attitude, education and heredity, and social pressure on the other. Selection in any one of these fields is accompanied by interest if conditioned by education or heredity, and is accompanied by diffuse strain sensations that give rise to the feeling of effort if the selection is controlled by duty. The act of selection is called attention when applied to sensations; it is called voluntary control of ideas when applied to recall ; and is called will when applied to action. So far we have considered explicitly only the control of sensation, although what has been said here of conditions and accompaniments holds of the other processes as well, as will be made clear in due time. It should be emphasised that the terms used to describe the fact are less important than the fact. The fact of selection is called will in many of its applications, as it has been called attention in this chapter. There should be no quarrel as to whether will or attention is the more important, as each is but a word used to designate different applications of this fundamental process with its conditions and accompaniments. The fact is essential, the name is a matter of usage. We shall make use of the fact in connection with all mental operations.

QUESTIONS

1 . Give an instance of the way sensations are selected. Do the sensations that are not selected enter consciousness? If so how do they differ from those which are selected?

2. What is the motive for attending to a musical selection? To solving these problems? To a loud noise? Why do you notice your own name whenever it is seen on a page? Trace the acts of attention to the conditions mentioned in the text.

3. Cite instances of attention that are due to each of the subjective conditions.

4. Are the movements which accompany an act of attention its cause or its effect ? Give evidence in favor of your opinion.

5. Is interest cause or effect of attention? What is interest? In what sense is it a condition, in what sense a mental state?

6. Answer the same questions for effort.

7. Outline the changes in the nervous system that explain selection. Are they the same for all conditions?

8. Is distraction ever favorable to mental work?

EXERCISES

i. Paste five bits of paper of different shapes and colours and four letters upon a square of cardboard. Show it to a group with the request to tell what colours they see. Note the answers. After an interval of half an hour ask what the shapes of the coloured papers were; then what letters were seen. Compare the percentages of objects seen that corresponded to the questions with those which did not. 2. Look closely at a point on an evenly illuminated and coloured wall. Can you distinguish any difference in the intensity or brightness of the point looked at as compared with the surrounding areas? Have an assistant strike several notes upon some instrument. Attend first to one then to another. Does the attending increase the apparent intensity of the tone or merely increase its clearness ?

3. Recall as definitely as you can some act of attention that involved effort. Can you analyse the components of the feeling of effort ? Lift a heavy weight that also requires effort. Is the quality the same as in the effort of attention ? Can you trace the feeling to any sense-organ?

4. Watch a small dot so far away that it can just be seen. Can you see it all the time? How many times a minute does it come and go?

5. Try to keep attention upon a dot when near enough to be seen easily. Can you watch it all the time? Keep a list of the memories or other sensations that come in to crowd it out. How many times will attention wander from it and come back to it in ten seconds?

6. Have an assistant prepare a set of cards with different numbers of dots upon them. Let him place the cards face down upon a table and show them one after another for an instant by turning them over and back. What is the largest number of dots that may be seen at a single glance ? Do you count them during the exposure or from memory later?

7. Try counting from 20 downward and at the same tune write the digits from i up to 20. Take the time. Take the time required for each separately. Compare. Introspect to explain the difference in time required.

8. Add a column of two-place figures while the room is quiet and all is favourable. Add a second column of the same difficulty while an electric bell is ringing continuously. Add while two people are having a conversation near you. Compare times and errors under the three conditions.

CHAPTER VI

RETENTION AND ASSOCIATION

The Materials of Memory and Imagination. Before we can regard our enumeration of the elements of consciousness as complete, we must consider those due to the rearousal of earlier experiences. With eyes closed and other senses unstimulated one still has conscious processes, and at all times elements not derived immediately from sense-organs mingle with the sensations. You may now recall an event of last year, although the sense-organ is now not excited at all. You can see the landscape in its original colours, can reinstate the temperature of a summer day although it is now winter, may in fact renew all of its features at will. These experiences in their ultimate qualities are of the same character as the sensations. The colours are the spectral colours, the tones are the tones of the scale, the cold is the familiar cutaneous sensation. They come now, however, not from the sense-organs, but are excited by the action of other central parts of the nervous system. To indicate the similarity in quality to sensation and the fact that they are due to the stimulation of one part of the cortex by another, these elementary components of memories are sometimes called centrally aroused sensations. A little observation and reflection show that in every case these processes ultimately originate in the senses. The object that you recall is the same object that you saw last year. On occasion you may compare the memory of the object with the object itself and assure yourself of the similarity. Even when the image represents nothing that has been seen before, the elements of which it is composed are of the same character as the sensations. The elements are merely rearranged in new combinations. The sensory qualities, whether peripherally or centrally aroused, are like the colours upon the painter's palette. They are relatively few, but from their combinations all the conscious experiences may be obtained, as the artist may paint any scene with his few colours. All the centrally aroused sensations, the elements of memory and imagination, come originally from the senses. They are retained in some way and reinstated on suitable occasion. An understanding of these centrally aroused sensations requires an answer to three questions : (i) how are they retained and where are they between the time of entrance and of their reinstatement? (2) under what circumstances do they return? (3) how do they compare in quality with the original sensations?

Theories of Retention. Theories of the nature of retention have varied, from the metaphor of the ancients that mind was like wax on which impressions might be made by a seal, to the equally crude physiological theory that each idea was kept in a single nerve-cell. The generally accepted theory at present is that retention is a physiological process allied to habit. Aristotle suggested that memories were due to the repetition on recall of the same movements that were made when the original experience was first received. Of course his knowledge of the physical organism was not sufficient to carry him very far in his theory, but, with allowance for our increased knowledge of the nervous system, his statement does very well to-day. Our present formulation is that memory consists in the rearousal of the cortical structures originally active, or in the reinstatement of the same activity that was involved in the original experience. Whenever a nerve-tract is aroused, some change takes place in it that predisposes it to act in the same way again. What is left in the nervous system is only this predisposition to renewed activity, not an idea or other conscious process. The idea comes only on the rearousal of structures as a result of the predisposition. Between the first appearance and the rearousal, the predisposition gives no sign of its presence. At this moment you are not conscious of the memories that might be recalled on suitable occasions. You are not at present aware, e.g. of the facts you learned last night in preparation for to-day's recitation, although you will be able to recall them perfectly when questioned about them.

The Cortical Seat of Memories. The memories probably have their seat in the same regions of the cortex that are active in the original perception. Injuries of a sensory area usually give rise to loss or disturbance of memories, as well as to loss of the capacity for sensations. In addition, injury to associatory areas may have an effect upon memories. It is possible that in some individuals the sense-organ is excited as well as the central nervous system, and that part of the memory comes from the retina, or from the skin where the impression was first received. The muscles originally excited by the stimulus may also be in slight contraction during the memory, may add their quota to the total consciousness. All of the structures active during the original experience may have their activity renewed in the recall. Since, as will be seen later, the order of occurrence determines the order of recurrence, it seems probable that the connections formed at the original experience make possible recall and that the change in the nervous system is in the synapse or point of contact between neurones.

Retention a Form of Habit. In this, retention is closely related to habit. Habits, as was seen, are due to the establishment of connections between sensory and motor neurones by a change that takes place at the synapse. After these have been connected frequently, the stimulus tends to reinstate the act whenever it appears. Retention of ideas has exactly the same basis. The cells involved in the ideas also act together, and this activity produces changes in the synapses. Whenever one of the ideas presents itself again, the other is, or tends to be, reinstated. Not merely the cortical elements are rearoused in memory, but the whole sensorimotor tract may be partially active. This brings the process still nearer to habit. Memory is an habitual response in which the greater part of the activity is in the cortex. The activities of the sense-organ and of the muscles are subordinated to the central processes, while in habit the whole sensori-motor tract is active in approximately the same degree. The tendency to repeat an action once made, or the tendency for neurones that have once been active together to act together again when either is aroused, is at the basis of both processes. Thus, when a stranger enters the room, I stand because the sight of a stranger has been closely connected with rising. But at the same moment I recall vividly a remark, made on another occasion, by a person of similar appearance. This remark has been connected with the sight of a person of this description, in very much the same way that the act of rising has been connected with the entrance of a stranger. The thought might have been spoken and, then, that also would have been a habit. The only difference when it is merely recalled is that motor accompaniments are left off. In all else it is as much a habit as any movement.

After-image, Memory After-image, and Memory Image. Retention may also be related to the visual after-image. The after-image is the effect of a stimulus upon the retina that persists for a short time after its cause has ceased to act. Cortical cells show a similar tendency to continue in action for a period. If you will glance out of the window for a moment and then close the eyes, you will notice that the objects you saw during the momentary glance persist for a few seconds with sufficient definiteness for you to note details that escaped you during the actual observation. This is the mental photograph mentioned in the chapter on attention as rendering possible the perception of more than one object during a very brief exposure. It has the same explanation as the positive after-image. Like the after-image it is the result of the persistence of activity in the neurones after the stimulus is removed. It is sometimes called the memory after-image or primary memory, or more recently the perseveration tendency. The ordinary memory, or reinstatement after the primary memory has lapsed, may be looked upon as a renewal of the same activity of the cells that was induced by the stimulus and that persisted during the primary memory. To-morrow when you recall what you saw as you looked from the window, you will induce in the cortical cells the same sort of activity that they showed when you were looking and during the memory after-image.

Recall always through Associated Experiences. The answer to our second question, how centrally aroused experiences are recalled, is found in the laws of association. These laws assert that all recall is due to the preceding mental process. This process is effective in calling back the ideas because of connections developed between them at some earlier time. The idea that was in mind a moment ago and the idea that it recalls now must have been experienced together at some time, if the one is to recall the other. The initiation of recall by these earlier experiences and connections may be seen in any train of ideas. If one will record the elements of an uncontrolled train of thought, it will be seen that each element is connected with the following by virtue of the fact that both have been experienced together at some time. A girl passing my window suggests the house I saw her going into yesterday. That suggests the stages in building the house; that, in turn, the sound of hammering that woke me this morning ; and this again the protest of one neighbour to another who had been frequently chopping kindling wood at an unreasonably early hour in the morning. A revery of this sort, when started, may run through successive links until disturbed by some duty or other distraction. A study of a train of ideas will show that each member of the train has been connected with the preceding and succeeding links at some earlier period. It is evident, however, that in the train just described, the connections are of different sorts and are due to different earlier connections. The first two associates are the result of observing two things at the same time. The last two turn about an element (the sounds of hammering) common to both of the terms, although the terms as a whole have never been in consciousness together. This difference makes necessary a classification of the forms of connection.

The Laws of Association. The traditional classification of association has been traced back to Aristotle. It recognises four laws of association : association by contiguity, by succession, by similarity, and by contrast. The first two classes have an altogether different explanation from the last two. The first two refer the connections to the relations at the time the connections were formed, the last two classify by the nature of the experiences at the time of recall. Association by contiguity means merely that if two objects are perceived at the same time, one is always likely to enter consciousness if the other presents itself. Association by succession asserts that if two ideas have been experienced in succession, the second will be suggested by the first whenever it comes to consciousness. In the illustration of the preceding paragraph, the girl suggests the house because I have seen them together. The best illustration of successive association is found in the ordinary rote learning. Words repeated in succession return in the same succession when the first word is heard. Association by similarity includes instances of recall, in which the idea suggested is in some way similar to the preceding. Such is found in the building of the house recalling the hammering that awakened me, or perhaps, more strictly, the connection shown when the hammering suggested the protest of a neighbour against a disturbance of a similar kind.

Association by contrast covers the cases in which the two ideas involve opposite qualities, as when black suggests white, or big, little.

The Neurological Theory of Association. These original laws of association are merely descriptive of the ideas that succeed each other and of the relations between them. The laws do not indicate the reasons for the succession or the causes for the entrance of the different ideas; they serve only to classify the connections. If one ask why an idea recalls the one that accompanied or succeeded it, one must be referred to the study of the nervous system. In its terms our law is that if two neurones are active simultaneously or in immediate succession, some connection is established between them of such a character that if one be excited in any way the excitation spreads to the other. The point of connection is, as has been said frequently, the synapse. Just as in habit, the excitation of two neurones at the same time or in close succession decreases the resistance of the synapse. This increased closeness of connection makes possible the spread of any activity from one to the other. When one learns the first letters of the alphabet, the impulse spreads from the neurones corresponding to ' a ' to the neurones corresponding to ' b/ and as a result of numerous repetitions the two groups grow together to such a degree that whenever ' a ' is suggested, the excitation spreads to the neurones that correspond to ' b/ and they are excited also. The change in the synapse as a result of use is the explanation of association, as of habit. Association by contiguity and succession is the expression of this simple and familiar neurological function.

Association by Similarity. Not so immediate is the explanation of association by similarity. Similarity is not itself a force, nor is it possible to find simple physiological correlates for it. The ordinary idea is not a simple element of consciousness but is a complex of many centrally aroused sensations. The mechanism of recall consists in replacing certain of the elements of the first idea by others to constitute the new idea. Thus the replacement of the idea of the disturbing hammering, by the idea of the neighbour's protest at another form of disturbance under the same circumstances, may be regarded as due to a shift of ideas about ' early-morning-noise-that-disturbs-sleepers ' as a centre. The elements that have to do with hammering in building the house, drop out, and the persisting elements that constitute the early morning disturbance idea, are retained. These by the law of contiguity or succession waken the remaining elements of the incident described by my neighbour. The whole process is the dropping out of certain elements, and the recall by those remaining of new elements that have been connected with them. The common element at once makes possible the entrance of the second, and gives similarity to the two ideas. If this be translated into nervous terms, the first idea corresponds to the action of a considerable group of neurones. The shift to the second idea consists, first, in the cessation or diminution in the activity of certain elements of the mass, while others continue to act with full intensity. The cells that continue active rouse to activity the other group of cells with which they have also been active earlier, and with that the incident of the protest against chopping in the early morning comes to consciousness. The simple physiological laws are the same here as in the earlier case; the only added feature is the dropping out of some elements, while the others continue active. Wundt has called this sort of recall association by identity, since it is the identical element in each idea that determines the course of recall James calls the process focalised recall, but both agree on the essentials of the process as given above.

Units for Thought, Complexes for Neurology. Both sorts of association involve the same principle, but there is a slight difference in its application. This is, that use tends to connect neurones, or that mental elements that appear together tend to return together. The apparent difference between the two classes serves merely to emphasise the fact that ideas are neurologically and psychologically always complex. The ideas that are recalled by contiguity or succession are not simple, but the mass of elements may be regarded as disappearing or appearing as a whole rather than as dissolving one into the other, as in the so-called association by similarity. In both cases one must distinguish between the unit for thought and the unit for physiological action. For thought, the idea is the unit; one is concerned only with things and with their representatives as wholes. Association on the contrary is always between the elements that correspond to the activity of neurones. Their connections alone determine the way in which ideas shall succeed each other, and how they shall dissolve, one into the other. The older laws oi association considered only the relations between the ideas as wholes ; any dynamic explanation must consider primarily the connections between the elements. They explained by similarity what the more modern men explain by the shifting of associates about some persisting element as a core. Both are true, but one is a description of the ideas after the recall, the other is the real explanation of the recall. Of the two sorts of association, it is probable that there is in every case something of the gradual disappearance of one idea, and the gradual reappearance of the other. In general the more mechanical sorts of recall, the effects of rote learning, etc., involve contiguity and succession, while the more intelligent forms of thinking make the association by identity more prominent.

Association by Contrast. Association by contrast of the older schools is also to be explained as due either to the frequency with which things that contrast are perceived together, or to the shifting of elements about some common unit. Probably each explains certain instances. The contrast in many cases would not be noticed unless the elements were in consciousness together. Dark is appreciated only when near light, rich only when experienced with poor. On the other hand, there is always something in common between contrasting qualities. Rich does not contrast with dark, nor light with small, because they have no common qualities. If one looks to the real causes of recall rather than to a description of the ideas that succeed each other, association by contrast is really an instance either of association by contiguity, or of association by similarity. All recall is due to the simple fact that ideas that are in consciousness together tend to return together. The various classes are but different applications of this one principle.

Selection in Recall. While recall depends upon association, it is still a question why one rather than another of the many possible associates comes to consciousness. Practically every idea has been connected at some time with a great many other ideas, but at any one time it will arouse only one of these associates. The selection of one from among these possible associates has approximately the same conditions as the selection of sensations in attention. Here again we may divide the conditions into two classes, objective and subjective. Among the more mechanical factors, corresponding to the objective conditions of attention, we find the influences that determine the strength of the physiological connection between the neurones. These are four in number: (i) the strength of the original excitation ; (2) the number of times the two have been active together ; (3) the recency of the original connection ; and (4) primacy, or the novelty of the experience. A first impression makes stronger associations than later ones. The intensity of the original excitation depends upon three factors: (i) upon the intensity of the physical stimuli that gave rise to the original experiences ; (2) upon the degree of attention that was given at the time ; and (3) upon the emotional condition of the individual at the time of learning. Your own experience will convince you that each of these has an effect. Two weak experiences will be less likely to be associated than stronger ones. Much more important is the effect of attention. Inattentive reading is only slightly effective. Attention at the moment of the original reading may make faint impressions more effective than intense impressions. In fact it might be questioned whether the intensity of the stimulus had any effect, except as it served to attract attention. The effect of emotion is very closely related to attention. If the original experiences are accompanied by marked emotion, the likelihood of recall is increased. The others of the objective conditions of recall require little comment. The strength of the connection grows regularly with repetitions, and falls away with the lapse of time. Of two associates, the one first made seems to have an advantage over the other. This is one explanation of the fact that events of childhood are more frequently recalled than those of later life. Each of these objective conditions is effective, because each helps to determine the strength of the connection between the different elements in the nervous system.

Subjsctive Factors. While these objective or physiological connections are essential to all recall, and play an important part in determining the selection of one from many associates, they cannot be the only determinants. Were they the only factors in the selection, the course of thought would show no flexibility and no spontaneity. Only one associate can be physiologically strongest at any moment. In actual experience we have an idea recalling now one idea and now another ; we are ever and anon preferring a faint associate to a strong, an old to a new. What gives this variety and flexibility to ideas is the group of subjective conditions. These are practically the same as the subjective conditions in attention. The first is the attitude or purpose of the moment. If you are solving one problem, the associates that are suited to that problem will be recalled ; if you are solving another problem and have the same idea in mind, it will recall another idea. For example, if you see in your account book two numbers written one above the other, you will add in one case, you will subtract in the other. Whether you add or subtract will depend upon the context, upon the problem that is set you by the earlier stages in the accounting. If you are dealing with two expenditures, you add ; if dealing with a balance and an expenditure, you subtract. In this case, the sum is one idea that the two numbers might suggest, the difference, another, and which shall enter depends upon the purpose of the moment. Similarly, if you read a series of adjectives to a person with the request to name opposites, you will get one series of associates ; if you ask him to give synonyms, you will get another series. Here you set the task, and it leads at once to the right associate. Probably in most cases the attitude is not at all conscious, is not appreciated by the thinker. When asked in a class in psychology what is a sensation, one at once thinks of the psychological definition. The same question by a child who was reading the headline of a newspaper brings to mind an entirely different answer. One is not aware of the psychological attitude, but it is suggested by the place. The sight of the newspaper gives the newspaper attitude just as certainly and just as unconsciously. James illustrates the influence of attitude by the effect of the context in two lines of verse. The same word, when it occurs in different lines, will recall different associates. Thus the word ages occurs in the two lines from Locksley Hall

" I, the heir of all the ages, in the foremost files of time " and

" For I doubt not through the ages one eternal purpose runs."

One does not, however, make a mistake and supply ' one eternal ' after the ' ages ' in the first line, nor ' in the . . .' after the ' ages ' in the second. The preceding words and the general purpose in quoting insure the recall of the right associates, whether strong or weak. The wider setting, the attitude or purpose, directs the course of recall.

Social Pressure as a Control of Association. Of the other conditions that were seen to determine the selection of sensations, education, social pressure, and heredity have their effect in the control of recall. Education is harder to distinguish from the preparation of connections here than in attention. Its most important influence is probably in grouping experiences that may be aroused later as units, and so constitute the basis for attitudes. An attitude or purpose is very largely just the response of an entire group of neurones that serves to facilitate the recall of all members of the group when the group as a whole is aroused. One's purposes grow out of, and are dependent upon, training and education. It is in preparing for these attitudes that education exercises its most important influence upon the selection of associates. Social pressure here, as in attention, is the most important element in enforcing duty. One is held to the disagreeable task by considerations of what others would think if the work be not finished, when it would be pleasanter to let the train of thought wander at will. A student in writing an exercise wanders away for a moment in a day dream, but as soon as he is reminded of the task, the ideas connected with the writing reassert themselves. The course of association is held to the task until the work is completed. The considerations that enforce this return to the unpleasant course of thought are primarily social. It is probable that heredity has some influence in directing the course of thought. Thoughts of a certain kind are pleasant because of the natural endowment of the individual, just as certain objects are pleasant. In brief, the conditions that select one associate from the many possible ones are approximately the same as the conditions that select one from among the many possible sensations that present themselves in the outside world.

The Physiological Basis of the Control of Ideas. The physiological explanation of the action of the subjective elements upon the course of recall must be found in the influence of masses of neurones other than those involved in the direct arousal of the memory. Let us assume that one is attending to a pencil, and that several associates have been connected with it. Let us assume that : A represents the neurones involved in thinking of the pencil, and connected with it are B, C, D, and E. B is the neurone group connected with the idea of graphite mines ; C, with the thought of a pen ; D, with the picture of a cedar forest ; E, with the memory of the shop where it was obtained, etc. Let us assume that the strongest connection, as a mere physiological process, is with the shop, but that you are writing of the crystal forms of carbon. The neurones corresponding to the means of obtaining graphite have been predisposed to excitation by the writing, the group B would be partially aroused. The preparedness of B for excitation from this other connection is sufficient to overcome the greater physiological strength of E, and you think of graphite mines, rather than of any of the other things that were possible. At any moment the course of thought will be determined by these antecedent and related thoughts, or by the physiological activities that correspond to them.

All recall depends upon associations that have been formed by the experiences of the individual. At any moment recall is limited to the ideas that have been connected with the idea then in mind. Of the many things that have been connected, that one will be chosen whose bonds are physiologically strongest or which is most in harmony with the purpose of the moment. In many cases of mechanical recall it is the strength of the association that is most important in determining the course of ideas, but in ordered thought the subjective conditions are more prominent. In a day dream the mechanical associates are dominant; in writing or hi speaking of a serious sort, the attitude and the problem will predominate. Even in connected thinking irrelevant ideas will frequently insert themselves. If these are carefully examined, it will be seen that the interjected irrelevant ideas are introduced because of the strength of the objective connection between them and the preceding idea in the train. The objective connections are sufficiently strong to prevail against subjective control. No idea can be recalled unless some idea that has been associated with it is present at the moment. One can reinstate ideas only through their natural antecedents. This causes no inconvenience, because one does not ordinarily feel the need of an idea without being able to recall it. The desire for recall or the occasion for the desire ordinarily serves as a sufficient suggestion to effect it. Given the old connections that make possible the recall of different ideas, the subjective conditions, attitude or purpose, social pressure, and heredity, together with the setting, internal and external, select from the possible associates the one that suits the need of the moment.

How Memory Images are Distinguished from Sensations. The elementary qualities of memory, imagination, and reasoning are very similar to the qualities of sensations. If one thinks of a red surface, one may have an image in every respect like the original perception. The colour is red, the texture of the surface is the same as the texture of the object; but while the qualities are the same as in sensation, there are nearly always sufficient differences to prevent one from mistaking a memory image, -or image of imagination, for the real object. That this mistake is not made more frequently is due to at least three factors : (i) centrally aroused sensations are ordinarily less intense than the real sensations; (2) they have certain characteristic qualitative differences ; (3) they do not harmonise with the objects that are seen at the moment. The first criterion is ordinarily sufficient, but fails when the images become very intense, or the external stimulus is very faint. Such great vividness of the images comes only rarely and usually in abnormal individuals or under abnormal conditions. Faint intensity of external stimulation may be obtained at will. In a series of experiments by Külpe, individuals were seated in a dark room and were told that at a given signal coloured lights might be thrown upon a screen. Sometimes these were shown and sometimes not. They were asked to say whether the resulting experience was subjective or objective and also to state how they distinguished the real colours from those merely imagined. Under these conditions, every observer made mistakes. Ordinarily the mistakes consisted in asserting that colours were seen when none were shown. The merely imagined qualities were mistaken for objective qualities. When questioned as to how they distinguished one from the other, the observers gave a list of the characteristics that aided them. The subjective processes were indefinite in outline, were thin or netlike, they moved at random, they persisted when the eyes were closed and moved with the eyes, they left no after-images. The real sensations were definite in quality and outline, vanished on closing the eyes, remained stationary as the eyes moved, and left after-images. The differences are on the whole insignificant, and even those that were mentioned were not constant for all individuals. In quality, images are not very different from sensations.

More important as a means of distinguishing one from the other in practice is the harmony of images with the preceding train of thought, and their lack of harmony with the events of the outside world. If one should look up suddenly and see what appeared to be the figure of a person known to be remote but whom one had been thinking about just before, one would at once appreciate the figure to be an image. This would be all the more certain if no footsteps had been heard, and the wall could be seen through the image. The figure would be seen to be a natural result of the thought processes but altogether out of harmony with the external events. Reference of a mental process to a central or peripheral origin is most frequently made in terms of the degree to which it fits into the train of events, although intensity and the peculiar penetration or vividness of the sensation nearly always contribute their share.

The Projection of the Memory Image. A third criterion is often furnished by the direction in which memory images are projected. For some individuals the image will be directed backward if centrally aroused, as opposed to the ordinary outward and forward reference of the real visual sensation. Objects when recalled may be seen as if they were on a surface some distance back of the head. Others project imagined objects to the right or to the left. Here they will not be confused with the sensory impressions. It is possible that images can be projected outward and forward so as to have a position among objects actually seen. One individual always sees remembered or imagined events projected in colours upon the wall of the room, and many can give these images any desired position in the visual field. These are mere personal idiosyncrasies. Where the central processes are thus habitually given a direction different from that given sensations, the direction is a result of the distinction that is made, rather than a means of distinguishing them from external objects. The decision as to whether the process is of external or internal origin is practically always immediate and without hesitation; one does not even appreciate that a decision has been made.

Memory Types. While the memory images are in general like sensations, they certainly have fewer qualities. The number of pure colours that an individual can recall is probably limited to a dozen or twenty, as compared with the one hundred fifty or two hundred that may be discriminated in the spectrum. The qualities in the other senses are similarly limited. Not only are the remembered qualities of any one sense relatively few, but most individuals are restricted for their memory material to two or three, and a few to but one of the senses. Most numerous are the individuals who remember in visual terms. A visualiser of the exclusive type will recall only the pictures of objects. As he thinks of the water running from a faucet, he can see the water fall, see it splash, but has no trace of the sound. The whole event is noiseless in memory. Everything that he remembers must be translated into pictures. More rare is the auditory memory. Individuals of this type lack all but the sounds in any memory process. An event will be recalled only in terms of the sounds that were connected with it. In other individuals memories are restricted to the movements that were made in connection with the events. These movements may be memories, or the movement may be partly reinstated. One might translate the sounds of the voice that one desires to recall, e.g. into the movements necessary to imitate them and so represent the voice to himself. Smell, taste, and the other lower senses alone would not suffice to recall all sorts of experiences; where present at all in memory they are subordinate to one of the forms of imagery just mentioned.

Verbal Imagery. Another method of recall which may be used for all purposes is by language. Practically every experience may be and is expressed in words, and most individuals use words very generally in thinking as in talking. Much of thought is anticipatory speech. This form of reproducing or imagining is known as ' inner speech.' Inner speech might conceivably be present in the form of words heard, auditoryverbal imagery ; of words felt as if they were to be spoken, mo torverbal ; or of words as seen in print or writing. As a matter of fact verbal imagery is mostly either auditoryor motor-verbal. It is too closely connected with the pre-reading age for the visual elements to be very prominent. There is .little connection between the concrete and the verbal imagery for most individuals. One may be visual in the memory of concrete objects while one's verbal imagery may be either motor or auditory.

Memory Types Usually Mixed. The traditional treatment of imagery states or implies that these types are mutually exclusive, that if an individual has a welldeveloped visual memory, he will not have auditory images, and vice versa. Recent results indicate that while this may be true for the occasional man, usually for the older men who have become well set in habits, most individuals have more than one sense represented in imagery. The same individual may use all the senses in recall as in perception. In that case he will use the imagery best adapted to the event in question. Most use two or more different forms of imagery and may in addition have a verbal memory of a different sense from that used for concrete objects. There are also marked differences in the degree of clearness of the type of mental imagery that is dominant. Of exclusive visualisers some can picture objects clearly, some only in general or vague outline, and it may happen that a man who uses visual imagery predominantly may not picture events so clearly as another for whom auditory imagery is dominant.

Imagery and Practical Efficiency. Obviously, there must be a fairly close relation between the accomplishments of the individual and his memory type. It would foe very difficult to imagine a painter who could not recall colours and forms, or a musician who had no memory for tone. As a matter of fact, most great musicians are of the auditory type and most painters are visualists. In more commonplace affairs the memory type plays .an important part. A pupil who has little or no visual imagery finds difficulty in spelling. The methods of learning, too, soon adapt themselves to the memory type. It should not be supposed from this that powers of observation are similarly restricted. One of the visual type may understand a lecture fully as well as his fellow of auditory mind; as he understands, however, he translates what is said into pictures and remembers these. Recognition of the voice may be as accurate, also. The visual-minded individual will know the voice of a friend when he hears it again, although he may not be able to recall it at all. Apparently, memory types may be trained, and undergo changes with age. Experiments in developing memory types that were originally weak have met with some success, although the course of training must be long. Imagery tends to become less concrete and definite with advancing years, particularly if the individual devotes himself to pursuits requiring abstract thought. Galton found that English men of science had very little definite imagery. Most thinking was in verbal imagery or in other more abstract forms of thought. It seems that the general tendency, as men deal more and more with principles and less and less with particulars, is toward a disappearance of detailed imagery, and its replacement by symbols. The objects are represented in memory by imagery that has less and less resemblance to them, but which is better adapted to the needs of quick and accurate thought.

Summary. Our third fundamental mental fact is that impressions received from the senses are retained in the nervous system as dispositions to re-excitation. They return when some experience that has been connected with them precedes them in consciousness. This recall is subject to the same laws of selection that are exhibited in attention. When these dispositions become realised, they constitute the elements of memory, imagination, and reason. They are similar to the original sensations, although much poorer in the number of distinguishable qualities. In the representation of objects, not all the elements of the original object need be present. One or more sense departments may predominate in recall to the exclusion of others.

The three general principles upon which all explanation in psychology must rest have now been outlined. The first is that all our knowledge comes originally from sensation. All of its fundamental qualities are determined by the character of the sense-organs, together with the nature of the external stimuli. There are some forty of these simplest qualities. These, by their interaction and combination, give rise to the complexes of qualities found in the concrete objects of experience. The second principle is that the order in which mental processes of any sort enter consciousness and whether any process does or does not enter consciousness, depends upon the nature of the individual rather than upon the forces in the physical world. The nature of the individual that determines the entrance to consciousness is itself derived from his earlier experience and heredity. This fact of selection is the deciding influence, not only in perception, but also in recall, and in the voluntary control of action. The third and last of these principles is that each experience leaves a disposition in the nervous system that tends to the reinstatement of that experience on suitable occasion. These three principles recur together again and again in the explanation of the concrete mental operation. Together, they suffice for the understanding of practically all mental processes.

QUESTIONS

1. What are centrally aroused sensations? What are the common names for some of the concrete processes which they constitute ?

2. How are experiences retained? Are they retained as ideas or as nervous effects ?

3. Can you see any relation between the nervous basis of the retention and the nervous basis of habit ?

4. What is the perseveration tendency?

5. How far are the 'laws of association' explanations and how far mere classifications?

6. What is the fundamental neurological process in association?

7. How can one explain association by similarity in nervous terms ? association by contrast ?

8. What are the 'subjective conditions ' of associations? How related to subjective conditions of attention?

9. Give possible explanations of failure to recall a well-known fact. 10. How does 'primacy' affect retention and recall?

ji. How do you distinguish between a memory and a real object as you see it? Which is centrally, which peripherally aroused ?

EXERCISES

1. Trace the similarities and differences between an afterimage, a memory after-image or primary memory, and a memory image. Look at a bright object for ten seconds. Close the eyes and describe or note the after-image. Take a momentary glance at the same object and note the memory image of the object that is obtained. Compare it with the after-image for clearness of

outline and quality. Recall some similar object that was seen yesterday and compare it in every respect with the other two. How are the three processes related nervously ?

2. Let your mental stream flow at random for half a minute. Write out the ideas that came to you in the order of their appearance. Can you trace the order to earlier connections of simultaneity or succession ? Are there instances in which one idea dissolves into another? Classify the associations in accordance with the text. Are the simple or the complex associations more frequent?

3. In the list above mark the connections due to primacy, to recency, to intensity, and to frequency.

4. Speak a word to an assistant with the request to say the first word that comes to mind. Repeat for twenty words. Note the sorts of connections as in the preceding exercise. How long does it take to complete the series? Choose a series of words that have easy opposites and ask the assistant to give the opposites. Take the time as before. How does it compare with that obtained for the first series? How often does the assistant think of a wrong word before the opposite comes? How does the second series illustrate control of association or recall?

5. Recall the last public lecture that you attended. Can you see the speaker ? Can you hear the words that he speaks ? Can you recall in any way the peculiarities of his voice? How? Can you reproduce the pressure of the programme that you held in your hands ? the strain from an uncomfortable position ? Do you have distinct memories of taste and smell? Can you grade the clearness of the memories from the different senses?

6. Do you project your memory images in the same direction as your sense impressions ? For instance, do you think of the speaker in the preceding exercise as in front of you, or behind, or to the right ? How large do you think the speaker to be in your memory projection? Do the objects have the same colour and the same background as the actual sensations?

CHAPTER VII

PERCEPTION

Perception Involves a Correction of Sensations. So far we have been dealing with general principles and the laws which hold for all mental action. In perception we begin to discuss concrete mental processes. We perceive things, not sensations or images, although in psychology we think of things when appreciated as being in some way made up of sensations and images. In the discussion of perception we must show how the laws and elements that have been discussed in the last three chapters combine and interact in the attainment of a knowledge of the real world. First we must see that there is a real problem here. We have become so familiar with seeing things and with hearing things that it seems now that objects in some way walk over into our consciousness with the same characteristics that they have in the outside world. As with any operation that has been frequently repeated, we soon come to overlook the various steps in the procedure, and it is necessary to learn in some indirect way what is actually done. In this instance it is doubtful if the individual ever knew the methods by which he attains a knowledge of objects. That his assumption that objects are like the effects they produce on the sense-organ is erroneous, a simple examination of the facts of perception proves conclusively. The sensations that are received are added to or changed to make them correspond more exactly to what from our different earlier experiences we know they must be. One always corrects the shape of the table top as it appears in perspective. The angles are right angles as we see them, although the image must have acute and obtuse angles. One also makes an allowance for distance in the size of an object seen. The same object is always given the same size no matter how far away it may be, while the image on the retina diminishes constantly as the distance increases. Evidently objects do not walk over into consciousness as one might suppose, but the percept is reconstructed according to certain laws. The problem of perception is to determine these laws.

Perceptions Involve Recalled Elements. The first fact we meet -is that perceptions often involve centrally aroused sensations or memories, as well as sensations. In feeling a rough surface in the dark, one recalls how surfaces appear that have given similar tactual sensations. If the arm is moved with the eyes closed, one ordinarily pictures from memory the different positions of the arms ; one does not feel the sensations from the arm that tell of the motion. Similarly, in any perception, the object is made up in part of memories and in part of sensations. In perception through any sense the same law holds. When a dog barks at a distance, the dog is pictured in its proper direction, visual memories are added to the auditory sensations. The memory additions can be actually discriminated under certain conditions. In Figure 22, taken from Jastrow, the shadows alone are drawn but one seems to see the lines which they suggest. They are a little faint, but are unmistakable and can be seen even under conditions most favourable for observation. In most perceptions there are similar additions from memory, although they are not always so easily distinguished.

Perception of Objects as Real. In many cases, however, the object that is seen is not supplied by any one memory, but from a number of earlier experiences. Thus no one has ever seen the table top as it presents itself in perception. When seen from one side it slants in one direction, seen from the opposite side it slants in the other direction. When seen from in front the sides

Converge toward FIG. 22. (From Jastrow : ' Fact and Fable in Psy

the back, and choiogy,' Fig. 2.)

even when looked at from a point directly above the centre of the top, the sides would not be straight, as we know from the fact that the retina is a sphere, not flat, and from direct observation under suitable conditions. In Figure 23, taken from Helmholtz, if you will look at the centre when it is held only an inch or so from the eye all the lines appear straight and the angles, right angles. The figure is drawn in such a way that the curvatures are just corrected by the change in the image that produces a distortion of straight lines as they are normally seen. Everything we see on the periphery of the retina is distorted in the direction opposed to this. While the retinal image must always have been distorted in some way, the object as we perceive it is rectangular and the edges are perfectly straight. Obviously factors other than the recall of some single earlier memory must have been effective in making the sides straight and the angles right angles. It is probable that some of this modification of memories and sensations is due to the results of tests in various actions. One has found that the table will fit into square corners, and that if one is to make a table that has the appearance of this, the ends and sides must be straight and all the angles right angles. All the uses and tests that have been made harmonise with the assumption that the table top is a square, and as a result of all of these experiences one sees it square, whatever the retinal image may be. The results of all of the various experiences cooperate in giving the object that is seen the appearance it has. To put it the other way, the object that is seen is the one that serves to explain the different earlier experiences ; it is the one that harmonises all of the uses and observations we have made of it in the past. By constant trial and use, a construction develops that proves true when tested in any way. This is accepted as the real object as opposed to mere sensations. Whenever the sensation presents itself, this developed object arises in consciousness.

Not only do constructions that have proved true on test replace the actual sensations that are true under only one condition of perception, but sensations that on test prove not to have external existence are overlooked altogether. Probably many readers of this book never saw an after-image until they read the chapter on sensation, although every visual sensation has its after-image. Again ordinarily you do not see the shadows cast on the rods and cones by the retinal blood-vessels, but if in the dark a candle be held a little to one side of the line of vision and moved about, the network of vessels will be evident. These shadows are overlooked because they have no meaning in the world without. In general, perception is always of real objects; sensations that do not correspond to real objects are always neglected. The character of the percept is changed to correspond to what has proved to be the real object. An object in its turn is real if it will stand the ordinary tests, will satisfy the different uses to which it may be put, and will harmonise with all the related experiences. What one sees is the object which has proved itself real as a result of the various earlier perceptions and which stands the test of all the various trials. Perception is different from sensation in three ways : (1) Memory images are always added to the sensations to complete them and interpret them. (2) The percept is not a mere sum of sensations and memories but an explanation of this and earlier experiences of the same or similar objects, developed by repeated experiences and tests of different kinds. This explanation or interpretation is frequently very little like any single group of sensations that ever has been received from the object. (3) Since the percept satisfies the different uses to which it has been put, it is regarded as real, while the actual sensations may be regarded as unreal or illusory. The Determinants of Perception. If perception is made up of memories as well as of sensations, it is evident that the object seen depends not only upon the sensations that affect the sense-organ, but also upon memories and the laws of association and recall. Where the right memories are lacking, there is no possibility of correct or complete perception. This is seen in the failure to understand or even to hear all that is said in a foreign tongue. One could not repeat accurately even a short sentence in French if entirely unfamiliar with the language, and this largely because the sounds would not be correctly supplemented. One sees much more in an instrument that one already knows something about. To go back to the beginning, it is probable that the child sees practically nothing in the world because it has nothing to bring to it in the way of earlier experiences. But as in the case of recall in general, what is seen depends not only upon having the memories, but upon being able to get them back at the right time. There is frequently a choice in the interpretation that shall be put upon an object. Under these circumstances what is seen depends upon the setting of the object or the attitude at the moment. Associations are subject to the same laws in perception as in recall in general. The drawing in Figure 24 may be seen, either as a flight of steps or as a cornice, according as one brings the right ideas to bear. The figure from Jastrow, Fig. 25, may be seen as a rabbit's head or as a duck's according as one thinks of one or the other. The same dependence upon attitude may be seen in more usual perceptions. If one is listening for footsteps at night, many sounds are likely to be interpreted as footsteps. As a preliminary statement it may be asserted that any perception depends upon (i) the presence of a sensation or group of sensations ; (2) the recall by these of sensations or objects earlier experienced; and (3) upon the mental attitude and more general influences which determine this recall. We may proceed to the discussion of the way these laws act in giving rise to the different forms of perception ordinarily recognised.

Perception of Space. Two properties or aspects of objects are sufficiently alike for all to be treated irrespective of the objects themselves. These are space and time. Space has been particularly thoroughly investigated. Following the usage of geometry, psychology distinguishes three phases of the perception of space : (i) the perception of position, (2) the perception of distance on the surface of the sense-organ, and (3) perception of depth or distance away from the sense-organ. Each of these illustrates the general laws of perception.

The perception of position on skin or eye is so simple and has been made so frequently that it is difficult to distinguish, directly or indirectly, the immediate conditions that give rise to it. If one touches a finger or the cheek, one knows at once what the point is that has been touched, but one cannot say how it is known that it is that point and no other. That the perception of position involves physiological and psychological processes is evident from the fact that the accuracy of localisation varies from point to point on the body. This may be demonstrated by two experiments. Have ypurself touched on the skin and try to indicate the point. You will make a mistake of a millimetre or more if the point be on the finger tip and of several centimetres if on the back or thigh. Or you may have some one touch you with two compass points and determine how far apart they must be before you can say that they are two rather than one. This distance is the * limen of twoness.' On the finger tip it is about i mm., on the back, 40-60 mm. Similarly for the retina, one finds a ' limen of twoness ' at the fovea of .oo4~.oo6 mm. or about the distance between the cones. The limen increases very rapidly with the distance from the fovea. The 'Local

Sign.' To bring these facts under our explanation of perception, it is necessary to find, first, some old experiences that were suggested when the point was touched, and second, the peculiar quality of the point that suggests them. Various theories have been held concerning the nature of both. One of the oldest is that there is a sign of position, the * local sign/ that is different for each point touched and for each point of the retina stimulated, and that this ' local sign * suggests the position. No one has accurately described the ' local sign,' however, and one cannot discover it when one seeks it. Another theory is that stimulation of each point on the skin tends to call out some reflex movement and that this reflex is different for each point. There is, on this theory, either a movement or a tendency to movement which is different for each point of the skin or eye. This theory is partly satisfactory; the main objection is that one can recognise position more accurately than one can touch points on the skin, and that the eye is constantly moving over distances greater than the least appreciable differences in position. Another suggestion for the perception of position on the skin is that the contact recalls a visual picture of the point. This is the only suggestion that can be confirmed by actual observation. The most that can be said is that perception of position is due to some peculiar quality or motor connection attaching to each point on the skin or retina. It is likely that position itself is an idea so frequently used that its nature has become very complex, and the elements are no longer analysed from the mass. It is made up partly of movements or tendencies to movement and partly of ideas derived from sight or touch as the case may be, but also involving a number of other elements. This notion of position, whatever its nature, explains all the various experiences and responds satisfactorily to all tests. With use, the completed notion has come to replace the different elements so entirely that they are lost in it, and cannot now be analysed from it. The stimulation of any point on skin or retina calls out the corresponding notion of position, and that is all that can be said with certainty.

Perception of Distance. The perception of distance on the surface of skin or retina is dependent upon the suggestion of a similar complex that has been no more completely analysed. The one element that has been discovered in the notion of distance is movement. Several illusions indicate that one appreciates distance on the retina by moving the eyes from point to point. Thus, vertical distances are overestimated as compared with horizontal distances, because the adjustment of the eye muscles makes vertical movements of the eyes more difficult than horizontal ones. Distances on the skin also tend to be translated into movement, and the mistakes made show dependence upon movement. In addition, it is probable that distances on the skin are translated into visual distance for interpretation, and that visual distances may more rarely be translated into distances on the skin. That there is usually reference from one sense to another is shown by the fact that where two systems of distance are independent and not corrected by comparison, large mistakes are apt to be made. This explains the large size that cavities in the teeth seem to have when felt by the tongue, as compared with their size when seen in the dentist's mirror. Space as perceived by the tongue is seldom corrected by visual space, while other tactual distances are constantly subject to that correction. Distance, then, is a complex of numerous factors that have been lost in a more general notion. This notion is aroused whenever one estimates distance by the eye, on the skin, or by the movement of the members. What it is in itself one can no longer say, if one ever was able to analyse all of the experiences that have gone to make it up or that have served to develop it.

Perception of the Third Dimension. The perception of the distance of objects from the eye illustrates all of the laws of perception even more clearly than the simpler forms of space perception. The striking fact in connection with perception of this third dimension is that, while the rays of light affect the retina only, the objects that reflect them seem to be some distance away from the eye. Evidently distance cannot depend upon how the retina is stimulated, because a point of light affects the retina in the same way whether the source be two feet away or as remote as a fixed star. That the actual distance makes little or no difference can also be demonstrated by the fact that objects within the eye and even within the retina, when seen at all, seem to be in the outer world, and at a distance from the eye that depends upon the adjustment of the eyes at the time. So, if one lie upon the back on a summer day gazing upward, one will notice little bright specks rushing over the sky. These are the blood corpuscles darting through the blood-vessels in the retina, but when the eye is fixed upon the sky they appear to be far away. The problem of the perception of distance is one of determining what in the character of the excitation calls out the idea of distance, and what the nature of that idea is.

The Physiological Factors. The factors which serve to suggest the distance have been pretty fully made out. They may be classified into eight groups, three physiological and five psychological. The physiological factors are related directly to the adjustment of the eyes. With one eye only, the most important element is the change in the contraction of the ciliary muscle that focusses the eye for different distances. If one looks at a distant object, the lens is flat and the muscle of accommodation is relaxed ; if one looks at a near object, the lens is rounded and the muscle contracted. One may feel the change in strain as one looks from a remote to a near object. This strain of accommodation gives an idea of the distance of the object. Slight strain means distance, increased strain means nearness. The estimation of distance by one eye is much less accurate than with two eyes, as can be shown by asking one to put his ringer through a ring held sidewise. With one eye large mistakes will be made, while with two eyes one can put the finger through each time. Muscular strain is also a factor in binocular perception of distance. When one looks at a distant object, the eyes are parallel; as one looks at nearer objects, the eyes converge, and the nearer the object, the greater the convergence. This can be seen directly in another's eyes. When he looks at a distant object, the white shows about equally on each side ; as he looks at an object only a foot away, considerably more white will show on the outside than on the inside of the eyes. This adjustment is made known to the observer by the strain sensations from the muscles which turn the eyes. These vary with the distance of the object. It is to be emphasised that none of these strain sensations are noticed for themselves. They are overlooked in the interpreting, and one appreciates the distance alone, not the strains that suggest it.

Double Images. One of the most important elements in the perception of distance is the different appearance that objects present to each eye. If one will hold any object before the eyes and look at it first with one eye, then with the other, it will be noticed that one eye sees more of one side, the other more of the other.

If both eyes are opened, it is possible to distinguish in the common view the contributions of each eye. The difference in the pictures decreases as the object moves farther away. The distance of the object is estimated from the amount of difference in the impressions on the two retinas. Similarly one can distinguish the difference in distance of objects by the degree of doubleness of the image of the one not directly converged upon. If one will hold two pencils at different distances from the eyes, it will be noticed that the pencil not fixated is double, whether it be nearer or farther from the eye. The distance between them is estimated directly in terms of the degree of doubleness of the images. As a result of these double images, every object in the field of vision gives an immediate sign of its distance. It is largely due to these double images that the whole field of vision is seen at any moment to have depth. The stereoscope makes application of this principle of double images to give the appearance of depth to pictures. The stereoscope slide has two photographs taken from slightly different positions. When the two pictures are combined, the result is a series of double images similar to those that would have been produced had the observer been standing where the photographs were taken. The difference in the pictures may be seen if one will compare the position of the same object in each. An object in the foreground will be seen nearer the right edge of the view in the left picture, and farther from it in the right picture ; in the background, the relation is reversed. These double images again are not noticed for themselves, either in perceiving actual distances or in the stereoscope. They are overlooked in favour of the distances they suggest.

Psychological Factors in Depth Perception. The psychological signs of distance are found in certain qualities of images which vary with the distance of their objects. The most important of these is the variation in size of the retinal image of objects as they change their distance. This is the element that the artist makes use of hi perspective drawing. He draws the more distant objects smaller than the nearer, and we interpret that to mean that they are distant. A second sign of distance is the haze and changed colour that come with distance. Distant objects are hazy, indistinct, and blue in colour, while near objects are clear and have their own colours. The changed colour and haze depend upon the amount of air intervening. In a very clear, dry air, estimates of distance are subject to large mistakes on the part of one who comes from a lower altitude and denser atmosphere. Distant objects show but little haze or change of colour, and in consequence are regarded as much nearer than they actually are. A third factor of some importance in giving an idea of the distance of objects is their rate of movement, either when they themselves move or when the head or body of the observer is moved. If the usual rate of motion of an object is known, its apparent rate indicates its distance. Far objects seem to move more slowly, near ones more rapidly. A distant railway train seems to crawl across the landscape, while the near one rushes past. As one moves the head with the eyes fixed upon the horizon, near objects are displaced considerably, distant ones very slightly or not at all. If one is looking at a near object and moves the head, objectsfar from the point of fixation move more, those near it less. One may measure the distance of the object by the rate of motion. A fourth, very simple sign of relative distance is superposition. Objects that hide parts of other objects are evidently nearer than the objects covered. Finally, shadows furnish a means of estimating the relative distance of parts of the same object. Bright parts of the surface are ordinarily nearer, shaded parts more distant. The interpretation depends largely upon the way the light is falling, but with any illumination lights and shadows give a means of estimating the distance of the parts. These five characteristics of the retinal image combine with the three factors mentioned above to produce our notion of the distance of seen objects. The idea of distance depends upon all taken together.

Theories of Depth Perception. If the suggestion for the distance is found in one or more of these factors, the question at once arises what the idea of distance is in itself. One of the early theories and one that still has many advocates is that the various signs of distance serve to recall memories of earlier movements which were necessary to reach the object. Movement, no doubt, contributes a large share to the general idea. It is certain that other elements enter. Estimates in terms of movement alone are more inaccurate than those in terms of vision alone. One, for example, has no accurate idea of the distance walked through in the dark, and walking in the dark, one frequently tries to think how great the distance would look. Certainly the visual estimate of a distance is ordinarily more accurate than the purely motor estimate. It is probable that the idea of distance is complex, made up of a great many particular experiences. In this, it is like the idea of position or of distance on the surface of the senseorgan. What elements have contributed to the total effect cannot now be determined accurately. But to movement must be added the appearance of the distances, when viewed from the side and from other angles, and all the various activities that are furthered and hindered by distance. Whatever this complex idea may be, it is at once suggested by the strain sensations, by double images, and the various characteristics of the image that constitute the psychological signs of depth. Each of these primary space ideas has special stimuli that suggest it, and is itself a complex idea that is like no single experience, but is derived from and explains many experiences. Space, as a whole, is only another general idea of the same kind and origin that unites and explains the several less general spatial ideas and which is related to each of them, or combined from them.

Perception of Motion. A second form of perception related to the perception of space and common to all objects is the perception of motion, particularly perception of motion by the eye. We may distinguish two ways of recognising motion. In one, we know merely that an object has moved; in the other, the object is seen to move. The first is illustrated by the second hand and the second by the minute hand of the watch; one can be seen to move, the other we know has moved only because it changes its position between observations. The former alone requires explanation. Apparently perception of motion depends uponthe after-images left on the retina by the moving object. If the hand is moved across the field of vision, it will be noticed that there is a streak behind it that persists for a brief time. The motion is perceived on the basis of this image. The direction of the motion can be determined from the fact that the image is most clear near where the object was last seen. We ascribe motion to an object in the moving picture because the pictures of the object in different positions combine to give an almost continuous streak of after-image behind the object and this is practically identical with the effect produced by the real motion of the object. Motion of the eye shows itself by after-images of all stationary objects. Where both eye and object are in motion, the motion of each must be inferred from the various after effects. The interpretation in each case is not explicit. As in most perceptions, the result alone is evident ; the occasion for the perception is overlooked. In many cases movement is ascribed to one object or another on the basis of probability. In this a mistake is often made. For example, when one is sitting in a car in a station and a train on the next track starts, one is very likely to believe that one's own car has started. This is because one expects the car to start, and also because one is not accustomed to seeing objects move which are as large as the side of the car. The retinal image is ambiguous, and motion is ascribed to the object which seems most likely to move.

' The Perception of Space by the Ears. Two problems must be considered in relation to the auditory perception of space, the appreciation of the distance from which the sound conies, and its direction. In both cases the reference is to sight. When one hears a sound, one at once gives it a place in the visual field. The problem in each case is to determine the characteristics of the sound that suggest one distance or one direction rather than another. The distance to which a sound is referred depends very largely upon the intensity of the sound, provided the actual intensity is known. The barking of a dog is appreciated as near or far according to its intensity as compared with the intensity of the sound when the dog is barking near at hand. Allowance is made for the bark of different kinds of dogs on the basis of the quality of the bark. Where the nature of a sound is misinterpreted, the distance is wrongly estimated. The buzzing of a fly very near is occasionally mistaken for some strange, loud noise at a distance, and similar mistakes in judging distances are rather frequent. The direction of the sound seems to be appreciated by the difference in the intensity or quality of a sound as it affects the two ears. A sound to the right affects the right ear more strongly, a sound to the left stimulates the left more intensely. The relative differences serve to indicate the direction of the sound. In the median plane, the plane midway between the two ears, the effect upon both ears is the same, and in consequence in this plane it is very difficult to say where a tone is. A pure tone directly in front may be referred to a point directly behind, or to any other part of this plane. While the different intensities of the tone as they present themselves to the two ears seem to be the important element in the determination of the direction of the pure tones, noises and complex tones apparently undergo some slight change in their quality with change in direction, which indicates position. This change in quality is due to factors that have not been altogether determined, but it seems probable that it is in part the result of the reenforcement of different components of the complex as the sound comes to the ear from different directions. The Space of the Blind. For the blind, the auditory perception of space is much more important than for the seeing individual. Not only are they more accurate in all of their localisations of sound, but they use sound to obtain an idea of the space in which they are walking, and of the distance of obstacles. The echo of the footsteps varies with the size and shape of the room, and the time between the echo and the original sound increases with the distance of a wall or other obstacle. Even when the echo is not noticed, it affects the quality of the tone. The blind have learned to connect this quality of the tone with the different distances of objects, and guide their movements accordingly. When the boys in a blind asylum were provided with felt slippers in place of their heavy-soled shoes, they could not avoid obstacles with their usual skill. The footsteps were noiseless, and they were deprived of their most important means of appreciating objects at a distance. It is said that the blind ordinarily refer their larger spaces to auditory qualities as we refer them to vision. In all respects perception of space by the ear follows the same law as perception by the eye or skin.

Perception of Time. Much less is known definitely of the perception of time than of the perception of space. Time is much simpler than space and has fewer components. The statement is often made that time has but one dimension, while space has three. The idea of time reduces to before and after, together with the notion of different points in the past. The most essential part of the idea is change, and the occasion for the appreciation of time is also change of some sort. Rhythmic changes in nature, the movements of the heavenly bodies or of pendulums, give the scientific means for the measurement of time. Psychological theories look to changes in the body for the explanation of our appreciation of time, of which two forms must be distinguished. The one applies to intervals of less than four seconds in length, the other to longer periods. Shorter periods ordinarily are referred to changes in strains, particularly the strain that accompanies expectation, and to rhythmic vital processes such as .breathing. One compares short periods of time on the basis of the relative strains of expectation. The strains commence at the beginning of the first interval and increase in intensity until the end. They begin again with the second interval, and when they have reached the same intensity as at the end of the first interval, it is said that the second is equal to the first. These periods of expectation do not ordinarily last more than three or four seconds without relaxation, and even at three seconds become very unpleasant. This is evident to any one who has watched the movement of a clock with a slow torsion pendulum or any similar slow rhythmic movement. The strain of waiting for the turn becomes unendurable after a short period.

Periods longer than three or four seconds are estimated in terms of the events that fill them. Intervals in which much happens seem long, while those which have few incidents or are filled with the monotony of routine acts seem short. A month of the ordinary life seems no longer than a week of travel. This law of dependence upon the number of events, holds primarily of time when considered in retrospect. When the time is passing, the greater the number of events, the shorter seems the time ; while empty time seems very long. The difference probably is due to the different ways of measuring time. While one is merely waiting or is bored, one is constantly aware of the strain sensations that accompany expectation. In other words, empty time seems long as one lives it through, but when one looks back upon it afterward, no events stand out and the time appears short. Time filled with the ordinary routine seems short both in passing and in retrospect. One is too much interested to notice the strains that mark the passage of time or else the strains do not get a chance to reach any marked intensity, because events succeed each other so closely, and there is nothing to stand out prominently in memory. The apparent decrease in the length of the years with increasing age is an expression of this law. In early life, every event is new and seems important ; as one grows older, less and less attention is given to the routine of life, and in consequence the days and weeks seem less full. Strain sensations or the events that fill an interval furnish a basis for the perception of time. The idea which they suggest is a complex of experiences, based primarily upon change, but involving many experiences of motion, and even of space, that have slowly combined with them in a consistent, unitary whole. So far as the idea can be analysed, it is on the same level as the idea of space.

Reading as an Illustration of Perception. The perception of particular objects illustrates the same three laws as these more general characteristics of all objects. One of the best illustrations of the perception of particular things is to be found in reading. Reading seems to be a process of taking words directly from the page to consciousness. Investigation of the reading process under various conditions has demonstrated, however, that one does not actually see all the letters or words that are read, but receives only suggestions of the words, and constructs or recalls them on the basis of these suggestions. In the ordinary connected reading the eye does not run slowly and regularly across the line as is usually supposed, but moves by jumps and all reading is done during a few pauses. The number of these pauses is greater with less familiar material than with more familiar ; there will be from three to six or more in the average length of line. The amount of material read at each pause is greater than can be attended to at a single glance. One must supply the rest. That misprints are frequently overlooked is also an indication that one receives but little from the page, and adds much from memory.

Three forms of reading may be distinguished ; these differ in the sensations that suggest the matter read, and in the material brought out to supplement the sensations. In one we read letters ; in the second we read words ; and in the third we read for sense, and neglect both letters and words. These three are frequently combined or mixed in practice. When reading the letters, as in proof-reading, or in reading separate words, one usually sees only part of the word, and fills out the letters seen by associates. Thus if ' t ' is seen, one tends to supplement by ' h,' and ' l ' is supplemented by ' y,' or other frequent associates ; which of these associates it is will depend upon the environment or setting of the letter. If the letter ' l ' is near the end of the word, it will be supplemented by * y/ while some 'other supplement would be more likely at the beginning. The other letters that have been read will also aid in determining what shall be seen. Even more general contexts will have a part in the process. If one is reading German words, one sort of associates will predominate ; if French, another sort. Often the word is read from its general form, and the letters known to compose the word are supplied later. One may at a second glance look to see if the letter suspected is actually present, and in the right place. Even in reading for letters, association plays a considerable part ; the operation is not one of seeing' alone.

Reading Words and Reading for the Sense. The associative processes have a more important role in reading words, whether in connected discourse or singly. Here, what is seen clearly is the form of the word with a few letters, and these serve to call up the whole word. That one usually reads words rather than series of letters is indicated by the fact that one can read short words more quickly than single letters. The word form, with or without the initial letters, suggests the word by the laws of association, but the associates are controlled by the context and setting. A form that in one connection suggests ' there ' will in another setting suggest ' these ' just as certainly and quickly. One selects the word that makes sense in the particular context, and, if one mistakes the context, may supply a word that is not present, or change the word that is seen to another which fits the context. The more usual form of reading, however, is neither of letters nor of words, but of ideas. As one reads one sees in the mind's eye the scenes that the author describes; the words are overlooked or neglected. This reading for sense or for meaning follows the same laws as other forms of reading. The visual impressions have been connected with ideas, and selection is made from the ideas in accordance with the context, with what has been read, and with the expectation of what the author intends to say. The fact that the same word may have different meanings in different contexts without any interference of one meaning with the other is an illustration, at once of the dominance of the idea, and of the importance of the context in selecting the idea. ' Lead ' is a verb in one context and a noun in another, but one never thinks of the noun when the verb is intended. The idea that is suggested is entirely different in the two contexts, and the idea alone is important. It is because one is so much more concerned with the idea than with the letters or words, that one so seldom distinguishes between what is actually received from sensation and what is added to interpret the sensations. One is intent upon knowing what the author is saying, not how one knows it; the ideas are appreciated, not the process of receiving them.

As this page is read, the eyes dart from point to point on each line, making perhaps five pauses to take in the general form of the words and an occasional letter. These sensations suggest familiar words or familiar ideas, and the suggestions are controlled by the context and the appreciation of what is to be discussed. As a result, you construct for yourself the ideas that I have in mind as I write. You are aware of the ideas ; it is only when some new word is introduced, or the statements are not clear, that you become aware of the words. All other perceptions follow these same laws. In listening to spoken words, you appreciate the ideas, not the sounds. Sometimes when one is listening to a language more familiar in print than in speech, one translates the sounds into visual pictures before one understands, just as in the early stages of reading one may translate the words seen into spoken words before they are understood. In both instances one usually translates into ideas at once. Other objects are perceived in the same way and by the same laws. Any object gives a few sensations that correspond to the letters or form of the words, while the object that is seen corresponds to the words or to the ideas that are read. The distinction between the mere sensations and the appreciated object cannot always be made out so clearly, but the same laws hold in the instances so far analysed.

Optical Illusions. One of the clearest demonstrations of the dependence of perception upon interpretation in the light of earlier experience is found in the fact and nature of illusions. In all forms of perception what is seen or heard frequently proves, on closer examination, not to have had real existence in the outside world, or to have existed in some other form than that in which it was perceived. The illusion is due to one of two causes. The sensations suggest the wrong memories or ideas, either because of close associations, or because the wrong context or setting is dominant at the moment. The influence of close association is most clearly shown in optical illusions of space.

One interpretation of a number of illusions is that they are due to a suggestion of perspective where it does not belong.

One of the most general applications of this law is the tendency to overestimate small angles and to underestimate obtuse angles.

Square surfaces are nearly always seen in perspective, which makes right angles appear to be either acute or obtuse. The most frequent association with these angles is a right angle, an overestimation of the small and an underestimation of the large angle. This association which has become fixed through the great preponderance of rectangular objects leads to error in many different cases. A circle with a square inscribed seems broken at the corners of the square, as may be seen in Figure 27. Where an oblique line cuts a plane figure or two plane figures, the sections of the line seem not to be continuous. (See Fig. 28.) Both illusions can be referred to the overestimation of small angles. A more complicated figure, that may be explained as due to the overestimation of small angles or more directly as a misapplication of a perspective interpretation, is the Hering figure (Fig. 29). In this figure, the oblique lines are taken to represent parallel lines converging toward a vanishing point; and as straight lines drawn on such surfaces would represent curved lines, the parallel lines are assumed to diverge in the middle. This, too, can be explained as a result of overestimation of small angles. In all of these cases, the figure has been closely associated with the wrong interpretation, and the interpretation replaces the actual figure. Other illusions are apparently due to a comparison of parts of the figure that are not directly involved. The best known of these is the so-called arrowhead or Muller-Lyer figure (Fig. 30). The distance bounded by turned-out arrow-heads seems much larger than that bounded by those that turn in. It is probable that one really judges the enclosed area, rather than the distance from angle to angle. The perspective explanation has been applied to this figure also, on the assumption that one figure represents a book opened away from the observer, the other a book opened toward the observer. This makes one line seem more distant and thus larger than the other. Another illusion due to the surroundings is the underestimation of the upper of the two identical figures (Fig. 31). The upper one seems smaller because one expects both to be bounded by the same radii; the failure to extend to that line makes it seem shorter than the lower. A very large number of optical illusions are due to the effects of associations similarly misapplied, and a large number may be brought under these two principles of misinterpretation of perspective, and of arousal of associates by the surroundings.

Illusions illustrating the same principle of the arousal of wrong associates may be found in any field. It has been said that one frequently ascribes motion to the wrong object. When standing on a bridge over a rapidly flowing stream, one can easily believe that the bridge is moving upstream and the water is stationary. This is due to the fact that the smaller object is ordinarily in motion, the ground or the whole field of vision very seldom. The interpretation more frequently associated with the sensations asserts itself against the less frequent. The overlooking of misprints in reading has the same explanation, as has the shadow lines in the letters in Figure 22, page 171. Many misinterpretations of common objects can be referred to the same law. Illusions due to the dominance of the wrong context or to the wrong attitude are also numerous. If one is expecting any object, anything at all like it may be mistaken for it. If one is listening for the footsteps of one person, any passer-by may be mistaken for him. When hunting for cows in the dark, any bush or dark spot takes on the form of the cow. Any preconception or situation that favours one interpretation is likely to arouse associates that constitute a misinterpretation or illusion. In general, illusions are due to wrong suggestions by sensations, either because of the greater strength of the inappropriate association, or because the wrong mental attitude is dominant. Illusions follow the same laws as perceptions ; the only difference is that in the illusion the interpretation is proved false by later observation under more satisfactory conditions.

Hallucination. Hallucinations are closely related to illusions. Hallucinations have a slighter basis in sensation than illusion, and derive more from association. An illusion is always a misinterpretation of an object, while in hallucination there is no apparent basis for the perception in sensation. It is probable that the absence of sensation is in most cases only apparent, and that the sensational basis may be found in some slight stimulation, as in the after-image for the visual hallucination, and in the circulation or some abnormal condition of the middle ear for auditory hallucination. Even in the insane, who are most subject to hallucination, there is considerable evidence that the presence of the false experience is determined by some obscure stimulation of a sense-organ which is misinterpreted and referred to the outer world. Thus a patient may insist that he is constantly hearing voices when no one else hears them, and with no apparent cause. On examination it is found that he suffers from a disease of the ear that produces a constant ringing in the ear, and this has been misinterpreted to give rise to the hallucination. The only difference between this and an illusion is that the illusion is excited by some slight objective sound as when one mistakes the rustling of leaves for an approaching car.

Summary. Perception in all of its phases, then, is due to the interpretation of present sensations by organised earlier experiences. The character of the perception depends upon the sensory stimulus, the developed ideas the individual has at his command, and the connection between these and the sensations. In all cases of perception, the result is accepted as a thing in the outside world, and this, the final outcome of the process, is the only part that is noticed ; all else is overlooked.

QUESTIONS

1. How is a percept different from a sensation?

2. What do associates add to perception?

3. Why do you see the same thing differently at different times? W r hat changes?

4. In what ways are things different from percepts? from sensations?

5. Is space a thing ? If not how are the two related?

6. What is a 'local sign'?

7. Describe the mechanism by which the lens accommodates itself to different distances.

8. Why are two eyes more accurate than one in estimating distances?

9. Do you see double images ordinarily? If not what influence have they in distance perception? If you answer 'yes' in what sense do you use the term 'see'?

10. How does the estimation of the direction of a sound differ in the two different planes : the vertical between the ears and the vertical through the ears?

11. Illustrate from reading the three processes of perception.

12. In what two ways do we estimate the length of a time interval ?

13. What are the possible misplaced associates in the MiillerLyer illusion ?

14. Explain the illusion in Figure 31.

EXERCISES

1. Move the finger in a circle before the face with closed eyes. Do you appreciate the motion in the arm or do you see it with the mind's eye ? How is the picture suggested ?

2. Have some one touch you on the wrist while the eyes are closed. Try to touch the point. Measure the error and repeat twenty times. Average. Is the first touch more or less accurate than the point finally decided upon? How do you know what point was touched?

3. Compare two lines 20 and 21 mm. in length. Can you tell which is the longer? Do the eyes move in the comparison? Can you compare with the eyes stationary?

4. Draw a horizontal line 20 mm. long. Without measuring try to place a point 20 mm. above one end of the line. Measure the distance. Repeat twenty times. Average. Explain result. Repeat, putting the point above the centre of the line. How do the results compare ? Explain the difference.

5. Wave a candle or incandescent electric lamp about to one side of the line of sight in an otherwise dark room. Note the shadows of the retinal blood vessels. Why are they seen outside of the eye? Can you change their apparent position by looking at different distances? Why?

6. Hold a bottle with a label on it about 30 cm. before the nose. Close first one eye, then the other. Note the difference in the images. Place the bottle six metres away. Compare the images as before. Where is the difference between the images greater? Can you see the difference in the images with both eyes open? What is the bearing upon the perception of distance ?

7. Hold the index fingers 25 cm. apart before the eyes. Look at the more distant finger and note the double images of the nearer. Close one eye. Which image vanishes? Look at the nearer finger. Which image of the more remote finger vanishes when one eye is closed? Look at a point 6 m. distant. Can you notice the douoie images ot nearer and more remote objects? How do the double images vary in distance from each other as they depart from the point of fixation ?

8. Have some one tap a two-second interval and attempt to reproduce the interval. How accurate are you? Can you notice strain or other sensations during the interval? Do they seem to affect the comparison?

9. Give a group of students an interval of about two minutes, first when doing nothing, and then while adding. Ask them which is longer. Explain.

10. Watch the eyes of some one when reading at the ordinary rate. How many pauses do the eyes make to the line on the average? Compare reading a newspaper with a page of an unfamiliar chapter of this text. Try when reading to detect misprints. In which instance are the words relatively prominent as compared with ideas?

1 1 . Draw a vertical line with an oblique line across it. Can you see the figure as a cross with the arm perpendicular to the upright, but in some other plane than the plane of the paper? What bearing has this upon the interpretation of the illusion of overestimation of small angles?

CHAPTER VIII

MEMORY AND IMAGINATION

MEMORY, imagination, and reasoning are related to simple imagery very much as perception is related to sensation. Each may be analysed into simple sensational or imaginal qualities, and each follows the laws of association. Each deals with things, is concrete, as opposed to sensations and images which are pure abstractions. Each is an attempt to understand the world and prepares for action in the world. The thought processes differ from perception in the time and place to which the event is referred. In perception it is actually presented to the senses at the moment ; in the three processes under discussion it is regarded as past or future or as having real existence in some distant place. The only other difference is that perception contains some sensational elements, while the others are altogether of central origin. Memory, imagination, and reasoning differ from each other, also, in the temporal reference and the attitude that is taken toward the object or event which they represent. Memories are all ascribed to the past, while reasoned and imagined events may be past, present, or future. Memories and the results of reasoning, again, are accepted as true, imaginings are without implication of truth. Otherwise they are not to be distinguished. Each may be made up of the same elements. One may imagine an event, later reason that it is sure to happen, have this conclusion confirmed by the outcome, and later remember it, all in the same imagery. They are all three suggested and determined in their course by the laws of association. Not the materials or the origin distinguish these states from each other, but the attitude taken toward them and the points in time and space to which they are referred.

The Phases of the Memory Process. We may begin our discussion of thought processes with memory. Memory is a reinstatement of an old experience, or a present consciousness of an old experience, with the knowledge that it is old. Four fairly distinct processes are involved in memory, learning, retention, recall, and recognition. These cannot always be distinguished in practice, but they require separate treatment if memory is to be understood. Any one of them would be valueless without the others. Learning without retention is almost a contradiction in terms. Retention without recall is equally futile. Retention, in fact, can be demonstrated only through recall. The knowledge stored in your brain at this moment gives no sign of its presence. You can be aware of what you know only by recalling it. Finally, if events when recalled were not recognised, recall would be valueless. If when an idea came to mind you could not say whether it was derived from a dream or a real experience, it would be merely confusing. Statements that you remember you have read but cannot refer to a definite book or time can be little relied upon. Each of these processes must be taken up in order.

Observational Memory. It is convenient to distinguish between memory derived immediately from perception and memory for the words into which a perception has been translated. The former is called observational memory. One constantly has occasion to recall and report upon events or objects seen when one had no intention of remembering them. All practical occupations involve memory of this type and success in many of them is dependent upon its accuracy. Numerous experiments have been made upon individuals of different age and intelligence to determine the number of objects that may be recalled and the percentage of mistakes that will be made in reporting. Aside from their general interest, the results determine the amount of credence to be given the statements of witnesses in the courts. In the experiments a group of objects or a picture is shown for forty or fifty seconds and after different intervals the observers are asked to write what they can remember. In other experiments which more nearly approximate court practice, a scene is carefully acted and report made upon that.

The Fidelity of Testimony. Recall in observational memory depends upon three factors : the accuracy of observation, the completeness of retention, and the adequacy of recall. The first depends upon the direction of attention, and the correctness of interpretation. Attention, of course, depends upon the earlier training and the momentary attitude. The observer sees what will give an answer to his specific questions or what earlier experience has shown to be important. The questions that are uppermost also depend upon the training, particular or general. One who has participated in many experiments knows what is likely to be overlooked and makes special effort to observe that. It is also an advantage to put the observations into words when they are made. If, for example, one count at the time of exposure the objects in the picture, the number will be correctly reported, while if one attempts to count from the memory image at the time of recall, mistakes are practically certain. The experiments show that all are more impressed by persons and their acts, by objects and space relations, than by quantities and colours. From eighty to ninety per cent of the first class are correctly reported as compared with forty or fifty per cent of the second. Younger children notice objects and persons and as they grow older appreciate space relations and quantities, and finally colours. Their reports increase in accuracy with age. Everyone, a child especially, is likely to make mistakes in perception by the addition through association of objects or parts of objects not really present. This error increases when one observes rapid actions or when one is under the influence of emotion.

True forgetting is relatively slow for material that has been put into words after observation. Two experiments show an increase in errors of one third of one per cent a day. Much more important are the influences that affect recall.. In writing the report there is always a tendency to add to the actual observation what is only inferred. These additions are supplied by suggestion and are mistaken for real memories. Questions greatly increase this tendency since they suggest objects which are either not observed or only vaguely remembered. When left free to describe an experience in his own way, the individual makes from ten to twenty-five per cent fewer mistakes than when questioned, even when the questions are as free from suggestions as possible. When the question is in any degree leading, the number is greatly increased. If one ask a class to give the colour of an object that is not in the picture, as many as twenty per cent may comply. Children are much more influenced by suggestion than adults and so their testimony is much less to be relied upon. The same holds of a witness on the stand. Cross questioning always decreases the accuracy, although it brings out points that would not be thought of unaided and so is necessary. It may also be added that subjective assurance is not a satisfactory warrant for truth. Statement under oath is only a little more correct than ordinary assertion.

Rote and Logical Memory. In everyday life we put most emphasis upon the retention and recall of events as described in words. Written and spoken words have so large a place in school and in social life in general that verbal memory is assumed to include all memory. In dealing with it we may disregard the errors of observation and emphasise the real memory processes. In all discussions, it is essential to recognise two distinct forms, rote memory and logical memory. In rote learning connections are formed between the successive ideas or elements to be learned, and recall is always from one to another of these elements. In logical learning, on the contrary, the material to be learned is connected with the organised knowledge of the individual ; it is understood, and learned because it is understood. Most learning in everyday life is of the logical sort. We acquire ideas, not mere words, and the ideas are assimilated at once with the ordered experiences. This is much quicker and more effective than rote learning. We must consider both forms in each stage of the memory process.

Experimental Methods. Practically all of the experimental work in memory, of which there has been a great volume in recent years, has dealt with rote learning. Nonsense syllables were chosen as the material to be learned in these experiments, since these were entirely new to all of the learners and hence should be equally easy. Nonsense syllables were made by placing a vowel between pairs of consonants and eliminating all of the combinations that made words. From these syllables series of from eight to sixteen were chosen and shown to the learner at regular intervals. The number of times the series were shown was recorded. Tests as to the amount retained were made after different intervals to measure the amount of retention, and thus to determine the relative value of the methods of learning. A large number of results have been obtained from these experiments, and we can profitably begin our discussion of the memory process by a summary of certain of the more important laws thus established.

The Laws of Learning. Learning, the first step in memory, is only a process of forming associations. Rote learning is primarily a process of forming associations between series of words or events, in the experiments we are considering, connections were formed between nonsense syllables. The experiments were devised to determine the best methods of establishing these connections. The results may be stated in a series of brief laws.

1. Learning is closely dependent upon the number of repetitions. If four repetitions induce a given liability to recall, eight will give approximately double the liability, and others in proportion. Probably the first repetitions are relatively more effective and after a large number the effect of each is relatively less, but between eight and sixty-four repetitions each has approximately the same value. It is important to note in this experiment that the series could be repeated without mistake after thirty-one repetitions. This means that after the learning is apparently complete, the added repetitions increase retention although at the moment no effect is apparent.

2. Capacity for learning increases with age up to the period of maturity, and then remains constant until the beginning of old age. The popular belief that children learn better than adults has no basis in fact. It is due apparently to the child's closer observation of routine events, and to the frequency with which events of childhood are recalled on account of their original interest. When tested in any accurate way, the child is found to learn less easily and to retain less well than the adult.

3. Distributed Repetitions more Effective than Accumulated. Learning is easier if the repetitions be distributed over several days, rather than accumulated on a single day. With twenty-four repetitions, two repetitions on each of twelve days are more effective than four repetitions on six days, or six on four days. Any distribution will be better than to have twenty-four on one day. In general the most effective distribution is one repetition every other day. This is due largely to the

fact that the change induced in the nerve-cells by learning increases during the period between repetitions. The new repetitions add more to the old when its effects have had time to 'set/ to become more completely incorporated in the nervous tissue. It is a common observation that a lesson is better learned if one will prepare it on one day and review it the next morning, than if one prepares it more thoroughly at the first sitting, an instance of distributed repetitions.

4. Learning as a Whole vs. Learning by Parts. In learning a selection, it is advisable to read through the whole from beginning to end, and to repeat the reading until all is learned, rather than to learn bit by bit. If one attempts to learn a poem line by line or stanza by stanza, one makes a number of unnecessary and misleading associations between the ends and the beginnings of lines that both waste time and interfere with the correct associations. Then, too, learning by parts leads to the repetition of the first portions more frequently than is necessary, since they are repeated with each of the later parts. The only objection to learning by wholes is that one is likely to lose interest in the work when no progress can be noticed, and to read more slowly than usual. This may be obviated by making pauses at the natural points of division without going back to the beginning. It is also advisable, after the selection is partly learned, to repeat the harder parts more frequently than the easier. These methods combine the marked advantage of learning as a whole with the greater interest that comes from observing progress in the task. When this rule was observed, some investigators demonstrated a saving of from twenty to fifty per cent in the repetitions required for learning.

5. Dependence upon Rate of Repetition. Learning is quickest if the rate of repetition is as fast as is convenient for the man who is learning. Slower repetitions waste time and permit distraction ; faster distract attention from the learning to the articulation. As many as two hundred syllables a minute have been found most advantageous for some individuals. When a student has been compelled to postpone preparation of a lesson to a short period before the recitation, unexpected results are shown for the time spent. Rapid reading is of less value for material that requires thought than for rote learning. Slower reading permits the formation of more associates ; rapid reading gives strong associates with the preceding and succeeding elements, but gives no time for others that might be important. Slow reading is better at first ; more rapid later, when the material has been partly learned.

6. Rhythm Aids Learning. Rhythm is a great aid to learning. It is difficult to avoid rhythm, and best results may be obtained from a rhythm adapted to the material and to the individual peculiarities of the learner. The strongest connections are made between the elements of the rhythmic unit. When the rhythm is changed or elements are given a place in a new unit, relearning or retention is much interfered with. The importance of rhythm is shown by the ease with which blank verse may be learned.

7. Learning is much quicker if the material is repeated with the intention of recall. Sanford found that he could remember very little of the Morning Prayer which he had read more than five

thousand times. With the intention of recalling, twenty repetitions should, at a conservative estimate, give complete learning.

8. Active repetitions are of more value than passive. If one tries to repeat from memory as soon as possible, fewer repetitions are required than if one continues passive readings. Witasek found that learning was quickest with six readings and fifteen attempted repetitions.

9. Associative Inhibition. Ideas learned in one connection seem to be more difficult to learn in another connection. If idea ' A ' has been learned in connection with an idea ' ,' it will be more difficult to learn it in connection with another idea ' C/ than if the other association had not been formed. Learning anything incorrectly makes correct learning more difficult. The wrong associations check the formation of the correct associations. Associative inhibition is present only when the first set of associates has not been completely formed. After complete learning, the one set of associations may make easier the formation of others of the same kind. If, for example, one has partly learned one style of typewriter key-board, it is much more difficult to learn another; but if the first has been thoroughly learned before one begins the second, the second will be learned more quickly than the first. The same holds in some degree of learning languages.

All learning, then, is a process of forming associations ; and all rote learning, with much of other learning, depends for its adequacy upon the use of suitable methods of repetition. To translate into nervous terms, learning is a process of producing changes in the synapses. This change depends directly upon the number of repetitions, upon the age of the individual, upon the time that elapses before one repetition is succeeded by another, and by the rhythm and rate of repetitions. Proper control of these factors and of attention gives the means of easiest and most complete learning.

RETENTION AND FORGETTING

If learning is the result of producing changes in the synapses, retention depends upon the persistence of the impression, forgetting, upon its disappearance. That the impressions fade and gradually disappear with the passage of time is obvious, but the rate of disappearance and the conditions that favour or retard the disappearance can be determined only by experiments. The same procedure that gave us the laws of learning has also developed a series of laws of forgetting. We may summarise these as before.

i. Rate of Forgetting. Forgetting goes on very rapidly at first, then more slowly, until finally there is no appreciable change even over long periods of time. Ebbinghaus found that with series of nonsense syllables, half of the learning was lost in the first hour ; two-thirds the first day ; while at the end of the month, less than four-fifths was forgotten. Radossawljewitsch obtained the same general law, but with a slower rate of forgetting for the shorter periods. In ordinary learning, details disappear very quickly, while the more general principles are remembered for a long time. Both in sense and nonsense material, traces of learning persist long after all possibility of recall in the ordinary way. In the experiments, the amount of forgetting is measured by comparing the number of repetitions needed for relearning after the lapse of some definite time with the number of repetitions used in the original learning. Thus, if sixteen repetitions are required for learning a series of twelve syllables, eight repetitions may be necessary to relearn at the end of the hour. After three days, no single one of the syllables can be recalled off-hand, but all can be relearned in ten repetitions. In much practical learning, the same rule holds. One may have forgotten all about a principle in arithmetic, but will find that it can be relearned in a fraction of the time originally given it. Not a little of the benefit of learning lies in this increased ease of relearning, even where nothing can be recalled spontaneously. Forgetting is much slower for sense material than for nonsense. Ebbinghaus found that half was retained at the end of twenty-four hours, as compared with one-third for nonsense syllables. He was able to demonstrate a saving of seven per cent in relearning poetry after the lapse of twenty-one years.

2. Retroactive Inhibition. After learning, the degree of retention is affected by mental activity of any sort.

If, after learning a series of nonsense syllables, one turns at once to learning something else or to any other form of mental work, retention is sometimes less complete than if one rests a few minutes. The new work seems to interfere with some continuing activity of the nervous system that is essential to the best retention. This * setting ' of the associations after learning is probably what makes distributed repetitions more effective than accumulated ones. It is also connected with the memory after-image, that has been mentioned in previous chapters (vide, p. 145). The nerve-cells continue to act for some little time after the conscious processes have ceased and the associations increase in strength during this period. New work interferes with this activity, and prevents the associations from reaching their full strength. This so-called retroactive inhibition is analogous to the retrograde amnesia of the psychiatrist. This technical term means that a mental or physical shock will destroy memories of immediately preceding events which may be assumed to be represented by associations that have not completely ' set.' A blow upon the head often obliterates the memories of events that have occurred for a half hour or more before. An emotional shock may have the same effect. In our present connection, hard mental work exerts the same influence in smaller degree. A lesson will be better remembered, if one will wait three to six minutes after finishing it before turning to another task.

3. Individuals who learn easily seem to forget slowly while those who learn slowly forget rapidly. This law holds if one considers pure rote learning. When learning sense material by logical connections, the man who learns slowly may have an advantage if he gives the added time to understanding the matter. In this case the evidence shows that slow learning is compensated for by retentive memory. The conditions and results are somewhat in dispute.

All learning and retention, then, are dependent upon the formation and persistence of associations. Learning and retention are never of ideas or things in isolation, but always of things in connection. The only laws that affect learning are the laws for the easy and quick formation of associations, and for preventing interference with them when they are formed. No new principles need be added to the discussion of association to understand rote learning and retention.

The Advantages of Forgetting. One is inclined to think of forgetting as altogether a disadvantage. A little consideration shows that on the contrary, if everything were remembered, it would probably be a great misfortune. Many of the trivial events of everyday life are very much better forgotten. Forgetting is an expression of the selective activities of consciousness, and is almost if not quite as important as attention in protecting the individual against the unessential events. Attention very largely determines what shall be selected, both for observation and retention, although it may work different results for each, since many things important at the moment are not worth recalling. Forgetting plays its part in permitting these to lapse into unconsciousness. A good memory involves a certain amount of forgetting, provided only the right things are forgotten. Not only is it an advantage to forget the trivial events but also to forget things that were learned wrongly. If one remembered everything, the bad would survive with the good. As it is, when a mistake has been made and corrected, the correction may be remembered, the mistake forgotten. On the whole, then, the fact that the memory trace in the nervous system tends to disappear is an advantage rather than a disadvantage. In some cases where no distinction is made between the important and the unimportant, the individual is rendered ineffective. Slavery to detail often leads to waste of time and effort that a bad memory might prevent. In the adequate use of past experiences forgetting is almost as important as remembering.

RECALL

The laws of recall, too, are primarily the laws of association. Just as everything that is learned must be learned in connection with something else, so anything that is recalled must be recalled because of the rearousal of an associate. This can be brought about only through the presence of some cue, some idea associated with the fact essential at the moment. One cannot recall an idea without the associated idea or sensation. It is impossible to get back the fact in any other way than through the appropriate suggestion. This suggestion may be furnished by the preceding idea or it may come through sensation. Fortunately nearly every fact has been associated with the occasions that make its return desirable, and in consequence one never suffers from or even notices the lack of more direct means of recall. The desire for recall brings its satisfaction, and that is all that can be asked. The laws of recall come into prominence only when they fail to be effective . Occasionally one is certain that one has a bit of knowledge that would be desirable at the moment, but which cannot be recalled. Under such circumstances, one of two factors is at fault. Either no association has been formed between the idea in mind and the idea desired, or the mental attitude is wrong for developing that association. These are the conditions for the return of associations discussed in Chapter V. The one can be obviated only at the time the associations are formed, is due to the nature of the learning ; the other depends upon the condition of the thinker at the moment of recall.

Certain and accurate recall depends primarily upon the methods of learning; it is only in part subject to control at the moment of recall. The only rule that can be given for the improvement of recall is to learn a new fact in connection with all of the possible situations that may require its application. Most learning is in one connection only or in a few at most. The value of a fact increases with the number of connections that it makes, for each new connection makes it available in a new place and at a new time. These valuable connections can be supplied by taking time to think of the various uses that a new fact may have, or, more effectively, by actually applying it. A formula in trigonometry will be impressed much more surely and will be recalled in many more appropriate situations if a number of problems are solved by it. Each of these applications, when they appear in practice, will suggest the principle; while without them, only the preceding statements in the text will recall it, and these are seldom present when the principle is needed. In general, learning any new fact in all its useful connections will insure perfect recall so far at least as it may be insured at the moment of learning.

Attitude Influences Recall. The other element in recall depends upon having the correct attitude toward the situation when it presents itself. If one does not properly appreciate the situation, the associates that might be used at the time will fail to be recalled. When one is looking at the problem from the wrong standpoint a number of solutions that harmonise with that attitude will present themselves, but they will not be solutions of this problem. Both sorts of failure to recall may be observed in any class recitation. When a question is asked, it should serve as a cue for the answer. In many if not most cases, the failure to answer does not depend upon lack of knowledge, as is proved by the fact that the answer will be recognised when it is given. What is wrong is the failure to connect the answer with the question at the time it was learned. It was learned in some other connection, and is useless as an answer to this question. In the second place, the question may be understood in the wrong way. The question may have been connected with the answer when understood in one way, but, at the moment, the student is thinking of the question in one way, the instructor in another. The result is that the answer suggested does not meet the problem that the instructor has put. Adequate recall depends, first, upon having the material; then upon having the knowledge associated with an idea or object present when that bit of knowledge is needed ; and finally, upon being in a suitable attitude toward the situation. The first two, learning and learning in the right connections, can of course be insured only before the time at which the knowledge is to be used. The attitude is the only factor determined at the time of recall, and that is not easily controlled. It depends upon the agility of wit of the thinker, and upon the things he has been seeing or thinking just before. The most that can be done in the control of the attitude is to teach the individual to look at a situation in many ways, and to trust his memory. Taking the right attitude is in large part due to native endowment, but training or practice has some effect.

Reproductive Inhibition. One factor similar to associative inhibition, that was considered in discussing learning, may affect recall. This is reproductive inhibition. Associates with the same idea, not only interfere with each other in the formation, but also prevent the recall of the ideas.

If one has learned ' A ' with ' B,' ' C,' and ' D,' and 'A' is in consciousness, the recall of any one of the associates may be prevented, or at least delayed. All associates tend to return, and each helps to prevent the return of the others. This mutual interference of associates is probably the explanation of many cases of mental blocking. Often when one is trying to recall a perfectly familiar fact, it refuses to return. It seems to be on the tip of the tongue, but cannot be expressed. Later, when the occasion for its recall has passed, it will return with perfect ease. It is probable that the cue was associated with several ideas, and that they mutually prevented the return of any one. When recall occurs, probably all but one of the associates have ceased to be active. Ordinarily some one associate will be much stronger than the others, or will be favoured by the context or ' mental set,' and the opposition of the others is ineffective.

Logical as Opposed to Rote Learning. So far, we have been discussing memory as if all associations were formed at once, and as if all learning dealt with entirely new knowledge. As a matter of fact, however, most learning consists in bringing the new material into connection with old knowledge, or in seeing old knowledge in new lights. When one is reading even in a new subject, one is constantly referring what is read to earlier knowledge, rather than taking the new as new. We can bring ourselves to read very little of what we do not understand, yet to understand means nothing more than to refer the new to old knowledge or old principles. What is understood is learned very quickly, even by a single repetition. A large part of the work necessary for learning was done when the principles themselves were learned and does not need to be done again. All that is necessary is to connect the new with the old, and the new then takes on the permanence of the old.

The advantages of logical learning are twofold. In the first place, as was indicated above, when one understands, the material is partly known already, and so needs fewer repetitions to be remembered. In the second place, there are many more facts than principles, and the principles are used so frequently in different connections that they become part of the permanent endowment. Specific instances may appear and be forgotten, but the general principles illustrated are used over and over and thus are given no chance to be forgotten. When the new fact or experience is understood by being referred to this system of principles, it, too, comes to partake somewhat of their permanent character. One may notice in the simplest affairs the difference between the bare unaided memory and this memory of general principles. In playing golf, for example, one may either remember in a vague general way where the ball has been driven, or may fix the place by specific reference to a prominent object. If one merely notices, one may at once walk to the ball with no other thought than that one is going in the right direction. Under ordinary circumstances this suffices, but if one is turned aside to hunt the ball of the opponent, or the stroke is bad and arouses an emotion, the pure, unmediated memory is destroyed ; one retains but the vaguest idea of the direction of the ball. If, however, one refers the position to some fixed point, refers it to a system, the position will be remembered in spite of distraction, and for a considerably longer time.

Logical Learning more Rapid and more Permanent. Nearly all of the experiments whose results have been formulated in the earlier sections, have been made with nonsense syllables. Similar experiments with sense material learned as one ordinarily does for ideas rather than for words show that the laws stated above are true for logical as well as for rote memory. The most striking difference between the two forms is the greater ease and permanence of logical learning. Ebbinghaus found that learning poetry verbatim takes less than half the time required for nonsense syllables, but memory for the sense of ordinary reading matter has a much greater advantage. Long passages that would require days for their verbatim, learning can be appreciated and the ideas retained with one reading. The rate of forgetting is also much slower. A fact thoroughly understood may be remembered for most of a lifetime. Accurate experiments on the course of recognition indicate that objects, that may be referred to standards or general principles, are recognised practically as well after a longer as after a shorter time, while sensations, to which no names can be given or which can be referred to no general principle, lose their value for recognition at about the same rate as that at which nonsense syllables are forgotten. What experimental evidence there is, together with the results of observation, indicates that logical learning is very much quicker than learning of nonsense syllables, and that the material is much more slowly forgotten. Most learning is of ideas, and ideas follow logical laws, are learned in connection with principles already known rather than by the bare laws of association. In consequence, the usual learning is much quicker and forgetting much slower than the results obtained from experiments on nonsense syllables indicate. The one important difference is that what is essential in logical learning is the formation of associations between the new and the general principles that explain them, rather than the formation of associations between successive elements.

Cramming. Recent investigations throw considerable light upon the old problem of cramming. Cramming is essentially a process of learning by accumulated repetitions. In recent experiments upon material learned for its ideas rather than for the words, accumulated repetitions gave as good results as distributed when tested twenty-four hours later, while the divided repetitions were much more effective after two weeks or a month. This harmonises with the common experience that material studied intensively just before one needs to use it can be recalled fairly accurately, but leaves no permanent impression; while the work learned by various repetitions during the term, even if it be no better recalled at the time of examination, will be remembered for a long time. Frequent reviews are very valuable for the permanent retention. Edwards found that four minutes' study of a short selection with two and a half minutes' review a few days later gave thirty per cent more correct responses than six and a half minutes' study at the first sitting. In addition to the probably physiological effect of divided repetitions, frequent return to a topic makes it possible to relate it to many different facts and thus increase the number of events that will arouse it. Then, too, the definite intention to learn anything for a particular occasion seems to give a tendency for it to be forgotten when that occasion is past. Cramming for these reasons gives only temporary retention. Lasting knowledge demands faithful work day by day and frequent reviews.

General Principles Retained Longer than Particular Facts. Evidence for the advantages of logical learning and the importance of the background of organised knowledge may be obtained from a study of the decay of memory. The more general ideas and those earliest acquired are always the last to be lost. The aged remember the events of childhood and general principles long after recent events and particular ideas have been forgotten. In brain diseases of different origins the same laws hold. Common nouns are remembered after proper names are forgotten ; verbs are remembered longer than nouns ; and gestures persist when words have been forgotten. The reason may be found in the greater chance for the general terms to grow into the nervous system. The general terms and general principles have been used hundreds of times where particular words are used once, and each use makes the impression stronger, and makes possible recall on new occasions. The same factors that make these fundamental principles useful and permanent in the memory of the normal individual make them last to disappear with the degeneration of nervous tissue in disease and old age.

Logical Memory Is of Meaning. Not only the methods of remembering, but the content of the memory image, are different in logical memory. One thinks of remembering as a process of reinstating an experience in its original form. As a matter of fact, however, one does not ordinarily have the same sort of image ; in fact, the image may not be at all like the original ; it merely means the same thing. The image is modified by all that has been seen in that connection since the former experience. One nearly always remembers the event, not as it actually was, but as it must have been in the light of what has been experienced before and after. One interprets the experience in terms of the system of knowledge, and the system modifies the images that are recalled. Reasoning and memory combine in the construction of the recalled image. Still more frequently, no very specific image is reinstated ; one remembers, not the event itself, but that the event happened. The imagery involved in remembering that a thing happened is perhaps some symbol of the event, or some general symbol plus the associations that connect it with a specific time ; the image is lost in its meaning, in the fact that it represents. The image itself is not attended to, and one cannot say, after the experience has been recalled, what the image was in itself. This sort of recall is closely related to reasoning, and the process can be understood better after the discussion of meaning in the next chapter. Suffice it now to say that the memory is usually, not of images, but of meanings.

RECOGNITION

Forms of Recognition. After recall conies recognition. Recognition may be defined as an awareness of the time and place of origin of the memory image. Both objects and ideas are recognised, and recognised in the same way. One meets a friend of earlier years, and immediately or after some thought can refer him to a definite place and to a definite time in the past. Similarly an idea may float into memory and either be recognised as a fact read in a school book, or be referred vaguely to the past without specific knowledge of its warrant or of its authority. The explanation of recognition is the same for ideas and for objects. The process can be studied most easily in connection with the delayed or indirect recognition. Frequently one sees an object, and is at first uncertain where it has been seen before or what it is. Gradually other ideas cluster about it. As the new object suggests old ones, the new begins to seem familiar, and finally is completely recognised. Then it takes its place with the ideas that have themselves been recognised. One may see an animal and feel that it is of a familiar species, but not remember what it is. The object suggests a setting in which it was seen before, and that may suggest the name that a friend gave to it at the time, or the picture of the animal in the volume in which it was looked up after it had been seen. A face may be recognised in the same way. The face seems familiar, but the name cannot be given nor the place where it was seen. Gradually a cluster of memories group about the face, the background of a familiar room where the man was seen, or the class room where he had been sitting ; then the name or other explanatory ideas come up. and recognition is complete. In general, then, this delayed or mediate recognition is always due to associates aroused by the object or idea, when it presents itself to consciousness.

Mechanism of Immediate Recognition. When recognition is immediate, one knows at once that the object is familiar, there is no evidence of the nature of the process. The idea or thing is accepted and that is all there is to it. This is the more usual sort of recognition. One knows nothing of how a close friend is recognised, or of how one tells his own text-book from his neighbour's. It is pretty clear from experiment and observation that the process is in part the same as in mediate and delayed recognition. Associates are aroused as before, but they come at once and do not attract attention for themselves. They give evidence of their presence only by the fact that the object is recognised. When the very familiar object presents itself, there is a rush of associates, or the opening of a. number of association paths that bring the recognition with them. To the rush of associates one may undoubtedly add a number of movements called out reflexly. One knows one's own fountain-pen by the fact that the movements that it excites are suited to trie pen ; there is no hesitation or false adjustment. When a friend's pen has been picked up by mistake, one becomes aware of the mistake by the awkwardness of the movements. The position of the fingers, that is best for the familiar pen, makes the new one scratch, or it fails in some other way to respond as the old one does. Part of the recognition of an object that is not handled or that does not give rise directly to movements is due to the fact that its uses are appreciated, that when it is recognised, one knows at once what to do with it and how to use it. As a result of the associates and of the smoothness in the actual and the intended or possible movements, the old object ordinarily arouses a feeling of pleasure, while the unfamiliar is nearly always unpleasant. Possibly one may assume a peculiar feeling of recognition in addition to the pleasure, but this is less ea:y to be sure of than the fact of recognition. Three factors contribute to the process of recognition. First, the arousal of associates ; second, the excitation of familiar movements ; third, pleasantness, a result of these two processes. \

Recognition a Reference to the System of Knowledge. One question that is at once suggested in this connection is why the arousal of old associates should tell what the object is and where it was seen before. Part of the answer is found in the fact that the associates themselves are recognised. If each associate must be recognised by other associates, the process would become interminable and compel one to run through the experiences of the individual from the time of the event recognised to the present moment. This is evidently never necessary ; at most one or two sets of associates suffice for complete recognition. The reason is that we make use of the system of knowledge in recognition as in learning and retention. One refers the new to the developed system. When the new arouses an element of this system, recognition is complete. In other instances what we call recognition is nothing more than reference of the new thing to a general class. We recognise a small animal as a weasel when we can classify it; there is no implication that it has ever been seen before. This classification is only a reference to our system of zoological knowledge. Similarly, prominent events in life constitute a framework for the recognition of new events. These may be the places in which one has lived, or the different stages in the school life which serve for the recognition of personal events as do the kings of England as points of reference for all other events of modern history, or the succession of reigns in Rome for ancient history. Any event is placed when it is known to have been related to or contemporaneous with one of these landmarks. To understand, and to recognise in this way are very closely related operations. Each consists in being referred to the framework of knowledge or to the system of prominent events.

Paramnesia. Paramnesia, an interesting illusion of recognition, throws much light upon its nature. One occasionally feels, when in a new place, that one has been there before. The whole setting and many of the details of the place are familiar, yet one is certain that this is the first visit. Plato described the experience and used it in support of his theory of the transmigration of souls. He argued that the recognition indicated that the place had been visited in an earlier existence. As a matter of fact, however, the explanation is to be found in a misplaced recognition. Some parts of the situation are similar to old situations. These serve to arouse associates which give rise to a feeling of familiarity, and this feeling extends from the part to the whole. The illusion illustrates the dependence of recognition upon association and related psychological processes. The old is not recognised where these processes are lacking, and the new seems familiar when by chance they are called out where they do not belong.

The Best Methods of Remembering. Since the ancients many attempts have been made to find easy and certain ways of learning and remembering, and in all ages there have been individuals who profess to have methods for improving the memory. All of these attempt to make use of special methods in forming associations. They fall into two general classes, methods of learning single things such as dates, and methods of connecting two facts or events that it is desirable to remember together. Systems for remembering single events attempt to connect them with symbols that will be more easily remembered. Numbers are remembered by representing each digit by several consonants and then making words that include these consonants. Thus one may represent 8 by /, 7 by g, and i by /. Then one can recall that Alfred came to the throne in 871 if the burned cakes suggest fagot, a symbol for 871. Similar combinations could be made to represent any date or number, and the word is easier to remember than the number. Where two events are to be connected in memory, it is possible to form nonsense or superficial connections between them that shall serve to recall one when the other is given. In one system it is suggested that one may remember that tele in French means ' head/ by connecting tete with ' potato ' ; that in turn with ' root/ since potatoes are roots, and this by contrast with ' head.' Similar series of words are suggested for many other pairs, and the system consists in forming them for all series of facts. It is certain, however, that when used extensively, any such system requires more effort and is less satisfactory than the ordinary means of learning. Mnemonic verses and similar devices have some value in remembering a few purely arbitrary facts, such as the number of days in the months, but the usefulness of the system does not extend far.

The best mnemonic system is the ordinary logical system of classification. The connections are not arbitrary here, and each series of associates holds not for one fact alone but for very many. In one sense, the classifications of the sciences are parts of a vast mnemonic system. Each general principle groups many facts about a single statement. Since the general principles are themselves more or less closely connected, they amount in practice to a system of associations in which a few things, if they are remembered, will serve to recall all the knowledge of the individual. As we have seen, this system of knowledge, when it has been developed, makes easier the learning of all things referred to it, makes their retention more permanent, and by giving them a place assures their recognition. It follows that the more one knows, the better is one's memory; the more one knows of any subject, the easier it is to learn new facts in that subject. Much better, then, than any artificial memory system is a patient, thorough learning and logical classification of facts. This not only makes easy the learning and retention of the fact in question, but prepares for the acquisition of related facts. Learning logically is like putting money at compound interest. The material is not only saved, but grows and makes easier further acquisition.

Summary. Memory, then, is not a faculty but a fact ; and on analysis it is found to be, not one fact or process, but four that together make possible the reinstatement and use of earlier experiences. Learning, retention, recall, and recognition are special phases of the laws of association, and of the interaction between the particular new events and the earlier accumulated and systematised knowledge. Although the fundamental principles of memory are found in the laws of association, special methods may be used to advantage in learning, retention, and recall. But above all special methods stands the one general principle that memory at each stage requires constant reference to systematised knowledge. This makes learning easy and rapid, gives permanent retention, assures recall on the appropriate occasion, and provides the essential conditions for recognition.

Rules for Learning. We may summarize the results of this chapter in a series of rules for study both for material to be learned verbatim and for the ordinary retention of ideas.

For rote learning :

1. Read over carefully the material to be learned, slowly at first, then more rapidly as it begins to be mastered.

2. Read always with the intention of remembering as well as with full attention.

3. Attempt to repeat as soon as you are confident of success and continue to repeat actively until the material is thoroughly impressed.

4. Do not attempt to learn all at once. Divide your repetitions. Repeat once a day, or on alternate days until mastered.

5. Read the whole selection through from beginning to end rather than attempting to commit bit by bit.

If parts offer especial difficulty you may well depart from this rule to impress them separately. These should be divided from the rest by an interval before and after. Reading through the whole once each day will master a selection of considerable length with little effort.

6. Rest for about six minutes after learning one selection before turning to other mental work.

For learning ideas most of the same rules may be applied. In addition :

1. Understand what you read. To this end (a) read always with a ' why ' in mind ; ask is this so and find good reasons for or against before you leave it. (6) Where possible refer each fact to its causes, (c) Think over what you read in its important connections. (d) The relations should be represented graphically in a diagram. In taking lecture notes, write an outline of the main logical heads and fill these in from memory immediately afterwards. Make a similar outline of each chapter of a book as you read.

2. Review as frequently as possible to obtain the value of divided repetitions. In reviewing, diagram again and bring out in this review diagram the relation between the different lectures or lessons.

3. Make as many active responses as you can during the studying. Apply what you learn in as many ways as possible. Work problems that involve the principles. If the material permits draw the objects described.

4. On the rare occasions when facts have no logical connections you may form arbitrary or nonsense associations. These should be used as little as possible and then only when they are obvious and unambiguous.

5. In both forms of learning trust your memory in recall. The first suggestion is probably correct and should be accepted unless you have positive reasons against it. Confidence aids memory, while doubt paralyzes recall.

Imagination. Closely related in many ways to memory are the processes grouped under the term imagination. This term is used in two senses, (i) It designates the process of forming images, the root meaning of the term ; (2) it covers all processes of construction, ranging from day dreaming to developing scientific hypotheses. The first use of the term is approximately identical with the formation of imagery discussed in Chapter V and need not be considered again here. The second term covers a wide field of operations closely related to memory and reasoning and in many respects intermediate between them in character. The ideas develop in imagination as in memory under the stimulation of some sensory process and run their course under the influence of associations. As distinguished from memory the products of imagining are not reinstatements of old experiences but are new. This does not mean that the materials are' new. As has been repeated frequently, all the central processes are, fundamentally, returned sensory experiences. In imagination, however, the materials are combined in new ways and thus make new objects or events.

The Course of Imagination. The same laws of association are apparent in imagination as in memory. The only difference is that an element from one experience recalls a similar element from another, or events that were contiguous or succeeded each other in one experience are transferred to other larger connections by virtue of common elements. In most constructions of the imagination, one may distinguish two factors, the functions of which correspond to recall and recognition in memory, the production and testing, respectively. The associative processes are constantly active, mental pictures occupy the entire waking life, but it is only now and again that the constructions are of value. It is not possible to obtain a particular effect directly. Usually a number of constructions will appear before one presents itself which fulfils the requirements and wins approval. The acceptance or rejection alone can be controlled ; what shall appear is subject only to the most general control. That one cannot even think of anew thing at will is made evident by attempting to draw as many different figures as possible. When examined all show many of the same characteristics, one element runs through them all. While a desire for one idea will nearly always induce something of the same class, more exact control is impossible, one can only wait for the desired construction to turn up and it may come soon or late or never.

Forms of Imagination. The products of imagination may be more or less like objects and events actually experienced.. It is customary to distinguish between reproductive and productive imagination. The productive imagination gives material that is very different from anything seen before, reproductive is more like memory. The difference is one of degree only and no great agreement can be obtained as to what is productive and what reproductive. It is said that Sir Walter Scott carefully examined even the minuter flowers in a setting that he had chosen as the scene of one of his romances thus taking much of what was to be a new construction from direct and detailed observation. This would certainly be reproductive imagination in spite of the newness of the events depicted. At the other extreme are certain descriptions of poetic fancy, Dante's Inferno for example, or the constructions of the mathematician or inventor. One approximates memory, the other reason. They differ in the attitude taken toward the product rather than in the product itself or the way in which it is attained.

QUESTIONS

1. How much of the accuracy of the testimony concerning ar accident depends upon attention and perception and how much upon memory?

2. What is the difference in the activities involved in observational and in rote memory ?

3. Is learning ever perfect? Is forgetting ever complete? What is the difference between learning half and half learning?

4. What is the ' setting ' process in learning ? How does it explain the advantages of divided repetitions?

5. What is retroactive inhibition? how dependent upon the perseveration tendency?

6. Why is cramming a bad method of study? Answer in the light of the laws of learning and forgetting.

7. What rules should be observed in studying to make probable a satisfactory recitation?

8. How does the ordinary recitation by question and answer illustrate the laws of recall? What is the question and what the answer in the terminology of memory ? Give some conditions that may make a good recitation impossible, even if the answer to the question is known.

9. Cite instances from your own experience of associative and reproductive inhibition.

10. What are some of the advantages of forgetting ?

11. Give instances in your own experience that illustrate the advantages of logical over rote memory. In what subjects do you use the first and in which the second ?

12. Trace the course of recognition in some instance in which recognition is delayed. Why should the mental operations that result make the object seem familiar ?

13. What rules suggest themselves for acquiring a good memory ? What are the limitations of the rules ?

EXERCISES

1. Show a group of students a picture with a few prominent highly coloured figures. Twenty minutes to an hour later ask the members to describe it in detail. Prepare a list of questions to bring out important points and request them to answer them. Count the number of objects that can be readily seen and find the proportion of these reported by each subject. What percentage of objects reported are not in the picture or are wrongly described ? Make a similar count of the questions rightly answered.

2. Select two bits of verse of eight lines each as much alike as possible in metre, ease of learning, etc. Learn one at one sitting, keeping a record of the number of repetitions and the time required

for learning. Read the second through twice each day until it is learned. Which method is the more economical?

3. Choose two other selections of eight lines. Learn the first as you naturally would, or two lines at a time. Learn the second by reading through from beginning to end. Compare the two results for the time and number of repetitions required. Unless the selections are well chosen, it may be necessary to repeat the experiment several times and average before positive results are obtained.

4. Relearn after twenty-four hours one of the selections learned for exercise 3. Relearn another originally learned by th same method after forty-eight hours. Compare the number of repetitions required for relearning each with the number required for the original learning. How can you use the results as a measure of retention or of forgetting?

CHAPTER IX

REASONING

REASONING has always been given a very prominent place among mental operations. To be able to reason is generally recognised as the mark of a high degree of intelligence, and to reason well is one of the most certain marks of exceptional mental development. The effectiveness of a man's reasoning measures in large degree his value to society, and his own possibilities of success. It has frequently been said that reason is peculiarly a human endowment. Wundt, for example, asserts that animals never reason and man seldom. If reasoning occupies this high place in the scale of human capacities, it is evidently desirable to know what distinguishes it from the other mental operations and so far as is possible to determine the laws that make for accurate and true reasoning. The definitions of reasoning show much diversity. A very simple definition is that reasoning is purposive thinking. But to constitute reasoning, thinking must be not only purposive, i.e. must have a definite end, but must also be true and be able to justify itself. Reasoning is a process of solving problems. The solution of the problem must be true, and must also be proved true. To define reasoning fully, it must be distinguished from imagination and memory when observed from the inside, and from instinct and habit when expressed in action.

Reasoning Distinguished from Other Mental Processes. Reasoning may be distinguished from memory and imagination, not so much by the character of the mental states or by the way they are obtained, as by the attitude taken toward them when they arise. The idea attained by reasoning may be exactly like an idea which on other occasions is merely remembered. The laws that govern the appearance of rational ideas are the laws of association, controlled in the same way as in memory or imagination. The three processes are different in that the results of reasoning are new and are accepted as true ; the results of memory are true, but not new; and the results of imagination are new, but not true. Belief is the acceptance of a construction as true, and may be said to hold the same relation to reasoning that recognition does to memory. When an idea is recognised and believed, it is remembered ; when believed, but not recognised, it is the result of reasoning; and when neither recognised nor believed, it is imagined. The distinction between memory and reason may be illustrated by the different ways of preparing a lesson in geometry. One student merely commits the demonstrations to memory and when called upon to recite repeats by rote the words of the book. Another does not commit to memory but reads over and understands each point made. When called upon to recite, he works out the problem for himself in large measure, following only the general lines of the book. He has made, not the words, but the ideas his own and is able to make new applications of the method when called upon to do so. He believes in his result because he can see that it fits in with the other propositions he has learned and with other things that he knows, but he does not recognise the conclusion or the construction when it develops in his mind.

Objective Criteria of Reasoning. If one were watching the actions of a man or animal and knew nothing of the thinking processes behind them, one would still decide on certain occasions that the individual was reasoning, and on other occasions that he was acting from habit or instinct, or from mere chance responses. As compared with habit or instinct, reasoned actions must be new, this must be the first occasion on which the movement has been made: as opposed to mere chance response, the reasoned movement is repeated unfailingly, and is not preceded by other responses. Lloyd Morgan illustrates the difference by the way his dog learned to carry a stick through a picket fence. His habits and instinct led him to pick it up by the middle. Of course it caught at both ends on the pickets. Only after many trials did he happen to hit upon seizing it by the end and thus succeed in dragging it through. If he had reasoned, he would have appreciated the impossibility of his first attempt without trial, or at the first trial. The trials would have been made in thought only, and action would not have been attempted until the problem had been solved mentally. Then one act would have been all that was necessary. Possibly, one would accept as reasoning an act that gives an adequate solution of a new problem, when no solution in thought preceded the act. On this the definitions divide. If one does include acts of this sort under reasoning, it would follow that animals reason ; if reasoning is always a matter of thought or first a matter of thought, then reasoning cannot with certainty be ascribed to animals, i Reasoning Involves Proof. One further step is often present in reasoning and by some is made essential to the definition. This is justifying the conclusion before it has been tried in practice. This is certainly not present in animals and most of what is ordinarily called reasoning in man has no explicit justification. Reasoning has also been restricted to thinking in general terms. While much of human reasoning is general, it would unwarrantably limit the term to exclude all instances of solving particular problems. If we bring together the characteristics of reasoning, we may say that it is a mental operation that (i) is directed to the solution of a problem, is purposive, not random ; (2) the results of the thinking must be a new solution that is accepted as true ; (3) the action to which the thinking leads must also be new and immediately adequate ; (4) the solution may be warranted, in advance of test, by reference to general principles or earlier experiences; and (5) the solution itself may be general, i.e. applicable to many situations, or it may be particular. The two most important new principles to be discussed in connection with reasoning are the nature of belief or proof, and thinking in general terms.

Belief the Test of Truth. The simplest answer to the question, what is true, is that anything is true for the individual which he is willing or able to believe. The simplest answer to the question, what can he believe, is that he believes anything that is in full harmony with his experience. Ordinarily there is immediate rejection of any statement that is not consistent with one's previous experience. Just as the normal man rejects an hallucinatory impression because it contradicts the conditions of his seeing and will not fit into his idea of the world, so a statement or conclusion out of harmony with the earlier knowledge is refused belief. The general rule is that one believes when there is no reason to doubt, when there is no conflict between new and old. The older experiences stand guard in the reasoning operations as in all mental operations, and when any construction does not agree with them, the unpleasant feeling of doubt arises as a bar to its acceptance. Many constructions pass without question, but when one is doubted, it must then be formally proved or given up as untrue. Doubt is the incentive to all of the formal reasoning processes, while belief makes them unnecessary.

Meaning and the Concept. One of the most striking facts in connection with reasoning is that the images employed are not important for themselves, but only for their meaning, for the things that they represent. In a demonstration in geometry, for example, the figure represents all objects of similar form, without reference to their size or the materials from which they are made. The statements will hold of pieces of paper or tracts of land, just as truly as of the figure drawn in chalk or pencil. In all reasoning the same phenomenon -is observed. When one plans a house, one thinks of lumber and of stone, but not of any particular boards or stones ; or, if one does think of a particular material, it is recognised that anything else of the sort may be substituted for it without injury to the plans. The image in question does duty for or represents all other articles of the same kind. An image used in this way to represent several things is called a concept, and the things that it represents at the moment constitute its meaning. Two questions naturally arise with reference to this representative function, (i) How is it possible for a single concrete image to represent so many different objects in thought? This is the problem of meaning. (2) What is the character of the imagery that represents the numerous particulars? This is the historical problem of the nature of the concept.

Meaning Involves the Principles of Recognition. The representative function of images is more closely related to the function of recognition than to any of the other principles hitherto discussed. When an object is perceived, it takes its value from the earlier connections in which it has been seen. If the object is not at once recognised, it will ordinarily soon recall other objects that are familiar. The process of recognition was seen to be due in last analysis to these partially or completely aroused associations. When the object is not recognised as a particular object or as an object that has been seen in some particular place, it may still be appreciated as a member of a class. I recognise a bird in flight as a robin, but not as the robin that has its nest on my lawn ; I recognise a tool as a hammer, but not as my hammer that has been missing since last week. This class recognition is sometimes called cognition, but it follows the same general laws as recognition. It, too, is dependent in part upon the connections that have been formed between many objects and one single name or type, and in part upon the arousal of old situations in which similar objects have been experienced, and of old uses to which they have been put. These associates prepare one to deal with the object when presented, and give it a peculiar conscious quality, a quality that changes with its classification.

The representative function of the image has the same explanation. When the image presents itself, it has a constellation of potential associations about it and these give it meaning. These connections tend to recall each of the objects represented and the uses to which each has been put. These association paths, partly aroused, make the image representative of each object and of each use intended. When it represents a single object, there is only one associate or group of associates ; when it represents a class, many associates are partially aroused. The feeling varies with the associates. Thinking goes on as if all the associates were in consciousness; instead of the single representative image. As the recognition of the object depends upon the associates that are partially aroused at the moment, so the meaning of the image is the expression of its partially or potentially aroused connections. When one recognises a man as a man, the same paths are aroused as when one has in mind a particular image of a man and knows that it represents all men of whatever kind.

The Concept. The image that represents the particulars, the image that has the meaning, is known as the concept. The nature of the concept has been much discussed in the history of philosophy and psychology. It has been argued that the image, which has a general meaning, must itself be general in form. Following out this line of reasoning, it has been asserted that the image of general meaning may be some bare outline of all the particulars that it represents, or that it may be a composite picture of all. My image of a dog would be a dog without colour or particular size or length of hair. My image of a man, a composite photograph of all the men I had ever seen. In any case it would be an image that was like each of the things it represents, but not identical with any of them. This sort of vague schematic image sometimes constitutes the concept, but it is not at all universal. It is no more necessary that the concept be represented by a general image, than that the object recognised as some sort of tool shall be general in form. What gives each its generality is the group of associates that cluster about it. In fact, the two most usual images of general meaning are, on the one hand, an individual object that has nothing of the general in its make-up ; on the other hand, the word, which is not at all like any of the things represented. When one thinks man in general, one is likely to think either of some familiar individual, or merely the word man. Each will represent perfectly all men or all human qualities, since what is important is not the imagery, but the associates that are aroused.

The individual image represents the different particulars in the same way that a model represents the different machines that may be manufactured under a patent. The model may be of wood, while the machines are made of different metals; the model is usually small, the actual machines are large; and numerous other changes may be made in the model, but it still is regarded as typical of them. Its meaning, like the meaning of the concept, is found in all of the machines that might be built on its lines. The model and the actual machines are often spoken of as embodying the same idea, in spite of the differences in size and materials. When thus associated with many particulars, an individual idea stands for them in thought, and the results of the thinking hold true for each of the particulars represented, as well as for the actual image. The word, too, represents objects in thinking because of its many associates. When the word is thought, the associates are aroused and colour the word, so that it seems to be not a mere word, but something much more real and vivid. The difference between the word as bare image and as representative of objects has been illustrated by James by asking one to stare at a word on the printed page for a few minutes as just a word. After one has looked at the word in this way for a short time, the meanings seem to drop away and the word image alone remains. The difference between this and the word as ordinarily used is very striking, how striking one can discover only by trying the experiment. In general, then, the image that is the centre of the concept is relatively a matter of indifference; the associates of the image are essential. The meaning of the concept changes from moment to moment as the connections change. Words change their meanings with the context. The English ' son ' and the French son have an altogether different feeling. The reason is that the partially active associates change as the context changes. Everything serves to emphasise the fact that the associates which irradiate from the concept are the important part, and the image from which they irradiate is relatively indifferent.

The Development of Concepts. The statement that the meaning of the concept depends upon the associates that have been formed about it is well illustrated by the way concepts grow, either in the individual, or in the development of knowledge as a whole. The child's knowledge grows through a process of developing and changing concepts. If one dare speculate on the nature of the first experiences of the child, it would seem that in the beginning all is chaos. It is only as concepts develop, about which the experiences may cluster and to which they may be referred, that any order is introduced. When, for example, a child sees a kitten for the first time, it has no meaning for him. It is a mass of sensations, that is all. Even what little appreciation there is, is in terms of older experiences that have become definitely established. The kitten resembles the mother's furs, its colour suggests coal ; each of its other qualities, if they are appreciated at all, are appreciated only as they are referred to known qualities and objects. When the kitten has been seen a few times, it becomes in its turn a centre of reference for new experiences. At first it stands as the type for all animals; the first dog seen is called ' kitty ' and any other animal receives the same greeting. The concept of the cat develops from this point in two ways. Each new kind of cat will increase the number of objects represented by the term, while each quality of the cat, or of any cat, will increase the qualities that may be ascribed to the animal. When the animal is seen to eat, a new point of resemblance to man is indicated. As the college student studies the anatomy and physiology of the cat, the concept is deepened and extended through the relations that are found between less fully developed animals, on the one side, and chemical and physical laws, on the other. Each of these experiences, either of new sorts of cats or of new qualities and responses of cats, serves to extend the concept. These individuals and laws and functions are all represented by the concept in thinking; and the greater the number of connections that have been developed with it, the wider is the concept, because the greater is the number of associates that are partially aroused when the image is called to mind. The concept is the point of reference of all that is known about cats.

The development of concepts in the race is even more interesting, and the development can be traced more completely. One of the most used is the system of numbers. As the word ' digit ' shows, counting was at first always on the fingers. The larger groups, five and ten, are the fingers of one hand and of two, respectively. Still larger numbers are multiples of ten, the largest number that can be counted on the fingers. After the habit of referring objects to the fingers in counting had been developed, the reference became less explicit, and finally all thought of the fingers was lost from the number idea. The number symbols developed and were capable of replacing the finger idea altogether. One may still see some evidence of the fingers in the Roman numerals, but in the Arabic symbols in ordinary use, there is now no evidence of any similarity to the fingers or to anything that at all corresponds to the values that are represented. The numbers gathered many associates, and each new sort of thing counted served to make the concept more general in its application, until the original reference and practically all imagery disappeared in the meaning or idea. One can trace similar stages in the development of any sort of concept. Words of abstract meaning were nearly all concrete at one time. The meaning first became very much extended ; then some one meaning, remote from the original, became emphasised, and the original one was forgotten, or what was originally the name of a substance or thing came to designate an abstract quality. Each of the fundamental ideas of science could probably be traced to some perfectly concrete object or idea that had been applied successively to many objects and so gradually lost all particular meaning. General notions like atom, molecule, ether, and force, have undoubtedly developed in this way. Now they are concepts that have value because they represent a large number of particular experiences.

Knowledge a System of Concepts. Laying aside for the moment the problem of the development of the concept, one may assert that practically all of the ordered knowledge of any individual is a system of concepts. The system of concepts contains not merely abstract and concrete things like atoms and ether, tables and trees, but general laws and principles, such as special laws of connections and the principle of cause and effect. All that one knows finds its place in the system of concepts ; the system of knowledge and the system of concepts are practically identical terms. These concepts and general laws have value, (i) because they are types and are in consequence more nearly true than any particular experience of the class ; (2) they represent a mass of particulars by virtue of the fact that each of the particulars has been associated with the concept, and, without detriment to the truth of any statement that is made, might be replaced by any one of the particulars. This system of concepts is an essential factor in each of the simpler psychological operations, as well as in reasoning. One ordinarily sees, not the group of sensations, but the developed type or concept of the object. Similarly any statement or thing can be remembered much more easily if only it can be connected with the system of knowledge already obtained. Ordinarily one recognises an object by referring it to the class to which it belongs, even when it may be recognised also as a particular member of the class. While concepts play an enormously important part in each of these mental operations, it is in reasoning that the concept attracts most attention. Here its importance cannot be overstated. Each of the reasoning operations involves reference to the system of concepts. The situation is judged by referring it to the system of knowledge, and to its particular concept. When a solution has been reached, it is justified or proved by a reference to the appropriate general concept, law, or principle. All processes of understanding and of proof are in terms of the classified body of knowledge, concepts.

The Stages of Reasoning. We have seen that the reasoning operation is ordinarily some bit of purposive thinking of which the conclusions are capable of proof. Reasoning comes when one has a purpose and is thwarted in that purpose. One has no incentive to accomplishment if one has no purpose, and no new operations are demanded if the old habits are sufficient to effect the purpose. Reasoning presupposes a thwarted purpose as its starting point. Three stages in the reasoning operation may be distinguished. First, the obstacle must be appreciated or understood ; second, some plan that will remove the obstacle must be developed ; and third, the plan that suggests itself must be proved, must be justified. The obstacle may block the progress, either of thought or action. But if the obstacle be to thought alone, it will probably be an obstacle to action at some time, and to remove it in thought will make action easier when occasion arises. The first of these steps, the process of understanding the difficulty, is judgment ; the second is inference ; and the third, proof.

One may illustrate the different parts of the process by any simple problem. Suppose two boys are canoeing, and it is desired to reach a distant place in a limited time. Suddenly the canoe scrapes hard on a rock. A moment later water begins to rise in the bottom. At first it is a question whether there is a leak or whether the water has been shipped. As it increases in amount, it becomes evident that the water comes from a leak. When this is decided upon, one has a judgment, a classification or interpretation of the trouble. Further explanation comes when the scraping on the rock is recalled, and a complete understanding is obtained when the canoe is turned up and the hole through the canvas is discovered. The next step is to decide upon a remedy. Someone suggests that a patch might be made of a handkerchief. This is probably rejected as soon as the thinness of the material is recalled. A second or added suggestion, that the handkerchief be covered with pitch from a spruce tree on the shore, is accepted by both and put to the test. Thinking of coating the handkerchief with pitch constitutes the inference. Were the suggestion of using pitch questioned by one, and successfully defended by the other, the process would be completed in proof. Proof comes only when there is preliminary doubt on the part of the man who makes the suggestion, or on the part of someone who hears it. Ordinarily the suggestion will be accepted without question. It will be believed at once and at once be put into practice. It is only when there is doubt before the test is made that one requires proof, and the full reasoning process is completed. In our case, one would justify the use of pitch on the handkerchief only when someone asks how that would help. Then the justification may be made in one of several ways. One may answer in the abstract that pitch is sticky and waterproof, or one may recall that the Indians used pitch in repairing or making canoes, or one may recall his own use of pitch for some similar purpose.

The Judgment. Of these steps in the reasoning process, judgment and the different forms of proof have received the most attention, particularly from the logician. The judgment may be denned most simply as the process of referring a new situation to its appropriate concept, or, as it is more usually denned, as the process of ' ascribing meaning to the given/ Each difficulty or obstacle has a different class in which it belongs ; it is understood in terms of a typical older experience, or group of older experiences, which usually has been named. When anything is understood it is referred to a familiar class or object, and this reference, in a sense, transfers the meaning of the old to the new. Each difficulty or obstacle has a class in which it belongs and when it is referred to that class it is in a fair way to be solved or overcome. At least the first step has been taken towards overcoming it. When an army engineer has been assigned the task of bridging a river, he must first measure and so classify the various features of the obstacle, must measure the width of the stream, the depth of the water, and appreciate the particular dangers to which the place is exposed. Each measurement is in essentials a reference of the new situation to a familiar class. When he classifies it in this way, he is ready to solve the problems, he knows what lengths of material to order and what type of bridge to construct.

Classes of Judgments. We arrange judgments themselves in classes or groups. For our purposes, they must themselves be judged. All are alike in that they refer the material or situation to be understood to its class, but the classes themselves differ widely. The object may be referred to its class as a thing. This is the simplest. Where two things are present that differ in any way, one may compare them as greater or less in each of the respects in which they differ, as to weight or length or breadth. This judgment of comparison is like the ordinary judgment in that the relation is referred to some typical relation of greater or less in each respect. Although comparison involves two objects, the comparison itself is a single process and consists in referring the particular difference to some standard difference or typical relation. The judgment of evaluation is the form most frequently used in everyday life. In this the object to be judged is referred to a scale of values or excellencies which an individual has acquired in the course of his experience. We judge all commodities with reference to their monetary value when buying them. We judge people with reference to their intelligence, their morals, their agreeableness, and the probability that they will succeed. All of these judgments are made by assigning the particular specimen to the point in the scale where he or it belongs. The standards are not usually definitely pictured. The one who judges may not even know that he has them until called upon to judge. The procedure prescribed by the army personnel board for grading officers asked the judges to think of five men who represented the best, the worst, the average and one midway between in each of the qualities to be judged and then to grade the man to be judged by saying which man he most resembles. This made the scale of standards fully conscious. Evaluation probably gave the name to the whole process, as it is what the judge does in criminal cases. He must first classify the crime and then decide on the severity of the offence in the scale of offences and assign a punishment accordingly.

The Verbal Judgment. In what has been regarded as the typical judgment by the formal logician, the process of reference is expressed in words. The form of expression is undoubtedly more variable than the formal logician will admit. In many cases, perhaps in most cases, the new situation is represented in the subject of the sentence or the proposition, and the general concept or principle to which it is referred is put in the predicate. When the water is seen to appear in the bottom of the canoe, one would say ' there is a leak/ in which the * there ' represents the general situation ; the ' leak/ the classification of the situation or difficulty. The particular present experience is stated in the subject; the concept that interprets it, in the predicate. Under the head of judgment are included, not only these interpretations of the present situations, but also many possible experiences that may need to be faced for the benefit of later action and disposition. Such are all of the descriptions and classifications of science, and all abstract explanations whatever. From one point of view this text on psychology may be said to be nothing more than a series of references of the mental phenomena to classes and laws that may enable one to know what to expect in the future, and to understand the thinking of the present and of the past. All understanding is a reference of the thing to be understood to the system of concepts; the thing to be understood is ordinarily represented in speech by the subject of the judgment or of the sentence, and the concept by which it is explained is expressed in the predicate. What for the psychologist is a reference of the new to a concept is, for formal logic and grammar, a combination of words, a succession of subject and predicate.

Inference. Inference is primarily a psychological process. Ordinarily one solves problems by casting around until the proper solution suggests itself. The suggestion follows laws of association, just as does memory or imagination, but the essence of the reasoning or inference is to be found, not so much in the way the suggestions come up as in the way they are treated when they come. The greater the fluidity of ideas, the greater the number of suggestions that arise, the more likely it is that the true solution of the problem will be obtained. The essential thing is that the true solution be recognised when it appears, and that all false suggestions be rejected. If the reader will observe his thinking while trying to solve a problem in geometry, or while trying to find some way to earn money for a vacation, or in any other problem, he will see that many different suggestions present themselves before one is found that is accepted as a probable solution. The problem of inference, then, falls into two distinct parts: first, how do the suggestions arise? second, how are the true suggestions separated from the false? The answer to the first question has been given in the chapter on association. The solution in reasoning is reached through the connections that have been earlier established, is controlled and directed by the purpose of the moment, the mental context. The more important second process, the acceptance or rejection of the solutions offered, is an expression of belief. When a suggestion in harmony with all that is known on the subject comes, it is ordinarily accepted and put to practical test. When a suggestion does not harmonise with some experience in consciousness at the moment, it is imme.diately rejected. When the response is in doubt, one must proceed to proof of some sort before either accepting or rejecting. It should be emphasised, however, that in very many cases no formal proof is necessary. When a suggestion is believed, it is at once acted upon without any preliminary proof. The outcome of the ; action is the only test required.

Proof. The process that has most concerned the logician is proof. In its essentials, the process of proving a statement or conclusion is one of producing belief in the mind of the thinker himself or of a companion. Doubt is necessary to call forth proof. The forms of proof are ordinarily divided into deductive and inductive. Deductive proof gives belief by referring the conclusion that is in doubt to some general principle or law already accepted. The new receives added credence from the old. Induction draws the justification for the conclusion from specific earlier experiences or from experiment.

The Syllogism. The most familiar form of deduction is the syllogism. In the syllogism, the general principle by which the conclusion is justified is ordinarily stated first; then the conclusion is referred to that general principle; and, finally, the conclusion to be established is stated. It may be illustrated in ' All metals conduct electricity : tungsten is a metal, therefore tungsten conducts electricity.' It should be asserted explicitly that the order of thinking is not the order of the syllogism, but that the conclusion presents itself first, and the rest of the syllogism is then developed to justify the conclusion. One would never make a series of statements of the sort, unless one had started to use tungsten to close an electric circuit and someone had questioned its value. The syllogism in practice is advanced to prove the conclusion, and develops after the conclusion has been hit upon and questioned; the conclusion does not grow out of the major premise. In actual everyday thinking the syllogism seldom makes its appearance. The conclusions ordinarily are rejected or accepted immediately, and no justification is required. When it does appear, it is usually expressed in a much abbreviated form. In the example given, one would say merely, ' tungsten is a metal, you know ' ; and this would suffice to suggest all that is important in the syllogism.

One question that might be raised is, why does the syllogism or the mention of the major premise constitute proof? The answer is that it serves to connect the conclusion with the system of concepts or general principles previously accepted. When one sees that the new suggestion comes under the old principles, the belief that has been developed for the system of knowledge extends to the particular instance. When established and accepted laws and principles are connected with the conclusion, doubt disappears. The process of reference to the system of knowledge, not merely justifies the old, but also increases the number of applications of the old. Each doubt that is resolved increases the belief in the principle, since it assures its connection with a new fact. It extends its application, and when the conclusion itself is confirmed in practice, the general principle receives new warrant.

Proof by Induction. The second form of proof, induction, consists in reference of the suggestion to the particular earlier experiences. When questioned about tungsten, one would not reply that it is a metal, but would point to an electric lamp, or recall some other instance in which it is known that tungsten wire has been used in electrical work. Or one might take the still more empirical course of actually testing to see whether it does conduct, and whether the resistance is low enough to make it useful in the particular application. It is probable that the proof from induction is much more closely related to the proof by deduction, than was assumed of old. The particular instances, by which the conclusion is justified, must be in some degree typical or they will be valueless. If the tungsten used before was mixed with some other metal, it might very well be that the results that held of that sample would not hold here. Unless again it is assumed that laws hold universally, no conclusion can be drawn from any number of particular cases. Each new case would needs be studied for itself and the results of one experience could not be applied to a later case. Again, as has been seen, older developed concepts are involved in any perception, so that in each of the particular observations principles, similar in kind to the general principles that warrant the conclusion in the syllogism, must have been used. On the other hand, there is always more or less implicit reference to particular experiences in the general principles that justify the conclusion in the syllogism. The difference between the two sorts of proof is one of emphasis only; the same fundamental principles are involved in each. In any case proof is found in a reference to experience. In one case the experience is formulated in concepts and the general is emphasised; in the other the particular experiences are in the foreground, the general laws only implied.

Analogy. Perhaps the form of proof most used in popular discussions is analogy. It involves something of the principles of each of the more formal types, induction and deduction. Analogy consists in pointing out the similarities between the statement to be proved and others with which the man to be convinced is familiar and which he is willing to accept. Thus, one argues that a man should invest in a new company by mentioning companies in the same line that have succeeded. One argues that it is possible to communicate thought without words, written or spoken by mentioning wireless telegraphy. Analogy is a satisfactory form of proof, provided only that the similarity is in essentials. Too often the resemblances are in non-essentials and the proof is seeming, not real. Thus the argument for the new stock is likely to say nothing of the relative financial standing of the two companies and attempts no comparison of the probable earnings. The argument for telepathy or thought transference without words neglects to mention the lack of transmitting or receiving apparatus. Where analogies are critically drawn, they approximate the validity of the syllogism; where the resemblances are only superficial, they may be completely misleading.

Summary. In brief outline, reasoning consists in solving problems, and in justifying the solution when it is obtained. The occasion for the reasoning is always a thwarted purpose. The first step in the solution is to understand the nature of the check, and this is accomplished by referring the present difficulty to some old principle, to some old concept. The second step is to obtain a solution. This is provided by the laws of association. Finally, this solution must be justified when questioned. The justification is, ordinarily, through reference of the suggested solution to the system of earlier knowledge, to the system of concepts. The whole process of inference is thus a series of interactions between the new and the old and ordered experiences. The old is constantly giving order and warrant to the new, while on their side the new are constantly extending and correcting the old experiences.

QUESTIONS

1. How may reasoning, memory, and imagination be distinguished? Habit and reasoning?

2. What gives an image meaning? What makes an idea a concept?

3. How does your abstract idea of a triangle differ from your memory of a particular triangle ? How do you picture to yourself 'machine' as a general term? Describe the mental content fully.

4. Can you trace in your own experience, or in the experience of some child you know, the growth and extension of meaning that a concept like force has undergone?

5. Enumerate five abstract terms in English which bear evidence of the development of the corresponding concept from concrete experience.

6. How is a science a system of concepts? How does such a system develop ?

7. Outline the steps in a reasoning operation.

8. Illustrate the three more important forms of judgment : of things ; of relations ; of values.

9. What do you mean when you say that you understand a mechanical toy? What does seeing your way out of an involved situation imply? How is the process related to judgment as it is defined in the text ?

10. How is inference related to action? What place has association in inference ?

11. When do we prove a conclusion ? How do you prove any conclusion or statement ?

12. Distinguish inductive from deductive proof. How are they related ?

1 3 . How do you know when the solution of a problem is correct ? How can you demonstrate its correctness to another?

EXERCISES

1. Stare at the word triangle for a minute by measurement and keep a record of the changes the word goes through during that time. Explain the result.

2. Prepare two weights of 10 and 10^ grams by loading empty cartridge shells with shot. Have an assistant lift first one and then another and judge which is heavier. What is the process? Does a type play any part ? .

3. Try to work out an original device of a simple sort ; e.g. find a substitute for a stairway in your dwelling. Record each step in the mental operation. Can you state the process in a single word?

CHAPTER X

INSTINCT

Instinct and Experience. One might conceivably treat man as an altogether passive, intellectual creature whose mental life is restricted to calm contemplation, and whose contemplation can be explained in terms of sensations and memories, and combinations and selections from sensations and memories. So far we have been emphasising this phase but it is far from being the whole story. To complete our description we must add a discussion of the active and feeling side of consciousness. Fundamental to an understanding of either action or feeling is a consideration of the different innate tendencies of the individual. These are his instincts. Man is constantly acting, not only in the light of his own experience and learning, but also in terms of various innate tendencies. They have an even more profound influence on the development of both feelings and actions. All through life they serve as a background for the acquired capacities, and they colour feeling and determine action. They often conflict with the acquired and explicit knowledge where that knowledge has been fully developed.

Signs of Instinct. Instincts may be detected in two ways. First, the organism at birth exhibits certain responses that cannot have been learned. These responses 267 show a very marked similarity in all infants. The babe expresses his disapproval of the first discomfort to which he is subjected by a violent outcry. He responds to the first opportunity for nourishment with the appropriate sucking movements. All of the immediate necessities of life are provided for by instinctive responses. Second, in the adult life there are many responses and feelings that cannot be explained by experience, that are in fact out of harmony with experience. These arise spontaneously and take approximately the same form in all individuals, although they need not have been present at birth. Under this head come the tendencies to self-assertion, the bashfulness of the adolescent youth, many fears, together with a host of movements not learned in advance of their execution. Instincts, then, fall into two classes. They are movements that are made at birth or are movements that show themselves relatively late in life, but which need no preliminary learning or practice. While the term is used most frequently in connection with movements, instinct also explains much of feeling and many of the intellectual processes. The disagreeableness of bitter and the pleasantness of sweet can no more be understood from the experience of the individual than the blushing of the maiden or the cry of the child. Fear, too, is at once a movement or a series of movements, and a conscious state. Under instincts we shall consider explicitly or implicitly both actions and feelings.

The Physiology of Instinctive Acts. We may understand the fundamental nature of instincts best if we consider what must be the inherited characteristic. If we turn back to our discussion of nervous physiology, it is evident that these movements must have a basis in the nervous system at birth. The part of the nervous system to which we must look for an explanation is the synapse, the point of connection between nervecells. We know that, when a habit is formed, there is some lessening of the resistance offered by the synapse to the transmission of the nervous excitation. In habit, the lessened resistance is due to frequent early connection. Since instincts present themselves at birth, the openness of the synapses must be inherited. In brief, instincts must be due to something physical. This physical characteristic is to be found in open connections between sensory and motor neurones. When the stimulus presents itself, the movement that constitutes the instinct is at once evoked. How feelings are transmitted is an unsettled question, but it is probable that part of the instinctive feeling is due to instinctive motor responses. Whether there are other predispositions to response involved in the dislike of bitter, for example, is as yet unknown.

The Origin of Instincts. Instincts are immediately explained by the inheritance of predispositions to response, the inheritance of open connections between sensory and motor neurones. The next problem that suggests itself is how these connections originated. This problem, like the problem of inheritance above, is entirely a biological one. Two explanations have been given of the origin of instincts. The simpler is that instincts are merely inherited habits. On this theory some ancestor learned a movement, and the habit was transmitted to his descendants and became a racial possession. Were the biologist willing to accept this theory, the explanation of the origin of instincts would be very simple. Unfortunately the evidence that a change wrought in one individual is transmitted to his offspring is not accepted by the great majority of biologists. Weismann has demonstrated to the satisfaction of many of his colleagues that the structures of the body are so completely set off from the tissues which are to continue the race that the changes in the body have no influence upon the inheritance of the offspring. The cells from which the progeny are to develop have in potentiality at the birth of the individual all the characteristics that they later reveal, they are influenced only by the factors that weaken or destroy the body as a whole. Whatever be the outcome of the biological controversy, it is necessary for the psychologist to construct a theory of instinct on the assumption of the accepted biological theory.

Instinct a Product of Natural Selection. On this theory of Weismann, instincts come not through a change in the habits of the individual, but through some chance change in the characteristics of the germ plasm. It is a fact that, while the characteristics of the parent are transmitted, they are not transmitted accurately, there is always variation in the characters. If one sows a thousand seeds from the same plant, the young plants will show a wide range of variation from the parent plant and from each other. The theory of the development of instincts assumes this same tendency to variation in the nervous system and in the instincts that correspond to the nervous connections. If this known fact of variation be accepted, all that is necessary for the development of an instinct is that some selection be made from the variations. This selecting agent has been found by all the evolutionary theories hi the environment. When a variation in response better suited to the environment than the older responses makes its appearance, the animal that shows the variation will be more likely to survive. If this variation is inherited, as it tends to be, the offspring of this animal will survive in greater numbers and in time will outnumber those with less adequate responses. In brief, variations in responses are constantly appearing as the result of changes in the structure of the germ plasm. The animal that has the more beneficial responses will live and its offspring will increase, while any animal that develops variations unsuited to the environment will be destroyed, or the offspring will be fewer. As a result of this variation in structure and response, with selection of the animals that show suitable variations, instincts become constantly more suited to the conditions of life, and also become more and more complicated. Variation and selection can account for any instinct, granted only a sufficiently long time for the variation to develop.

Suppose, for example, that we have a large number of rudimentary organisms with all possible combinations of two responses. Assume, e. g. that certain organisms in the mass seek food and flee dangers, that others flee from food and seek the dangerous stimulus, that a third class flee from both food and the dangerous stimulus, while the fourth seek both. Of the entire group only the first class will long survive, the others will either starve to death or be eliminated by approach to dangerous stimuli or organisms. Each variation of the primary responses in the progeny will lead to similar elimination, or, as the responses become more numerous and more adequate, a greater proportion of the generation will survive. In time, we would have a set of instincts that would serve to protect the organisms from the more evident and usual dangers. The whole process of development of instincts is thus due to the development of the physical structures upon which these responses depend. But it does not follow that instincts are necessarily simple. Many instincts even of comparatively low animals are extremely complex. The egg-laying instinct of the Yucca moth, cited by Lloyd Morgan, is a case in point. The eggs of the moth are always laid in the seed pod of the Yucca plant, and after they are deposited, pollen is gathered and placed in the hollow pistil and fertilises the seeds. It is a movement that could never have been learned and the moth can have no idea of its purpose, for the moth dies at once after the process is completed. The continuance of the species of both the moth and the plant depends altogether upon the accurate performance of the act. The larvae when they hatch need the developing seeds for food ; the seeds of the plant would not be fertilised and consequently would not develop without the aid of the insect. In such a case the instinct has all the outward signs of intelligence, but must have developed without the aid of intelligence.

Forms of Human Instincts. While instincts are more striking in animals and, in the lower forms, are more easily distinguished in animals, they are very numerous and important in man. Professor James asserts that man has more instincts than any other animal. A complete list would require too much space, but it will prove profitable to enumerate the more important classes with some of the more striking instances under each head. Instincts may be conveniently classified as individual, racial, and social. Individual instincts make for the welfare of the agent, racial for the continuance of the species, and social for the preservation of the group or society. It is not always possible to draw a sharp line between classes, but the broader lines of distinction are clearly marked.

Individual Instincts. Among the individual instincts, we may distinguish those that care for the essential movements of the child. Here come in order the vocal protests against discomfort, the early and later movements of taking nourishment, the movements of selfprotection, the early locomotor movements. Under this head fall all the simple movements that the child is called upon to make to meet the demands of the environment. Many of them are not pure instincts or do not long remain pure. An instinct may lead to an awkward or vague movement, but when, as is usual, the movement is improved in performance by some chance variation in its character, that desirable variation is likely to take the place of the original movement. Probably in most of the later movements, habit and instinct are inextricably confused. Whether learning to walk, for example, is altogether an instinct or not is still an open question. Most likely it has an instinctive basis, as is shown by the alternate movement of the feet of an infant when they are lightly stimulated, but a very large part of the development is due to habit formation. Instinct and habit cooperate in this as in many of the other simpler acts.

Another striking group of the individualistic instincts may be seen in the fears. Every child and many adults evidence fears that could not have been derived through experience and many that are in direct opposition to knowledge. The infant shows a constant succession of fears that appear, last for a few days or months, and then disappear, to be replaced by others. Fear of moving things, fear of living things or of soft things, fear of the dark, fear of men alone or of women alone, of children but not of adults, run their course one after another in the first few years of the life of the child. They seem to appear without reason and to vanish equally without reason. If the fear is confirmed, it may persist for a long time ; if groundless, it will ordinarily vanish as quickly and as unexpectedly as it came. Apparently each fear is the concomitant of a certain stage hi the ripening of the nervous system. When the right stage appears, the instinct shows itself; when that period of organic transition passes, the instinct goes. Certain instinctive fears persist into adult life. Here one has the fear of high places, the fear of reptiles and other small animals, the fear of death and of the dead, fear of the strange and unexplained, including the supernatural. These fears are probably present in some degree in all individuals whose daily life has not forced them into frequent contact with the source. One may assert lack of fear, one may even feel that the fear is absurd and unintelligible, but when occasion arises, the proper response makes its appearance. One may assert boldly, even haughtily, an entire disbelief in ghosts and the supernatural, but not be able to pass through a cemetery alone at midnight without feeling in some slight degree uncomfortable, unless, of course, such promenades have been frequent. Again one cannot hold the finger relaxed against the glass of a cage while a rattlesnake strikes at it, and that in spite of positive assurance that no harm can come from the act.

In the third class of individualistic instincts one finds a large group of activities with a wider social reference. Under this head come pugnacity and the various selfassertive instincts; here, too, fall the instincts for collecting and secreting valuables. These are evidenced by the small boy's pocket and in the tendency of the miser to accumulate without reference to use. Closely related to this is the instinct of emulation or rivalry. This is probably a mild form of the fighting instinct, and may be regarded as the basis of the collecting instinct so far as that has a social reference. Piling up a vast fortune may be an expression of the collecting mania on the one hand, but it also has in it a large measure of rivalry. To these may be added the hunting instinct with its attendant cruelty, then love of cruelty itself, which finds its expression primarily in those slightly disturbed mentally. To these James would add curiosity, which may be transformed into a desire for information and made a strong stimulus to education, constructiveness, and even cleanliness, in the form of an abhorrence of filth. As in the first group, it is difficult to decide how many of the tendencies grouped under these various heads are really instincts, and how much they have developed as habits or have been transformed in part by habits and experiences of various sorts. Probably something of each is instinctive, but it is always given direction by habit and social influences. The Racial Instincts. The racial instincts are also very numerous and are highly coloured by emotion. In the lower animals they are very widespread and very striking for their definiteness and adequateness, in spite of the slight knowledge of their purpose that can attach to them. The egg-laying instincts have already been illustrated. The nest-building instincts are almost as numerous and require greater complexity of response. Race instincts in man are equally important and have as little of their real purpose revealed in the consciousness of the individual as corresponding instincts of the lower animals. The innocent adolescent youth is as surprised at his thrills as he gazes upon the beautiful object of his first love and may be as ignorant of their cause and purpose as is the beetle that is laying its eggs, or the robin that is building its first nest. Even when the instinct is understood, there is little reference to that knowledge at the moment and the emotion is not controlled by it and not altogether appreciated in its full bearing. Similar instincts without consciousness of purpose and in advance of practice may be seen in the coquetry of the young girl. It apparently makes its appearance as naturally as the unfolding of a leaf, although the art may be perfect when measured by the most mature standards. To these various love instincts must be added jealousy, which may be as spontaneous and unreasoned as any of the others. More lasting are the parental and filial instincts and the brotherly and sisterly affection. These are important elements in holding the family together. They insure the care of the infant during the helpless stage, and the protection and care of the parent during old age.

Social Instincts. The social instincts have even a wider range. They vary from fear of a single individual actually present, to fear or consideration for the mass of men of the same nation or race, even including those known only by reputation and tradition. The most obvious expressions are seen in the bashfulness of a child or youth in the presence of strangers. Several recurrent eras of bashfulness may be distinguished. Apparently the young child ordinarily goes through two or three stages in fairly close succession. It has a period of being distressed by any stranger, then becomes indifferent or pleased by people, then suffers another attack of bashfulness. Usually there is a later increased susceptibility to bashfulness about the period of adolescence. Stage fright and the fear of man in the mass under unusual conditions persist through life and apparently are overcome only by much practice, and then only for the one situation in which adaptation has developed. The opposite instinct, sociability, is almost as striking and shows itself during the whole life of the individual. From a very early age, the child resents being left alone, and the desire for the companionship of friends is always very strong. When long deprived of the society of his kind, one develops an actual hunger for social contact and conversation.

The wider, more pervasive social instinct of sympathy is equally manifest. One cannot see the suffering of another without in some measure suffering oneself. When one gives a coin to the beggar on the street corner one does it not so much to relieve the beggar's suffering as one's own. If under the influence of the teachings of sociology one refuses to give, the thought of the refusal will produce for some time an unpleasant emotion. The instinct asserts itself in spite of the belief that the man is an impostor and may be better off than one's self. Much has been made of this instinct by certain of the modern schools of ethics as the source of all altruistic action, and no doubt it deserves a very high place among the forces that make community life possible. Closely related to sympathy, if not merely other expressions of the same instinct, are the instincts that lead to self-sacrifice for the larger group. The soldier when he enlists exhibits these together with the fighting and hunting instincts. Every instance of self-sacrifice is the expression of one or the other of the social or racial instincts. If one asks how an instinct that leads to the possible destruction of the individual could have survived in the struggle for existence, one must find the answer in the survival of the group rather than of the individual. Gregarious animals are on the whole more likely to live if the stronger are ready to fight for the preservation of the weaker. The male deer, that are said to form a circle about the females and the young when attacked by wolves, make possible the continuance of the species even if a large proportion of them succumb to the attack. And in the early stages of human development those tribes would survive in which each member would be willing to lay down his life for the welfare of the whole. Gregarious animals survive in the group, not individually. Complexes of Instinct Play. Two other instincts have sometimes been ascribed to man, play and imitation. It is probable, however, that these are not true instincts or at least are not single instincts. If one will watch the games of the boys or girls upon the school playground, one will observe that each game is the expression of an instinct or of many instincts. Emulation or rivalry enters as a factor in almost every contest. Sociability and the advancement of the welfare of the band arbitrarily formed can be traced in many of the sports. One may even see evidence of instinct in the content of some of the games. Playing with dolls is undoubtedly an early development of the parental instinct. In general the favourite games of each sex show evidence of instinct. But the games in their specific forms are also influenced even more by the environment and by the activities of parents and friends. The only thing that can be said to be common to all forms of play is the tendency to some sort of purposive activity, the inclination of the child to be always in action. This is not so much an instinct in the ordinary sense as a physiological law, that surplus energy will find expression in action. Various instincts and habits guide this expression. Play is the expression of a law of the physical organism, and so far as it is instinctive, it is the expression of a number of instincts, not of a single one.

Imitation. Imitation must fall into the same general class. If we look upon instinct as an inherited connection between sensory and motor neurones, it will follow that an instinct can be nothing more than a tendency to make a single response or a group of responses upon the presentation of a single stimulus. Imitation, on the contrary, must always involve a very large number of responses to many stimuli. Imitation in general can be either the result of many instincts or something other than instinct. As a matter of fact, it is now one, now the other. Some imitative acts are instinctive, others are the result of habit and learning. Even where learning is involved, there is an instinctive element in the interest that one has in the doings of other people. This general social instinct causes one to observe the movements and, where the results are desirable, to make an attempt to learn them. In infancy, the observation of any movement in another makes the same movement interesting when it is made by the child himself in the course of chance responses. Whatever the explanation, imitation in man leads to more rapid learning, even where it is not an instinct proper. Both play and imitation have an instinctive basis, but neither is an instinct in the same sense as are eating and fear.

Habit and Instinct. It should be added and emphasised that instinct and habit can seldom be altogether distinguished. In man at least, instinct is always relatively unstable and vague. An act at its first performance purely instinctive is soon modified by learning, and a response better suited to the conditions is pretty certain to develop sooner or later, and then to become fixed in habit. This may be seen in the nest-building instincts of barn swallows that must at some period have built their nests in natural objects. It can be seen in the control of fears in man and in most of the other instinctive acts. In very many instances, too, what is instinctive is not the act so much as the attitude toward its result. One dislikes suffering and will take any known means to get rid of it or to avoid seeing it ; the feeling, not the act, is instinctive. The end of removing the unpleasant or of obtaining the pleasant may be attained in a number of different ways, and the particular means to be used in attaining the end is determined by habit or by intelligence. Instincts of this latter sort are not stereotyped, as are the earlier, more primitive acts of instinctive origin.

Not only are instinct and habit difficult to distinguish in practice, but habit is constantly repressing and changing the instinctive tendencies. Instincts that have developed in one environment are not suited to another and, as was seen in the nesting instinct above, may be replaced by habits more appropriate to the surroundings. More often in man the instinct comes into conflict with tradition or convention that again has probably developed because better fitted than the raw instinct to advance the welfare of the social group. It is bad form to show greed, it is not polite to exalt one's self. The man of good breeding restricts these impulses to the limits set by his fellows. The racial instincts are controlled by the laws of marriage and divorce, the individual instincts are limited by customs and statutory enactments. Both of these checks probably take their force from the social instincts. The fact that man seeks social approval, and fears or avoids social blame is probably largely due to his instincts. Certainly, to command respect social disapprobation need never have expressed itself in physical violence or the infliction of bodily pain. The need for group solidarity has become embodied in an instinctive respect for the opinion of our fellows that is at the basis of what we called social pressure in the discussion of attention, and is the effective force behind both statutory enactment and convention. The social forces that curb and equalise the individualistic and racial instincts are themselves instincts or have a basis in instinct. It is a social instinct that receives its content from tradition and custom. One instinctively respects custom or convention, although it may have grown up through habit and tradition.

Instinct and Reflex. If instinct is closely related to habit and cannot always be distinguished from it, it is also closely related to reflex. In fact, the definition given of instinct as an act dependent upon an inherited nervous connection will also apply without change to reflex. The infant draws back the hand when burned because of an innate connection between the sensory neurone that receives the stimulus and the group of muscles that contract in response to it. The two terms are confused in popular speech. As a matter of fact in psychological usage there is much uncertainty about the exact line that separates them. In general one speaks of a single response as a reflex, of a complicated series of responses as an instinct. Winking is a reflex, the complex series of acts involved in nest-building is an instinct. The swallowing movement aroused when food touches the back of the throat is a reflex, the whole group of processes involved in nursing is an instinct. Again reflexes often can be easily reduced to a series of mechanically determined responses to a stimulus or series of stimuli, while the stimuli for instincts and their relation to the responses may not be easily discovered. One can understand why one starts if one steps upon a tack, but it is not so evident why one starts at a motion in the grass that later consideration shows might have been a snake. One does not know at all what stimuli lead a bird to fly south in the fall but one can see a purpose in the action ; it is an instinct, not a reflex. Finally there is ordinarily more consciousness attaching to the instinct than to the reflex. One does not know why one gives money to the beggar, but one is conscious of doing so, and would feel uncomfortable were it not done, but the eye winks several times a minute with no appreciation of the dryness that stimulates the movement or of the movement itself. In some reflexes the act and the stimulus are conscious after the act, but the act itself is not preceded or guided by consciousness. In most instincts all is conscious but the reason for the act. Instinct and reflex are to be distinguished in terms of the simplicity of the reflex and the complexity of instinct ; by the fact that the reflex can be understood from the mechanical activity of the nervous structures, while the instinct can be referred to its purpose alone ; and in terms of the amount of consciousness that attaches to the instinct. No one of these three criteria would hold accurately in every case, but taken together they give an idea of the nature of the two processes.

Instincts as Connate and Delayed. It should be added in connection with the differentiation of instinct from reflex and from habit that the distinction cannot be made on the basis of the time at which the process or activity makes its appearance. Reflexes may be distinguished from habits by the time of their appearance. Reflexes are present at birth, are connate, while habits require experience for their development. Instincts, on the other hand, may be either connate or delayed.

They may be present at birth or may appear only when the nervous system has attained a certain stage of development. It must be said that more of them fall in the latter group than in the former. One may recognise at birth the rudiments of the food-taking instincts, the vocal protests of discomfort, but relatively few others. The great mass of the individualistic instincts and all of the racial and social group are noticed only after the nervous system has ripened, and as has been seen, one instinct after another will show itself as the organism develops. The appearance of one fear after another in the infant is to be explained by the fact that part after part or function after function of the cortex is developing, and at each stage the corresponding stimulus calls out the reaction of fear. But while instincts may not be connate, unlike habits they are assumed to be innate. The nervous system at birth contains the germ from which they are developed, and while they make their appearance after some experience has been acquired, it is not because of the experience. Classified with reference to purpose, instincts are individual, racial, and social ; classified with reference to the time of their appearance, instincts are connate and delayed.

Summary. Instincts are movements, or feelings which may or may not be the result of movements, that come because of inherited connections and dispositions in the nervous system. In function, on the one hand, they serve to keep the infant alive until he may be able to learn for himself, on the other, they enforce general lines of conduct essential to the preservation of the individual, the race, and the social group. As opposed to habits and rational activities, instincts, of the latter class at least, are vague and prescribe only the end to be attained, not the precise means. Even the first group of instincts to make its appearance is soon modified by habit, or is repressed. Instincts cannot be set apart from habits and other intelligent movements in the adult ; all that can be said is that certain acts are more largely instinctive, others more largely acquired on an instinctive basis. The advantages of an inheritance of the vague outlines of action only with much left to individual learning are evident, ii one will but consider the relatively small number of movements that may be inherited and the great number of situations to be met, not to mention the great possibility of change in the environment. Were an organism to be rigidly limited to a few forms of response to predetermined conditions, it would soon find a situation for which it was not prepared and be eliminated. Or if the environment should change in some way, the organism could not long survive. An endowment of few and relatively indefinite innate responses with much capacity for learning at once relieves the necessity for multitudinous predetermined responses and assures the preservation of the organism until it has time to learn.

QUESTIONS

1. Which of the following acts are instinctive, which reflex: Sneezing; jumping when lightly touched on the shoulder; the nursing of a child ; nest-building ; drawing back from the edge of a precipice ?

2. What is the neurological basis of instinct?

3. Enumerate five instincts that you have exhibited during the day.

4. What were the conscious accompaniments of each of the above acts?

5. In what sense is play instinctive? imitation? Do they presuppose one or many instincts?

6. Give instances in your own responses of elimination of instinct by social training.

7. Illustrate from your own experience a conflict between individual and social instincts. Which won?

8. A dog has been taught to beg for food. One of her pups goes through the begging movement without having had any opportunity to see its mother make the movement. Is this an instinct? Could it have been developed by training the mother?

9. If instincts do not develop through habit how do they arise?

10. Why do individuals differ in the instinctive response to a given situation?

11. Give an instance of an instinct that has been modified as a result of learning, but is still retained as an instinct in the broad outlines.

CHAPTER XI

FEELING

Feeling as Equivalent to Selection. One of the

most striking and practically most important features in the behaviour of men and of animals is the preference for certain objects or stimuli. All animals from the protozoa up show a tendency to avoid certain objects and to seek or to remain near certain others. The amoeba withdraws its processes when stimulated by some substances and extends them towards and actually enfolds others. In the higher animals a response which gives one result will be repeated until the act becomes habitual, while others will be made but once. Movements of the second class are accompanied by excess movements, usually movements of withdrawal which may or not be useful in the particular environment. Such are the shrinking of the dog at sight of the whip and the wry face of the child when the medicine bottle is brought out. These are typical of the process of rejection as others are of the process of acceptance. Common observation indicates that most stimuli and most situations fall into two classes : those which evoke movements of approach or cessation of movement, and those which induce movements of withdrawal. This selection is probably the most important single factor in determining the animals' habits and man's entire experience.

Like all of the other facts of behaviour, this selection or seeming preference may be approached from two sides. From the outside it has been described above in terms of approach or quiescence if in contact with the object or of violent excess movements and of lack of movement. On the conscious side the one is accompanied by pleasure, the other by displeasure. As a conscious process the difference between pleasure and displeasure seems to parallel many of the most important distinctions in our lives. The movements that are learned, objects that are sought, ideals that are accepted, all are pleasant, whether the pleasure be cause or accompaniment we need not at present consider. If we treat pleasure and its opposite as causes or concomitants of causes they would be, like attention, important agents in determining the course of consciousness and of action. Unlike attention feeling is effective in deciding between actions and the results of action rather than in selecting stimuli. If an act has a pleasant result it is repeated, or if one expects a pleasant result from it the act is performed. The control of thoughts and of sensations is not so direct and complete. One may seek pleasant ideas but is not always able to exclude the unpleasant, and both pleasant and unpleasant stimuli affect consciousness more readily than indifferent ones of the same intensity. Obviously, pleasantness and unpleasantness require careful treatment. Before we attempt to investigate their influence upon behaviour we will describe them as conscious processes and assign them their places among other mental states.

Uses of the Term. The term feeling is used in many different senses. It is made to cover all sorts of mental states, from tactual sensations to the vague intellectual appreciations of truth. We ' feel ' with our fingers, and we ' feel ' that certain things are true when we are unable to prove them by any formal methods. Feeling indicates at different times and for different people all the vague experiences. The sensations from the skin are regarded as less definite and precise than those from sight and hearing. In the other fields the same use is predominant. The organic sensations are popularly classed as feelings, as are the psychological processes, like recognition and belief, which have not been definitely analysed.

Obviously it is not possible to discuss all of these different states in one chapter or in one connection. As used, feeling stands_for_the unclassified^ in_eyery_JkkL. Wherever we have been able to group facts about certain typical phenomena, there are other similar facts that seem to belong in the same group, but which cannot be definitely ascribed to that class. These constitute the feelings in the broader sense. Because they have not yet been reduced to types or forms, they cannot be described or defined. They are the limiting terms of our science. Whenever they^cease_ to be inde_scribable__apd tfl.ke_nn_ definite form, they cease to be feelings. Evidently, feeling in this broader sense is something that cannot be discussed ; when it is possible to discuss it, it is no longer feeling. Another objection to treating feeling in this sense is that there would be, on this definition, as many different sorts of feeling as there are different classes of experience. The feeling of belief is no more like the feeling of discomfort from bodily illness than the sensation of contraction is like a syllogism ; the feeling of recognition no more like a feeling of moral virtue than a memory image is like a voluntary act. If one were to attempt 'a discussion of feelings in this sense, a separate treatment of each would be necessary, and it would be most convenient to discuss them in connection with the experiences of the same group that already have been analysed and reduced to laws.

Feeling as Pleasantness and Unpleasantness. Pleasantness and unpleasantness are the only definite mental states to which the term feeling is applied. A description of them is as difficult as of any simple process, but there is no doubt what is meant when the word pleasantness or unpleasantness is used. Pleasantness and unpleasantness are general and are found in connection with practically every other state. They may be induced by impressions from any sense, and by memories of many different qualities. They are found as the accompaniments of different actions, in fact are attached to all sorts and conditions of mental processes. Pleasantness and unpleasantness are really distinct mental qualities and deserve a special name, whatever it may be. Psychologists are agreed in calling these two qualities feelings, no matter what other qualities they may add to the list. We can decide arbitrarily to regard pleasantness and unpleasantness as the feeling qualities and omit the others, not because they are unimportant in themselves, but because they are not feelings on the same level. So far as a discussion of them is possible, it is carried on to better advantage in connection with other subjects.

Differences between Feeling and Sensation. Even if we grant that pleasantness and unpleasantness are peculiar states of consciousness, the question is raised whether they are distinct from sensations. Ordinarily^ feelings arise through excitation by some stimulus and are closely connected in origin with sensations. But we may have both feelings and sensations from the same stimulus at the same time and can always distinguish^, them. The two are never confused! Many formal arguments have been de vised to show 'that they are really different sorts of mental content. Perhaps the most striking is the general dependence of the feeling upon the individual and his peculiar experiences. When the same stimuli affect us, we see approximately the same things, but we feel very differently at different times. What pleases at one time may displease at another. What one feels r|p|wwjgjipon tl^inrhViHiiqLand hj s mood_ at the moment, as opposed to the nature of the external stimulus which determines the nature of sensation. Feeling is as much subjective as attention, while sensation is dependent altogether upon the physicaLemdron^ ment. It is in this sense that feelings are subjective, sensations objective. Coupled with this subjective character is the further fact that an experience when recalled does not always have the same feeling as at first. What pleased at one time as a boyish prank may cause mortification in maturer years. In the same way an early social blunder that occasioned keen chagrin at the time may now excite nothing but mild amusement.

The individual has changed in the meantime and the feelings change with him. That feelings__undergo change between the actual experience and the recalj has led to the statement that we cannot remember them. It is true that we cannot recall the pleasantness in all of its warmth, but we do recall the sensational elements and receive the same feeling as if they were experienced at present. We undoubtedly remember that we were pleased or displeased, or there would be no question about the change in feeling. The remembrance is in words or other conceptual terms.

This subjectivity or dependence upon the nature of the individual and his momentary mood is the most striking characteristic of feeling. Closely related to it isjlslack of anything that partakes of definiteness or of a conceptual character. Feelings seem to vanish when one attempts to describe them or even to attend to them. Any attempt to analyse the characteristics of pleasure brings about a diminution if not the disappearance of the pleasure. Even to ask whether one is really pleased or not has much the same effect in smaller degree. Pleasure vanishes when examined carefully. The mood of analysis is not conducive to pleasure and in less degree is not conducive to displeasure. These general characteristics of the feelings seem sufficient to mark them as distinct mental qualities. Pleasantness and unpleasantness must be regarded as belonging in a different class from sensations.

The Quality of Feeling. Feeling is much less rich in qualities than sensation. The qualities upon which there is general agreement are pleasure and displeasure, or pleasantness and unpleasantness. They are both opposed to indifference. Indifference by some authors has been made a distinct class in addition to pleasure and displeasure. Indifference, however, is probably merely the lack of feeling and is applied only to the stimulus or to sensation. An indifferent stimulus is one that does not give rise to feeling ; there are no indifferent feelings. There are but two qualities of feeling, although stimuli that arouse feelings may be opposed to indifferent stimuli or sensations. The intermediate position is more suggestive if we consider the degrees of pleasantness and unpleasantness and their relation to the intensity of the stimulus. Pleasure and its opposite vary in degrees in both directions from just appreciable to very intense feelings. Wundt early suggested that there was a constant relation between the intensity of the stimulus and the nature and degree of the feeling. Faint stimuli are ordinarily pleasant and become less and less pleasant as they increase in intensity, becoming first indifferent and then unpleasant. Slightly sweet substances are indifferent or disagreeable. As the degree of sweetness increases, the substance becomes pleasant, while the intense sweet of saccharine is unpleasant. This relation holds approximately for some senses but it cannot be regarded as a general law.

Feeling and Affection. It has often been asserted that there must be different feelings for each sense department, and even for each sense quality. This depends upon the fact that one does not distinguish between the feeling proper and the accompanying sensations. The sensations in the complexes are different and make the whole complex different. The feeling proper is not discriminated from the sensational colouring. The elementary feeling process is often confused with the complex, even in psychological writing and thinking. To avoid the confusion it has become usual to apply the term ' affection ' to the mere pleasantness and unpleasantness apart from the sensational components, and to keep the word ' feeling ' for the complex. For example, in a toothache we can distinguish the sensation pain from the reaction against the pain. It is this reaction that we call the unpleasant ' affection.' The disadvantage of using ' affection ' to designate the element is that it has such a widely accepted popular usage as the name of an emotion. However, we shall find it convenient to use the term in default of a better one. Accepting this usage, we may assert that all affections are of two kinds, pleasant and unpleasant, and that all differences in feelings are due to the different concomitant sensations. The difference between a toothache and a headache lies in the localisation of the pain sensations, and perhaps in some of the accompanying organic sensations.

Sensation of Pain and Unpleasantness. Particularly close is the relation between the affection, unpleasant, and the sensation, pain, which is nearly always unpleasant. The affection and the^ sensation are combined^sp _a^ single feeling that frequently they are not the term pain is used in two senses, to designate both the affection and the sensation. Pain sensations may be pleasant, as in the pain excited by the biting cold of a clear day when one is in good health. The displeasure caused by a sudden pain is altogether distinct from the pain itself, although they are fused into a single complex. The quality of unpleasantness apart from its setting is the same in each case. We may conclude that there are but two qualities of affection and that differences in feeling come from the sensational elements in the complex, not from the affective components.

Sensory and Intellectual Feelings. Other suggested distinctions are between higher and lower, or sensory and intellectual feelings. In general the two classes overlap. Intellectual feelings on the whole are supposed to be higher ; the sensory, lower. The difference between the intellectual and the sensory is very much the same as that between the different sorts of sensory feelings discussed in the preceding paragraph. In the intellectual, the cognitive components are largely memory processes and products of imagination. Mental accomplishments of all kinds give rise to pleasure ; defeat or failure to perform a mental operation resolved upon causes displeasure. The resulting pleasure or displeasure is the same in each instance; the difference is in the occasion alone, the non-affective accompaniments of the pleasure. Between the higher and lower pleasures the distinction is largely in terms of ethical or social values, rather than in the quality of the affection. The higher pleasures are those that are important for the welfare of society and correspond to activities not deeply ingrained by instinct.

Society has given an indorsement to the pleasures of the one class because of their benefit to the social whole, while the pleasures of sense are regarded as strong enough to take care of themselves. The pleasure from a good dinner is apparently no different in its quality from the consciousness of a good deed, but the pleasure attaching to a good dinner is sufficiently vivid and the instinct to eat sufficiently strong to need no bolstering from society, while the instinct to perform a good deed is so weak that social approval is necessary to insure its performance. Society therefore expresses its approval by classifying the one pleasure as higher, while its disapproval of the other is expressed by classifying it as lower. Neither of these classifications has reference to the affective quality, and so makes necessary no change in our earlier statement that affections have but two qualities, pleasure and displeasure.

Bodily Accompaniments of Feelings. The bodily accompaniments of feelings have been made much of in psychological descriptions and discussions. Many bodily signs of pleasure are apparent to the casual observer. When one is pleased, the face is flushed due to the enlarged capillaries, the eye is bright from the dilation of the pupil and the slight secretion of tears, the carriage is erect. In displeasure the opposed responses are seen. Attempts have been made to determine accurately the different component physiological changes that give rise to the psychical condition, but at present the results are conflicting. No exact opposition can be shown between pleasure and pain in the accompanying heart rate, in the size of the capillaries, or in the strength or rate of breathing. All of these processes undergo change in any sort of feeling, but one cannot connect the nature of the change with the quality of feeling. All that can be said is that the changes are more marked in displeasure than in pleasure. The belief of the earlier investigators that they had discovered a definite relation between the bodily responses and pleasure and displeasure does not harmonise with the results of recent investigations.

Theories of Feeling. Three theories have value as an explanation of the nature and origin of feeling or of the affective component of the feeling. These are: (i) the evolutionary theory which is oldest and probably fundamental for the other two; (2) the theory that relates feeling to association and attention; and (3) the theory of smooth-running and checked mental operations. Each has its place and must be considered separately. The first asserts that pleasure is the accompaniment of stimuli that have in the long run proved beneficial to the race; displeasure, the accompaniment of stimuli that on the whole have proved injurious. We like foods, we dislike substances that are unfit for food. There are obviously many exceptions to this rule, but they arise largely from the fact that man has evolved, not to meet each specific case, but to meet the general conditions. Thus sugar of lead might be mistaken for cane sugar and be considered pleasant, but to avoid all sweets would be more injurious to the race than to eat all and have the few die who chance upon the poisonous sweets. Similarly medicines are proverbially unpleasant, but man was not evolved to take medicine. They are of value only in exceptional conditions. On this theory, man's action has been adjusted to the environment, and, as a part of the process, there has been developed a conscious foreshadowing of the effect of certain substances upon him. The promise of benefit from a stimulus constitutes its pleasantness; the warning of injury its unpleasantness. The feelings come in advance of specific experience. They are of value in planning action. In many instances the idea arouses pleasure before the action is begun, or even before the stimulus is received. If the anticipation of the results of an act is pleasant, it is executed, if unpleasant it is inhibited. Metaphorically, one may regard the feelings as organic memories of the effect of stimuli upon the race as a whole, come to light in the individual as a member of the race. As a matter of actual fact, all that this can mean literally is that all individuals who felt anything other than pleasure from beneficial stimuli, or other than displeasure from injurious stimuli and ideas have been eliminated. Evolution and elimination have found expression in tendencies to action and in feelings that now signify for all individuals the general relations of the stimuli to the benefit or injury of the organism.

The Experience Theory of Feeling. The first of the psychological theories of feeling seeks to explain the changes that feelings undergo as the individual grows. One of the most striking phenomena in connection with feelings is that they change their character with the experience of the individual. An unfortunate experience with a particular dish may make it unpleasant long after the experience itself has passed out of mind. Some pleasures, too, are the direct expression of association. A national anthem arouses a pleasure in the patriotic citizen entirely incommensurate with the artistic value of the music. Wundt carries the theory a step farther and relates feeling to the activities at the basis of attention. The accumulated experiences largely determine the character of attention. The character of feeling depends upon the experiences of the individual. These two statements may be combined in the theory that feeling is the outcome of attention. The ultimate quality of the feeling as pleasant or unpleasant must still be explained by the evolutionary theory. There is nothing involved in attending to a pleasant object that is not also involved in attending to an unpleasant one. Accumulated experience only serves to transfer the pleasure and displeasure, derived originally from one experience, to others with which they were not at first connected. The pleasure of a song may at first be due to the social instincts that have their source in the community of spirit with fellow-members of the group. Later the pleasure returns when the song is heard. All goes back to the appreciation of benefit and injury, but appreciation is rendered more certain and accurate by the later experiences. The evolutionary quality or character is extended from the immediately pleasant stimuli to other and related stimuli and qualities of sensation.

The Furtherance-Hindrance Theory. The third theory is favoured by Stout and Dewey in slightly different forms. It makes pleasure the accompaniment of any smooth-running, uninterrupted activity ; displeasure, of thwarting and interruption. If one's heart is set upon the accomplishment of any task and the task is interrupted in its performance, displeasure is the result. Whatever furthers the progress of the task gives pleasure. What the task is matters not. It is as truly pleasant to progress toward the solution of a problem in mathematics when that is the aim of the moment as it is toward the acquisition of an automobile or the worldly wealth v/hich that signifies. There is undoubtedly a very close relation between pleasure and progress toward a desired end. The possibilities of pleasure are dependent largely upon desires. This theory applies immediately, however, only to relatively active processes or operations. The application is extended by the use of many similes. The more general asserts that there are many more movements than one ordinarily assumes, that movements are called out in relatively obscure muscles and organs that one would never suspect to play any part in the operation. Lipps has suggested that these movements are evoked by sympathy, that we personify inanimate objects and then suffer or rejoice with them. A column that seems to be supporting a load beyond its strength excites our sympathy because we put ourselves in its place. Many geometric figures excite our compassion and so are unpleasant, others are pleasant from their complete adequacy.

All Three Theories are Needed. Each of these theories has its applications. The more fundamental activities and reactions must find their explanation in the evolutionary feeling. Fundamentally, the organism requires satisfaction in certain ways, and there is apparently a predisposition to respond to certain stimuli by the feeling of pleasure, to others by displeasure. Under this head come the sense pleasures. The associatory theory will explain the many transfers and changes in feelings in the course of our life, and the attachment of feelings to many objects that are themselves indifferent to our well-being. On the contrary, the oppositionfurtherance theory is best adapted to the explanation of the active pleasures, both physical and mental. Most pleasure from games finds its explanation in accomplishment ; and the pleasure that accompanies success in any undertaking has the same explanation. Feelings cannot be explained by any one theory as there are different sources of pleasure and displeasure. All three theories must be combined if feelings are to be understood in their entirety.

QUESTIONS

1. Distinguish feeling from affection. What is the popular, what the psychological meaning of each word?

2. Find cases which prove or disprove the statements (a) that sensations are objective, affection, subjective ; (6) that sensations are clearer with attention, affection less prominent ; (c) that sensations have a definite sense-organ, affections have not.

3. How can you remember an affection ?

4. What are the qualities of affection? of feeling?

5. Can you give pleasantness or unpleasantness a definite bodily seat as you examine any simple experience ?

6. What is the real distinction between higher and lower feelings? Is it in the qualities of the affection?

7. Is the pleasure recalled in Question 2 instinctive, the result of training or experience, or an expression of furthered or successful activity ? Recall different pleasures that can be explained by each of the theories.

8. Give instances in which pleasure has not been a satisfactory guide to conduct. How do you explain?

EXERCISES

1. Sometime, when much pleased at some happening, turn around upon yourself and try to analyse the state into its elements. Can you distinguish the ' affective ' elements in the total state from the sensational components ? Does the pleasure disappear during the analysis?

2. Try to recall some pleasure of last week. Do you reinstate the pleasure or remember that you were pleased ? In your opinion is the pleasure as intense as in the original experience? Do you recall the pleasure in its vividness, or merely the sensations that were connected with the experience ?

3. Make a list of twenty events in your past that were strongly pleasant or unpleasant at the time. What is your present reaction to each ? Is there any law as to change in tone ?

4. Watch the pupil of an assistant as you stimulate first with pleasant then with unpleasant odours. Record direction of change in size.

Count the number of breaths for a minute, first under pleasant, then under unpleasant odours. Is there a difference ? Record any checking or quickening of respiration after stimulus is given.

5. Prepare a series of crosses with an upright an inch long and cross-bars three-fifths of an inch long. Place the cross-bar on one one-tenth of an inch from the top, the others each a tenth of an inch farther down. Ask ten or more individuals to arrange them in order of pleasantness. Which is most often preferred? Can you explain the choice by any of the theories of feeling?

CHAPTER XII

THE EMOTIONS

The Place of Emotion in Consciousness. The emotions stand as mental states, intermediate between feelings and instincts and the higher intellectual operations. From one point of view, they are very intense and diffuse feelings aroused by complicated situations. Pleasure is the result of a mild response ; delight, of a response of the same general character but more intense and diffuse. Emotions, too, are related to movements. It was said at the beginning of the last chapter that stimuli which were accepted frequently aroused slight diffused movements or were accompanied by quiescence, while stimuli that were rejected nearly always induced vigorous movements of a different character. These incidental and apparently useless movements not merely indicate to the observer the likelihood of continued and repeated acceptance or rejection, but also give a definite colouring to the accompanying consciousness. When surprised, one starts ; when one thinks of some definite action to perform, one executes it. In this respect emotion is different from voluntary action since the movements in an emotion have no necessary relation to the outside world, but find their goal within the body. Injemotion, action ends with facial expression or diffuse organic responses ; in action of the .voluntary sort, the end of movement is some change in the world outside. In one sense emotion, like feeling, is an expression~of instinct. All emotionsjhave an instinctiyejrasis ; movements in emotional expression are the outcome of instinct. So true is this, that the emotion has been denned by Dewey and MacDougall as the conscious side of instinct. For instance, fear is instinctive, but fear is also an emotion. Jnstinct is the process viewed from the outside, emotion is the same process viewedjrojii. within. Every emotion has its instinctive side, every instinct its emotional side. Emotion is concerned primarily with the responses that end altogether within the body; impulses are the instincts that lead to action directed beyond the body and will be discussed in the next chapter.

Ancient Theories of Emotion. The ancients always spoke of the emotions as having their seat in the viscera. Courage was in the heart, jealousy in the liver, and several of the other emotions had their seat in the abdominal region. Study of an emotion whether during immediate experience or when recalled shows that many of its components are sensations from the various parts of the body. In sorrow there is pressure about the heart, in joy a feeling of lightness in the chest. The lump in the throat, the dryness of the membranes of the mouth, all contribute some part to the total emotion. Organic sensations constitute a large part of what can be described or remembered of the emotions. These have a definite bodily seat in the chest and abdomen, and seem to be more or less closely related to the vital organs.

This fact explains why the ancients ascribed the emotions to these organs.

James-Lange Theory. The recent discussions follow the same general tendency. The prevailing modern theory was developed independently by James and Lange. This theory makes emotion the subjective accompaniment and the natural outcome of instinct. When a stimulus affects one, it calls out numerous responses because of the inherited paths of discharge. These are the occasion both for the bodily attitudes as they are presented to the outside observer, and for the consciousness of the emotion as it is revealed to the man himself. Professor James insists that ordinarily there is no awareness of the emotion until the action has been completed. For instance, he asserts that as a small boy he was playing with blood without knowing what it was. Suddenly he fainted. Nothing in the experience suggested the act or gave any indication that he was about to faint. He generalises this fact in the assertion that the consciousness of the emotion always attaches to the act after it has been completed. " One sees a bear and runs away. One is afraid because one runs away ; one does not run away because one is afraid." The act comes instinctively as part of the stimulus ; no thought intervenes, no elaborate working over of the material is possible before the responses which constitute the expression and give rise to the emotion as mental process.

Emotion as Instinctive Response. The theory of emotion in terms of the instinctive response is very generally accepted. There can be no doubt that most of the vividness and life of the emotion depends upon the bodily expression. One is not really afraid unless one feels the general quaking and motor insufficiency together with the sinking feelings about the heart. One is not really angry unless one is going hot and cold and has lost control of the muscles to some degree. A man who could face a crisis and know it to be a crisis with none of these organic responses would not really feel an emotion, no matter how complete intellectual appreciation he had of the seriousness of the situation. The emotions take their colour^ from the bodily reverberation, from the sensations that arise from contracting^ .muscles. These contractions are aroused by the instinctive connections between the stimulus and the muscles. Up to this point the character of the emotions is determined instinctively. That the emotions would not have the qualities they do have without these instinctive responses is demonstrated by the observations of the pathologists, that when an individual has widespread anaesthesia of the body muscles, no emotions are felt or at best the emotions are not of the same character as in the normal individual. v The deep-seated motorjresponsc is an integral part of the emotion ; the emotion disappears or takes on an entirely different character when the response is lacking.

Evidence for the James Theory. Sometimes the objection is raised that one does not feel the emotion when it is merely feigned, although this may include making most of the movements involved in the ordinary emotional expressions. This suggestion led James to ask actors whether they felt the emotions;they depicted. As might have been expected, actors divided into classes.

Some felt the emotions they portrayed, others were left practically unmoved. Moreover, one could not say that there was any relation between the strength and accuracy of the acting, and the degree to which the part was felt. Great actors were left cold and equally great ones felt the emotion. The difference arises probably from the fact that some individuals must feel the part to express it, others are able to mould the features without having the complete bodily reaction aroused. It is probable, too, that in many cases an actor can separate the more superficial from the deeper responses; he can control the muscles of the face and the larger muscles of the trunk without making the associated contractions of the deeper-lying muscles. The amount of feeling depends upon the number of such deeper-lying muscles that are contracted.

Specific Physiological Responses in Emotion. Important in this connection are the recent more detailed studies by Cannon and others, of the physiological responses. James, after all, left the statement of the nature of the bodily responses in very general form. He did not attempt to determine what bodily organs were involved in the complex response but was content to let each man observe them for himself. One by one experimenters have added to the list of known changes and, while it still cannot be regarded as complete, we have definite evidence of a large number. Among the first discovered were changes in the digestive tract. Strong emotional excitement checks the flow of saliva and of the digestive fluids in stomach and small intestine as well as the peristaltic movements of the whole alimentary canal. One may observe directly the dryness of the mouth in fear or grief and the increased flow of saliva in various pleasurable states. The disturbances in the alimentary tract are the cause of the discomfort that follows eating when much excited, and can be directly observed in animals under experimental conditions. These changes prepare the animal for exertion by withdrawing the blood from the abdomen for use in the muscles, the organs directly involved in action.

Adrenal Secretion in Emotion. Still more striking are the recently discovered activities of the adrenal bodies whose function it is to secrete into the blood a chemical known as adrenin. Cannon has shown that the substance is present in increased quantities during intense emotion of any kind. The presence of adrenin has three effects, (i) It causes the liver to release its stored glycogen or sugar, which provides an easily assimilable food for the muscles and other tissues.

(2) It increases the tendency of the blood to coagulate.

(3) It produces a constriction of the small blood-vessels. These together prepare the body for vigorous action. The glycogen rapidly restores the fatigued muscle, and the constriction of the vessels increases the blood pressure and thus increases the irrigation of the muscle by the blood. This washes away the fatigue products more rapidly and so diminishes the effects of fatigue. The increased coagulability and the constriction of the blood-vessels diminish bleeding in case wounds result from the fighting which usually follows emotion in animals. One may look upon the entire group of responses as factors in the preparation of the body to meet the demands of a crisis and the emotion as the awareness of these changes.

Responses Common to Pleasant and Unpleasant Emotions. One result of these experiments is not altogether in harmony with the James theory of emotion. That is that approximately the same effects are produced by pleasant and unpleasant emotions. Secretion of adrenalin is increased both in the dog that attacks a cat safely protected in a cage and in the cat. Fear and anger induce the same effect. In man the excited spectators of a football game show an increase of glycogen just as do the contestants or as do students taking a severe examination. The changes in Jbreathing^Lnd, circulation are identical in pleasure and in displeasure. Secretion of tears is also increased both by pleasant and unpleasant experiences. The reactions of the alimentary tract probably take opposed forms in mild emotions of the two types, but on the whole these fundamental physiological responses can be looked, to onlyJorthe source of some conscious process common to all emotions. For the physical correlates of the mental qualities which characterise different emotions, one must look to the more external voluntary muscles. The facial expression certainly differs from emotion to emotion and probably similar differences may be found in the muscles of the trunk. One must then think of the emotion as a response of the organism to a critical situation, a situation which offers possibilities of great benefit or of serious injury. This situation arouses a mass of instinctive responses. One group ,of JLhese prepares the body to meet the particular situation and may be regarded as characteristic of the situation. The other prepares for action of any type, increases the capacity of the organism in general. The first varies as the situation demands running or fighting, as the outcome promises well or ill, and is accompanied by a consciousness that changes with each element in the situation. The second group is common to all emotions and its mental accompaniment is excitement which is also common to all emotions.

Distinction between Emotion and Impulse. One further limitation of the definition of emotion as the consciousness that accompanies an instinctive response is that in the emotion the movement has no end outside of the body, while in instinct proper the end of the action is to be found in the world without. Anger is anger in the strictest sense only when the emotion is not vented on the object. Fear is fear in this sense only so long as the contractions are restricted to the body of the man in fear. Flight ordinarily relieves the fear and is classed as an impulse rather than as an emotion. If we bring together the characteristics of the emotions, we find that they are distinguished from the feelings by the fact that emotion^is always a^oinrjlex response to a very complicated situation, while the feeling is relatively simple and aroused by a single_stimulus. A pin prick is unpleasant, but if on examination you find that one whom you do not like is pricking you, you become angry. Emotion nevertheless usually contains something of pleasure or displeasure. ^Emotions are distinguished from instincts or impulses by the lack of objective end for the action, the movements are confined to vague contractions of the body muscles. An emotion is related to both feeling and impulse, and at the extremes may easily be distinguished from either, although the exact line of division is not always easy to draw.

The Origin of Emotional Expression. Much interest attaches to the problem of why the movements in emotion take the course they do. The responses are common to all races and to most individuals, in spite of the fact that many seem to have no great utility. Darwin proposed a theory in his " Expression of the Emotions in Animals and Man " that is still as satisfactory as any that we have. He based his explanation upon the assumption that all facial and bodily expressions must be regarded primarily as survivals of once useful movements, whose usefulness has disappeared. In the early stages, crying makes for the preservation of the child, because it attracts attention when it is lost, or when injured or otherwise in need of assistance. The response persists after it has ceased to be useful. Aside from expressions that have been directly useful at some time in the development of the species, there are transfers of expressions from the original connection to others in which they are useless. Darwin recognised two principles of transfer. First, expressions that have once been useful in a given connection are transferred to other similar emotions. The sneer of a man is the remnant of the unsheathing of the teeth in an animal. The man feels as the dog does in preparing for the attack. He expresses himself in the same way, although it is no longer customary to fight with the teeth. The nod of affirmation is a metaphor that has been transferred from the motion of the head that the child makes in taking food into the mouth ; the shake of the head in negation, a transfer from the child's act in moving the head quickly to avoid taking unwelcome food into the mouth. Darwin's second principle, that opposed emotions are expressed in opposite ways, is of rather less general application. His best instance is the expression of delight or friendliness in the cat. When the cat is angry, it lashes its sides, and crouches for the attack so that it is as inconspicuous as possible. When pleased, the attitude is just the reverse, the back is arched, the tail is held erect, and everything is as conspicuous as possible. In addition Darwin has a group of expressions left unexplained which he refers to the mere nervous overflow for instance, the turning grey of the hair from fright (if the fact be accepted), and the standing on end of the hair. Of these principles, the second and third seem less well established. The metaphorical transfer of emotional expression is accepted in some form by practically all and has many applications. The more general principle, that expression is the survival of instinctive responses that were once valuable, is fundamental to all theories. The expressions are slight remnants of movements once important for the survival of the individual in the circumstances which now call out the emotion.

The Classification of Emotions. The problem of the classification of emotions has occupied philosophers and psychologists since Descartes, and no entirely satisfactory grouping has yet been made. This is partly because there are a number of different principles of division that cut across each other, partly from mere lack of knowledge. Since the emotions are the subjective side of instinct and at the same time definite bodily responses, one might base a classification either upon the instincts or upon the bodily reactions. Neither is quite satisfactory since the bodily responses, so far as known, are frequently the same for more than one instinct, and the instincts are classified on the basis of the ends they subserve rather than by the nature of the responses. The general lines may be suggested. Three definitely distinct emotional expressions are found in love, anger, and fear. One is pleasant, the other two unpleasant; and of the latter fear is passive, anger, active. These fundamental emotions vary in quality as they are aroused by different stimuli or subserve different ends. Thus fear is different from disgust and shame, both in the reference and in the bodily response ; jealousy in the same way, from anger, and pride and joy, from love. Anger is different from rage, in the intensity of the emotion. Some, as shame and pride, have a subjective reference, while fear and love have an objective. Again we classify in language with reference to the time of the event that arouses the emotion. Thus dread and hope are the future forms of fear and love, respectively ; regret and satisfaction, the past forms. Language supplies many minor shadings which are difficult to fit into any logical scheme. Another difficulty in the practical classification of one's own emotions is found in the fact that emotional response to the same situation varies greatly with the intellectual attitude toward it and this changes often while the situation remains the same. Hope changes to fear and fear to anger in rapid alternation. When one recalls the situation one is apt to overlook the changes and call the whole response one emotion, which one depends upon the final outcome.

Emotional Control. Control of emotion or of emotional expression is largely in terms of the attitude one takes toward the stimulus or sensation. A caress from one person may please or be a matter of indifference, from another may cause anger; what occasions anger in one mood may give pleasure in another mood or attitude. The attitude is in large measure under one's control. From the nature of the organism and its inheritance, certain objects or stimuli must call out one response, and one alone. But aside from these most fundamental instincts invariably evoked by certain stimuli alone, sensations and stimuli are susceptible of different classifications, and when classified, arouse the emotion that belongs to the class. Whether a remark falls into the group of jests or of insults is often largely a matter of chance, and dependent upon circumstance. The emotions may be controlled only in so far as it is possible to vary the classification of the stimulus. The classification depends very largely upon how one attends.

Does Expression Relieve Emotion? One frequently hears the statement that free expression relieves or reduces an emotion, while a pent-up anger or grief grows stronger. There is some evidence that a ' good cry ' assuages grief. Of interest in this connection is a theory of the Austrian physician Freud that many of the disturbances of mental life come from conflict between emotions that leads one instinct to suppress another. A recent report of Rivers on the nervous disturbance of shell-shock would trace the origin of the disease to a conflict between the natural instinct of fear and the social pressure that prevents a man from showing it. Curious paralyses and disturbances of sensation that prevent a man from subjecting himself to danger sometimes present themselves in these cases. Eder quotes the case of an Australian soldier at Gallipoli who was firing through an embrasure when bullets struck several times near his head. He could no longer see with his right eye, although the tissues were perfectly normal. It was interpreted as an instinctive protest against further danger. Whether we accept all of the phases of the Freud theory or not, it seems probable that many of these disturbances can be traced to such conflicts in emotional tendency.

Can Conflict and Repression be Avoided? It has been argued from these theories and facts that all conflict in instincts should and possibly could be avoided. We are told that a child should always be permitted to act out his instincts and that he should never be compelled to suppress the emotional expression that corresponds to them. This recommendation is an ideal, but one which can seldom be attained in ordinary practice. Were one to consider the individual alone and then only to insure perfect mental health, the prescription would probably provide a means to that end. But the fact that individuals live in society, and that the social

Instincts conflict with the individual makes complete compliance with the rule impossible. Certain emotional conflicts are necessary. There are many cases in which others would suffer did the individual vent his emotions freely and the individual who must live in society would suffer did he form the habit of disregarding others completely. In practice, one learns to compromise emotional conflicts. So much of the rule may be followed as implies not raising unnecessary conflicts for the child or for one's self. The puritan rule that one should practise self-denial for the sake of moral training and against the time when necessity for repression may arise may well be disregarded in favor of avoiding conflict, but in the many cases in which essential desires and emotions conflict, discipline must be maintained, the social forces must be given a hearing.

Self-Control. A large part of what is ordinarily called self-control is really "control "of" the emotions. Lack of self-control arises from conflict of emotions, and of the ideals and instincts that cause emotions. Usually either one has disagreeable emotions that are unnecessary or expresses too freely the emotions that one does have. Unnecessary discontent arises from failure to attain to one's ideal standard and this may be due either to having too high ideals, or in not working hard enough to attain them and then wasting effort in regret that might better have been spent on accomplishment. It is necessary, too, to keep in mind human limitations and so not to expect too much of one's self. A cure for any of these evils is not emotional repression, but elimination of the fundamental causes. The cure is to be found either in reducing one's ideals or increasing one's accomplishment by better methods of work. To reduce ideals is difficult, more difficult than one thinks. If it were too successful it would reduce efficiency by diminishing effort. A well-balanced soul may attain the same end by accepting the difficulties and at the same time striving for the end. To regard all effort as part of the day's work, with no stigma attaching to failure and not too much credit coming from success, is the ideal attitude, although if not in harmony with temperament it can be attained only as a result of long habit. Even in this prescription there is danger that it may lead to a cynical depreciation of the advantages of success that destroys ideals or on the other hand that it may merely repress the emotion, either as a pose that will have unpleasant social consequences, or if the repression be real that it may incur the dangers emphasised by Freud.

The other alternative is to permit one's self free expression at all times, to be perfectly ready to face the facts and willing to experience the emotion that logically or instinctively follows from them. Where one is dealing with misfortunes that are real and inescapable as in the death of relatives and friends or the loss of one's health and capacity for work, free expression is the only rule. Here, too, the emotion may be diminished by occupation of mind and body which will distract from the emotion. In certain cases the emotion may be transformed and find a useful outlet in something that symbolises one's own grief as in charitable work. The usual rule of looking on the bright side has much to recommend it, provided only that it does not lead to falsification of the event and so store up new troubles for the time of realisation or lead to suppression and the consequent mental and physical ills. Usually a grief boldly faced yields to the development of new habits that replace the old ones disturbed by the misfortune, and the formation of new ideals and complete readjustment follows. Readjustment must come some time and the sooner the better. Perfect honesty with one's self as with others is best in this field as in all others.

Transfers of Emotional Response. That reactions may be carried over from one situation to others similar to or in some way connected with it is proved by experiment and by observation in normal and abnormal individuals. The Russian physiologist Pawlow obtained evidence of these transfers in a number of striking experiments on dogs in which he used accurate measurements of the secretion of saliva as an indication of the emotions. As is familiar to every one, sight of food starts a secretion of saliva. If the food was given a few times simultaneously with the striking of a bell, the sound of the bell alone came to evoke the secretion. Evidence of similar transfers is abundantly supplied from common experience. Much of the pleasure or its opposite obtained from the articles of daily use is derived from their associations. So marked and so frequent are these transfers in the mentally abnormal that one school of psychiatrists sees in them the prime evidence of mental disease. The disturbances are connected with emotions aroused by memories of early crises, but the memories themselves frequently do not come to full consciousness ; they are assigned to objects that have become symbols of the event. Thus in one case reported by Dr. Morton Prince, a woman was profoundly depressed by the sound of church bells and could not account for the effect. Careful examination by special methods disclosed the fact that the sound had been closely related to the death and burial of her mother, which had occurred under peculiarly distressing circumstances. Such instances of transfer of emotion from one object or event to others only indirectly related to them in the life of individuals are suggestive of the possibility of a similar transfer of expressions from one event to others of the same class during the long course of evolution.

Emotions Dependent upon Intellectual Appreciation. Not all emotions can be explained directly by this theory of instinctive response. Certain emotions, it is true, come without preliminary consciousness and the response may be contrary to desire or even opposed to all rational expectations. James' fainting at the sight of blood is typical of this class. For them the theory outlined suffices. But we have many emotions which arise only after interpretation, which are influenced by contemplation as much as by the stimulus. Many times one does not become angry until one sees who is playing the trick; one is not afraid until the full list of circumstances is taken into consideration. One sees a snake and at first feels only curiosity. Later when the markings are noted or the rattle on the tail, one begins to grow cold, to shiver, to feel a sinking in the abdomen, and all of the other symptoms of fear. The reflection .upon the stimulus, not the stimulus itself^ seems to be the cause of the reaction. This does not mean that the bodily response is not an essential part of the emotion, even that it is not the most important element in colouring the emotion; but it does mean that in addition to the instinctive contractions or as a cause of these contractions, one must consider the wider intellectual setting if one is to give a full explanation.

The Intellectual Emotions. Two classes of emotion may be distinguished in which these intellectual factors are important. In one, interpretation consists in referring the stimulus to a known class. When the reference is completed, the instinctive response is immediate. Fear of the snake or anger at the trick is delayed until the reference is made, until the situation is understood, then the instinctive response comes at once. In the second class the situation threatens no immediate danger, and promises no immediate benefit and the response could never have been of survival value in a similar situation in the pre-human stages of evolution. MOSJL of our emotions in peaceful civilised life are evoked by winning or losing prizes of symbolic value only. One is elated over school or social honors, one worries at loss of money or of the social prestige that goes with money, one grows angry at deprecatory remarks about one's self or one's family. No one of these can be explained directly as vestjgial instinctive responses once of value in protecting the individual. Itjs__the_jcuk that emotions are now due to success or failure in the

Attainment of ideals established by social convention^. Originally they might have been connected with the attainment of ends of survival value, but in many cases the connection has become very remote. The organic response in these must be thought of as transferred from a similar situation in which it was fitting. In our present life situations seem to have been grouped into conventional classes, each class with its appropriate response. Unjust deprivation of anything becomes a cause of anger and the response always comes, it matters not whether the thing of which one is deprived is a dinner or an intangible something regarded as an element in the total reputation. The insinuation that a pet theory is not all that one has thought it may cause as violent a reaction as a physical injury. The transfer of the response from situations where they might be of value to those only remotely similar may be regarded as metaphorical and as expressions of Darwin's first law mentioned above. Iru discussing emotion, then, we must consider the knowledge and ideals of the individual as well "as" his instincts. Emotional responses are evoked by a total situation in the light of intellectual appreciation rather than constituting instinctive responses to a single stimulus. With this addition, emotion may be defined as the awareness of the instinctive response. It is the consciousness of the reaction of the individual as a whole to the situation as a whole.

Mood. Closely related to emotion are mood and temperament. Two uses of the word mood must be distinguished. The first designates an emotion of long duration and of slight intensity. A mood is an affair of hours or days. In the second sense mood is rather a predisposition to an emotion or group of emotions than the actual emotion itself of which one may not even be conscious until the emotion comes. Usually, however, one is conscious of the predisposition in advance of the emotional outburst. So one finds one's self in a cheerful mood in which everything pleasant has a definite appeal, or in a depressed or angry mood in which anything whatever is likely to arouse an emotion of anger or a state of depression. One is ' set ' for an emotion of one kind or of one general class, and as a consequence it is very much easier than usual to arouse an emotion of that class. At times one has an incipient emotion with no apparent cause. One may feel mildly cheerful during a day in advance of any emotion and irrespective of particular stimulus, but mood is not necessarily conscious in advance of the stimulus that excites the emotion. The mood may owe its origin to some particular stimulus or group of stimuli, or it may be due to the state of health. A piece of good fortune induces a pleasant mood that for a long time makes pleasant emotions easy ; any misfortune tends to reduce the capacity for enjoyment and increases the liability to disagreeable emotions over a period of hours or days. On the other hand, perfect health and a bright day are sufficient to induce a pleasant mood, while nothing is so conducive to low spirits and unpleasant moods as bad health. Temperament. Temperament is a mood that is permanent. Individuals are born apparently with tendencies to look on the bright or dark side of life. If it is not certain that the temperament is innate, at least it has become permanent in early life and seldom changes completely after maturity. The psychology of temperaments leaves much to be desired. With the whole of the psychology of individual differences, it has received more recognition for its importance than labour toward its development. One may pick out quite easily from his acquaintances individuals who are particularly prone to emotions of one kind or another, but to determine what the most striking features of the temperaments are and to group them in a satisfactory way is by no means so easy. Psychology is still accustomed to make use of the classes of the ancients, phlegmatic and sanguine, melancholic and choleric. This classification is modified by Wundt to designate the strength and quickness of the individual, not the permanent mood or susceptibility to emotions. The sanguine individual combines quickness with weakness ; the choleric, quickness with strength ; the melancholic is slow and weak ; the phlegmatic, slow and strong. While these qualities are the only ones made explicit by the classification, there is implied in the terms as ordinarily used a predisposition to different emotions and tendencies to be easily pleased or displeased. The melancholic individual is undoubtedly predisposed to grief or low spirits, as is the sanguine individual to pleasant emotions. The choleric individual is predisposed to anger, as the phlegmatic to calm, even amid temptations to excitement. This classification, old as it is, can be regarded as no more than a beginning in the study of individual differences. Much more remains to be done and could be done with relatively little difficulty. It is sufficient to indicate that men are differently disposed toward different emotions, and that some respond easily, others with difficulty. JWhat . emotion shall be excited depends fully as much upon the individual as it does upon the stimulus.

EXERCISES

1. Give an instance of an emotion and of a feeling. How are they different ?

2. Recall some strong emotion. How did it affect the accuracy of your thinking ? The efficiency of your acts ?

3. What are the characteristics of the James theory? Can you think of any objections to it ?

4. Can you recall any instance of true emotion without bodily reactions ?

5. How are the motor responses in anger different from those in fear? In joy from those in hate ?

6. Distinguish the physiological effects common to all emotions from others peculiar to certain emotions.

7. Do the bodily expressions precede or follow the emotion as a mental process?

8. Can the emotion or its expression be repressed or modified? Does experience change the original character of the emotion or its expression? How does it resemble instinct in these respects?

9. Why does sorrow over failure to win a social honour have the same bodily expression as sorrow over losing a bit of food ? Why does loss of a sum of money have the same effect?

10. Describe the facial expression in anger, in joy, in sorrow. Does the facial expression contribute anything to the quality of the emotion ?

CHAPTER XIII

ACTION AND WILL

Action the End. The most important practical problem in psychology is the control of action. Almost all thinking and very much of feeling and emotion are of value to the organism only as they lead to action of some sort or other. Action is very closely related to thought and feeling. Much of action grows out of thinking and we appreciate action only by means of the sensory processes. As was asserted in connection with the discussion of the nervous system, all action is sensori-motor ; it begins in sensation and ends in muscular contractions. One may complete the circle by the assertion that when the muscles contract, they arouse processes in the sensory ends in the body of the muscle, and these sensory processes, in their turn, give the only evidence to consciousness of the contraction of the muscle. A muscle moves only on the excitation of some sensory neurone, either directly by the senseorgan or indirectly by memory, and the movement of that muscle can be known only through the stimulation of the sensory ends in the muscle that contracts.

Evidently, the various problems in connection with

action are problems of the control of thoughts and of

sensations, and of the connections between thoughts and

sensations, and actions. The classification of actions

must be either in terms of the accompanying mental processes, or in terms of the nature of the connection between the movements and the ideas. Each of these criteria has been used in the generally accepted classification. In terms of accompanying consciousness, actions are classified as impulse, reflex act, and voluntary act. In the technical psychological vocabulary, any movement that grows out of sensation or memory image is called an impulse. In the complete impulse, sensation is followed by movement, and that is followed or accompanied by a kinaesthetic sensation which informs the agent that he is moving or has moved. In most of the frequently repeated movements, consciousness falls away. Reflex action is often not appreciated ; both the stimulus that calls it out and the sensory processes that accompany it may pass unnoticed. One winks without being aware of it or of its stimulus. In other instances, as when one draws back the hand on being pricked with a pin, one is conscious of the stimulus and of the movement, but only after the response has been made. Reflex action is distinguished from impulse by the fact that the conscious accompaniments either disappear, are reduced in number, or enter consciousness after the movement has been executed. The more complicated acts may all be regarded as modifications of impulse. Voluntary acts arise when several ideas each with corresponding impulses are present. In consequence, consciousness is more complicated than in impulse. Each idea has its own natural outcome in movement, and each of these partial movements adds something to the total consciousness. In automatic acts, the consciousness that at first accompanied the movement has disappeared, and the movement is run through without definite knowledge. This is true of walking, talking, and of most of the more complicated habits. If automatic acts are to be defined as impulses that have lost some or all of their conscious accompaniments, volitional acts may be defined as acts performed after a conflict of impulses. The consciousness is more complicated than in the impulse, because each impulse adds something to the total consciousness.

One may define acts, however, not merely in terms of the accompanying consciousness, but also with reference to the time at which the connection between thought and action was established. On this basis impulses may be classified as inherited and acquired. The former are due to connections between sensation and movement established before the birth of the individual. The child is born with the synapses between certain sensory regions and certain motor regions already open. Inherited impulses may be divided again into reflexes and instincts. As was said earlier, reflexes are simple and can be understood in terms of the mere physiological connections, while instincts are more complex and at present can be explained only through an appeal to their purpose. Acquired impulses, on the other hand, are only potentially represented in the individual at birth ; they are the outcome of connection? made or confirmed by action during the life of th individual. If we combine the results of the two classifications, we find that inherited impulses are more likely to be unaccompanied by consciousness than are acquired, although acquired impulses with practice rapidly lose their conscious accompaniments. It should be remarked that movements are always excited by sensory stimuli, whether these are conscious or not, and that there are always many more stimuli involved in the control of the movement than are conscious.

New Movements Learned by Trial and Error. Obviously, the first problem in connection with movements is to determine the methods by which they may be learned. The first experiments on learning that proved fruitful were performed on animals. An animal was confined in a box, provided with a door closed by some simple device, and the methods by which the animal learned to get out were recorded. The results demonstrated that learning was by chance. The cat would struggle vaguely, trying all of its acquired and inherited responses one after the other. It would bite here, there, and everywhere, would scratch at each projecting part and at each crevice, until finally some one of the movements happened to open the door. When returned to the box at another time, it would run through the same series of random movements, until the successful act was repeated. Gradually the time required would become shorter until, with frequent repetition, the sight of the cage would at once call out the correct response for opening the door. Nervously this means that the movement, arising at first by chance, is established by repetition. The synapse traversed frequently by this stimulus may be pictured as becoming more and more permeable, until, when learning is complete, the sensation leads at once to the appropriate motor discharge.

Human Movements also Learned by Selection.

The same general law has been shown to hold as well for human learning. One of the best instances of this is to be found in the way a man solves a mechanical puzzle. He may merely think it through and, after solving it in thought, test the solution in practice. Even this solution in thought is, as was seen in the chapter on Reasoning, a process of trial and error. Suggestions appear one after another until some one comes that is approved. But unless very familiar with other forms of puzzles, he will proceed just as the cat does to get out of a box. If the problem is to take apart two constructions of wire, he will try to put one through each place that seems possible, and will keep trying until he succeeds in the attempt. When he gets them apart, the chances are that he will have no very clear idea of how it was done. He will, at most, remember in a vague way the point of least resistance, but ordinarily he must solve the puzzle more or less accidentally several times before he can remember exactly how to do it again, or be able to succeed at the first trial. Practically all unfamiliar complicated acts are performed in this way. Random movements, with stamping in of the accidental success hrough frequent repetition, is the universal method of human as well as of animal learning. In this and all similar contexts chance movements mean movements of unknown cause. Each movement made is determined by the external stimulus and the connections established at birth or acquired. Where we cannot trace the connections we speak of them as made by chance.

The Child's Learning. This law is illustrated still more completely by the child. At birth the movements of the child are all pretty well tied together. When the child moves one hand, the other moves in the same way and about as far. If you watch the feet, you will see that they ordinarily move in harmony with the movements of the hand. Any stimulus calls out many more movements than are needed. Even at the age when a child learns to write, the different members are still more or less bound together. The boy follows the movements of his hand by sympathetic rolling of his tongue. The process of learning is one of waiting until these diffuse motor discharges bring a pleasant result, and then of repeating the movement that gave that result until it is thoroughly connected with the appropriate stimulus. After this, progress in learning is largely a matter of separating the particular element desired from the complex in which it first originated. Learning to speak is an illustration of the method. The child of six months to a year spends much of its comfortable waking time practising vocal exercises. At first the results are altogether indefinite and uncertain. All sorts of noises come out of the vocal organs. Whenever one that pleases the child's fancy makes its appearance, it is repeated, more or less accurately, until thoroughly learned. Learning words follows the same laws. When a sound is hit upon that is similar to a word uttered by the parents, it pleases the child. It is repeated and the results of the repetition, in the pleasure of the parents and in obtaining the satisfaction of its desires, serve to increase the pleasantness of the movement and to renew the struggles. The words that are heard do not serve as the stimulus for their repetition, but set a pattern toward which the child may strive, or merely make the word interesting when by chance it is uttered. Each of the other motor accomplishments is acquired by the child in the same way.

Learning as Transfer. After a fair number of movements have been learned, the first attempts at a new movement are more nearly successful. If the child has had some experience with a pencil in drawing, the first attempts at writing will not be so awkward as the first attempts at drawing. The movements will all resemble the desired result. At this stage, the known movements most like those to be learned will be used first. Still, the method of modifying the old to obtain the new follows the same laws as the original learning. One first makes some similar familiar movement, and then tries to vary it until the end is attained, but the modifications are struggled for in the same random way as in the original learning. Many trials and numerous discouraging failures are usually required before the desired modification presents itself. When it comes once, it can be called out a second time only after numerous trials. Each success makes new successes more likely, but perfection in any movement comes slowly. When one begins to learn the golf stroke, one ordinarily has a number of similar movements at command. One has swung an axe, or has cast a fly, or practised hitting at pebbles with a stick. One calls upon some one of these on the first occasion for hitting the ball. The probability is that the first attempts will be inaccurate; certainly they will be feeble. The process of transforming the familiar habits into adequate new ones is one of constant trial and slow selection of the successful variations. In the more complicated and delicate movements of this sort, one frequently does not know what it is that makes the stroke successful. The conscious antecedents of the successful stroke seem 4 o be very little different from those present in the unsuccessful, but practice brings the successful stroke more frequently. Assuming, then, that an individual has a large number of impulses under control, whether they have been established by earlier practice or are instinctive, we find that new movements are learned by slow and painful modification of these responses.

The Acquisition of Skill. Closely related in explanation and in practice to the learning process is the acquisition of skill. When one has mastered trie separate movements necessary for the accomplishment of some important end, the process of combining them and controlling them in such a way as to give rapid and accurate accomplishment offers much that is of interest psychologically, and also much of practical importance. Many investigations have been made of the methods of acquiring skill in telegraphy, in typewriting, tossing balls, and in various other games and occupations. The rough results show striking agreement among the different investigators, and for different sorts of learning. Learning has a characteristic course. One may represent it by curve i, showing the rate of learning to write upon a typewriter, given in Figure 32. It will be seen that progress is step-wise all through the test. First, there is a rapid increase in skill during the period when the elements are being learned, then there is a period without progress, then another rise, and so on. There are alternations of rapid improvement with levels of practice /ithout improvement. These level parts of the curve have been called the plateaus. It should also be noted that in the first part of the experiment the curve is much steeper than later. One gradually approaches, but never absolutely reaches, the highest performance of which the individual is capable.

The Curve of Learning. The mechanism of learning and the explanation of the course of learning are also fairly well agreed upon. In the first place, methods by which improvement is made are seldom conscious. One falls into good habits and gives up bad habits with no knowledge of how or why. The man does his best all the time, and at times he improves, at times he continues upon the same level ; he himself cannot tell how the improvement was brought about. He does not ordinarily plan out the improvement ; he hits upon it by chance. More interesting and consequently more discussed is the explanation of the plateaus in the learning curve and the occasion for rising from one level to another. All seem to agree that, during the period of no improvement, associations are being formed that are to be useful at a later stage of learning. One can advance to a certain stage only on the basis of one definite group of habits. When this stage has been reached, no further advance is possible until new habits have been thoroughly established. During the time one keeps to the plateau the habits are being stamped in. After they have been thoroughly established, it is possible to go on to higher acquirements. Apparently, the learner works just as hard when he makes no progress as when he is advancing. And while the effects of the work do not show in the accomplishments, something is being gained all the time that will tell finally in new progress. Very interesting is the question of what gives the sudden rise in capacity. Sometimes, apparently, it is the result of effort. It is said by Bryan and Harter that a telegraph operator may stay for years at a small office and make no appreciable gain in his sending or receiving rate, but when transferred to a larger office where more demands are made upon him, he will suddenly increase in skill. In this instance, progress is the result of effort, and effort of increased incentive. But effort does not always lead to increased accomplishment. If one strives hard for a new advance before the habits are ripe, the result usually is not advantageous; one is more likely to disturb the ordinary habits and lose efficiency than to gain new skill. Effort is necessary for the rise to a new level of speed, but effort is harmful before the necessary amount of preparation has been made by fixing old habits. The advance may be accompanied by relaxation of effort ; the work seems easier when the advance begins. Another element of value is to become clearly aware of the details of the movements that are made and of what parts are essential. It is the rule, in learning new and effective combinations, that they are hit upon blindly, and only later become consciously recognised. With the recognition, one is apparent!}prepared for a new advance. But the actual improvement that gives the advance is ordinarily some new chance combination that develops unintentionally, and is not appreciated when it comes. In some cases the plateau seems to appear when certain parts of the complex movement are being learned separately, and the sudden rise is apparently due to success in uniting them into a single whole. Still another factor that is probably as important as the acquirement of new combinations is the disappearance of bad habits. Failure to advance may be due to the persistence of some unfortunate habit acquired early in the task. In the course of time this bad habit may disappear, and the record will jump up suddenly to a new level. Both the development of a new and advantageous habit or set of habits, and the disappearance of some bad habit that has been retarding advance may be unnoticed. They are not planned in advance of their appearance, and are not recognised when they appear. All that can be said of the method of acquiring skill is that one must continue to work up to his best capacity, and must be constantly on the lookout for any new method that may promise advance; but, in spite of one's best endeavour, there will always be periods of apparently fruitless effort, plateaus of no advance, and the advance to new levels will come unexpectedly and for no assignable reason.

All learning is by the same law of chance trials and selection of the suitable movement when it is hit upon by chance. The first learning is by the selection of movements connected as overflow discharges with the original instincts. When a fair number of these have been fully established, new movements are acquired by chance variations from those already learned. Finally, when all of the movements involved in a complicated set of activities have been learned and one desires merely to combine them in the best possible way to obtain speed z and accuracy, the combinations and connections are again developed by chance. Ordinarily one does not know, either before or after, how the various advances in skill are made. In learning one can only keep trying and be alert for the appearance of the satisfactory movement or combination, when it makes its appearance. This, with constant striving to obtain some result and to repeat the result when obtained, is all that can be done toward learning. In time it is bound to be successful. It should be added that learning must be spontaneous. Unless the movement is made by the individual, no learning results. Movements forced upon an animal or man by a trainer or by electrical stimulation are not learned. To be learned, movements must be hit upon in the course of intentional effort. There is no short cut to learning.

Control of Movement. The second question is how movements are controlled when once they have been learned, why one movement rather than another is made on any occasion. It follows from the law of the connection of motor and sensory nerves that control of movement must always be primarily control of idea or control of sensation. The process of learning is to associate movement with a sensory process ; when the connection has been established, the movement results whenever the related idea or sensation dominates consciousness. The immediate antecedent of a movement is ordinarily an idea. In speech, the expression follows upon the thought of the words. In repetition of spoken words, the expression comes when the word to be repeated is heard. Similarly in writing from dictation, as one hears the words the hand traces them upon the paper. The writing may go on fairly accurately when no attention is given to the words. The student in a lecture may take notes without knowing much of what he is writing, while thinking of the next foot-ball game, or of other extraneous matter. The connection between the auditory region and the motor region serves to keep the hand writing properly, whether all attention is fixed upon the movement or not. The immediate antecedent of the movement is always some idea, but, in addition, two other groups of sensory processes must cooperate in the control of the movement. These are, in James's terms, the remote sensations, sensations from the eye or ear, and the resident sensations, from the muscles and other parts of the moving member.

Remote Sensations. As one writes, the pen is guided by the sight of the movements that are made. If the pen wanders from the line one sees it and brings it back. With the eyes closed or in the dark, writing is very uncertain. In speech, the ear takes the place of the eye. The voice is modulated by the ear. When a discordant sound is started it is checked and the vocal mechanism adjusted to give the desired quality. The deaf speak in monotonous, badly modulated tones because they cannot know what sounds they make and so cannot change them. Children born deaf are dumb because they have no incentive to speak and no means of appreciating the sounds they make. They can learn only when they are taught to control the movements of the vocal organs by touch. Education of the deaf in the art of speaking is necessarily a slow process. They must be taught to reproduce the movements of the teacher's mouth and larynx as they feel them with their fingers or see them in the glass. Otherwise learning follows the usual laws. After they have reproduced the movement by chance and know through touch that they have made it, the idea of the word, however it may be presented, will lead to the reinstatement of the movement. Later they substitute the sensations that come from the moving muscles for the tactual sensations. This never becomes as adequate as the control that is exerted by the ear of the normal individual. The deaf child always is deficient in intonation and modulation.

Resident Sensations. In addition to these impressions from the higher senses, sensations from the moving member serve to control all movement. The best evidence of this statement is the fact that when the kinaesthetic sensations are lacking, control is inadequate. Tabetic patients, whose Columns of Goll and Burdach in the spinal cord have been destroyed by disease and who in consequence have no sensations from the muscles, may tend to make a movement and have the appropriate idea, but the movement will not follow, or will be weak, or entirely misdirected. A child whose sensory nerves in the organs of speech have not developed will not learn to talk unless special methods are devised, and then will learn slowly and imperfectly. The sensations from the muscles and the moving parts are constantly coming in to exert an influence upon the amount and character of the motor discharge. They adjust the movement to the position of the member at the moment, and exert a general guidance upon the movement.

The Incentive to Action Takes Many Forms. Each of these directing and controlling factors may be explicit, or it may be implicit ; it may be conscious or unconscious, or vaguely conscious. It has been asserted at different times that the initiating idea must be a kinaesthetic memory of the act, that it must be a picture of the member in a certain position, and that it may be any one of several definite ideas or images. The more the antecedents of action are observed, however, the more evident it becomes that the directing idea may be any sort of image whatever. In many cases, the imagery is very indefinite, seems to be very largely lacking. It may be a mere thought that it is desirable to do a certain thing ; it may be any part of the act to be performed. In other cases, one may make up one's mind to do a certain thing at a certain time, and when the time comes, it is done with no appreciable idea whatever. The expected sensation starts the movement decided upon without any idea or intention intervening. Thus, at the moment you read these lines, we may imagine that you decide to underline them. You may think of the position your hand should take to bring the pencil to the proper point on the page, and you may think of this position in kinaesthetic imagery or in visual imagery; again, you may think merely in words, ' I'll underline that,' and draw the line with no further imagery whatever. Again, you may have decided at the beginning of the reading that you will underline the important passages, and now think nothing more than, ' this is important,' and the movement starts at once. The general rule is that there is more imagery the first time a movement is made, and that the imagery decreases in amount the more frequently the movement is repeated. In general, too, each part of the movement is at first preceded by a separate idea, while, after several repetitions, all that is necessary is to think of some part of the movement or of something that makes the movement desirable, and it is executed without further outlining of the details. Such a general thought as, ' that is important,' is the usual cue for the more familiar movements. Controls often Automatic. The controlling sensations, resident and remote, act even less consciously. As one underlines, one is aware through the eyes of the course of the movement ; one sees the lines grow, but does not realise that these visual impressions play any important part in the control. The control is not conscious and deliberate. One does not first appreciate the visual sensations, and then decide in terms of them how the pencil must move to make the line straight. One occasionally notices that the line is getting crooked and consciously corrects it ; but, if all goes well, the only way of being sure that sight is guiding the movement is to find that one cannot draw a straight line with the eyes closed. The influence of sight is effective, not only in determining the direction and character of the movement, but also in determining its force or intensity. One of the most striking instances of this is the illusion of the pound of lead and the pound of feathers. A pound of feathers seems very much lighter than a pound of lead, because the large bulk calls out a strong motor discharge for the feathers, and the small bulk of the lead, a slight motor discharge. In consequence, the feathers are lifted very rapidly, the lead very slowly. The weight that rises more rapidly than was expected seems light, the weight that rises more slowly than was expected seems heavy. For our present purpose, the important phase of the experiment is to show that the motor impulse is controlled in amount by remote sensations. Sensation may overcome knowledge. If one is told in advance that one object is light, the other heavy, the illusion persists on lifting. Even when told that each weighs exactly a pound, the large mass still calls out the larger impulse, and is raised the more rapidly. Given only the intention of raising the weight, the motor impulse is determined primarily by the visual appearance of the object to be lifted ; other sources of knowledge will be disregarded.

The same sort of control by vision may be seen in many other movements. In speaking, one unconsciously adjusts the loudness of the tone to the distance of the listener, the size of the room, etc. In making a golf stroke, the force of the blow is guided by the sight of the green, together with the unexpressed estimate of the distance. In each of these instances, the strength of the movement is closely adapted to the visual impressions, and the only requirement for the adaptation is that the weight to be lifted or the object to be hit be definitely looked at, or have been observed just before the movement. The control by the kinaesthetic sensations, the resident sensations, is similarly unconscious. One never thinks of them unless attention is especially directed toward them, and even then one is more likely to be conscious of the visual interpretation, to think of the motion of the member in remembered visual images, than in terms of the kinaesthetic sensations themselves. One misses them when they are destroyed by disease, but does not appreciate them when present. Three elements, then, combine in the initiation and guidance of a movement, (i) The general idea or intention to move. This is found in the thought of the movement or of the end to be attained. (2) The remote sensations from eye or ear. (3) The resident sensations from the moving member itself. These resident and remote sensations control the direction and force of the movements.

Not All Ideas Produce Movements. If, as has been said, the immediate antecedent of a movement is an idea, the question naturally arises why all ideas do not lead to movement or, more particularly, how it is possible that one may think of a movement without making it. One may think of saying something and not say it, one frequently thinks intently of an act without performing it. This problem has been much discussed but has received no very definite answer. The probability is that there is no particular process that comes invariably to set off the movement after it has been decided upon, but any one of a number of different circumstances may serve as the final determinant of the movement. Of these, the most important is the wider setting in which the idea presents itself. If everything else in the situation favours the movement, it will be made ; if the idea of the moment is altogether out of harmony with the act, it will not be put into execution. Thus, if one has been waiting for the summons to dine, one goes immediately to the table when it comes ; if the summons comes in the midst of writing a sentence, the movement will at first be thought of vaguely, but nothing will happen. Sometimes a contending image or idea may interfere with full attention to the movement itself, or other considerations may make the act undesirable at the moment. When these disappear, the act results. It is probable, when everything seems ready for the movement but it is not made, that the explanation is to be found in some inhibiting process, some vaguely conscious consideration that blocks the path.

The Release of the Movement. One of the best places to study the play of these forces and considerations is in getting up in the morning, which is made much of by Professor James, and which, for its difficulty, seems to have universal appeal. When the alarm goes off, one intends to get up, one even thinks of the movements that are to be made in their order, but nothing happens. Sometimes one suddenly recalls the task that must be finished early in the morning. That gives the required impetus, and the various habitual movements are begun. Often, however, one thinks of nothing new ; there seems no particular incentive to the movements just before they begin , one finds one's self dressing and that is all that there is to the whole matter. In such cases it is probable that the act begins when some inhibiting or blocking idea disappears or is forgotten, that the movement is due to the removal of a check rather than to the appearance of a new force. In brief, the movement is induced, not merely by the idea regarded as the motive, but by the entire mental context at the moment, by a large number of elements that constitute the situation and the attitude toward the situation. In any case the release of the movement does not follow upon any definitely assignable mental content, but is i he outcome of a whole mass of considerations that combine to make the act desirable.

Will and Choice. The rudiments of action are, then, comparatively simple. One acquires the possibility of moving by random movements that give a certain result, and the connection between the idea of the movement and the movement itself is established by frequent repetition. At all later times, the movement may be made whenever the idea comes to consciousness. The more complex problems of action are really problems in the control of ideas. What one ordinarily calls will is exerted primarily in the control of the course of thought, and action follows when the proper thought presents itself. The most striking instance of voluntary control is the decision between alternative courses of action. Frequently two courses present themselves which seem equally attractive or impelling. Decision in these cases is made by selecting one of the two possible ideas, the idea of the result of one course of action or of the other. This may lead in turn to the thought of the movement necessary to realize that end. Always what is chosen is not the movement as such, but an idea ; either the result, or the thought of the movement dominates consciousness at the moment of choice. When either completely dominates consciousness, the action results. Control of action offers nothing that has not been earlier discussed in connection with the control of ideas, or with attention, the selection of sensations. The importance of action, however, makes it desirable to study the old laws in the new application.

The Mechanism of Choice. When making a choice between two courses of action, one thinks of the probable results of each and chooses the one which offers the greater probability of a desirable outcome. If after class it is a question between going home or to a shop, you do not think of the movement as such, but you decide that it is necessary to finish the task at home at once, while your purchases may wait until later in the day. When this decision has been made, the necessary movements are begun at once. The same holds of the more complex life problems. Choice of a profession, where there is opportunity for choice in the matter at all, is a choice of ends. The advantages and disadvantages of each profession are weighed and compared with the difficulties that must be overcome in obtaining a preparation for each. When a balance has been struck, it finds expression in some phrase, such as, ' this will be my lifework ' ; from that time the first step toward the entrance upon the profession is kept in mind, ready to be translated into action when occasion arises. The idea, and the idea alone, is chosen at the moment ; translation into action may be delayed for years.

The Conditions of Choice. If we turn back to ask what it is that makes one line of action attractive and the other repulsive, we can do no more than enumerate different elements in heredity, education, or present mood. In action as in attention, two classes are to be distinguished, one due to interest, the other to social pressure. The one is said to be in accordance with desire, the other to arise from duty. Desires grow out of hereditary tendencies and experience, and change with the mood and attitude. Duties, on the other hand, come mostly from social influences, from ideals, and are relatively permanent. The actions from desire promise immediate satisfaction ; actions from duty are attractive from their more remote results. The outcome of the line of action decided upon always seems at the moment of choice to promise the greatest amount of good, immediate or remote. The only difference is that the preliminaries are in the one case irksome or even disagreeable, while in the other they are pleasant even though the final outcome be not so pleasant. The conditions of non-voluntary attention are also the conditions of desire; the conditions of voluntary attention are the conditions of duty.

Choice Determined by Instinct and Experience. Concretely, if one ask why last night one continued at a game instead of turning to work at the accustomed hour, the answer would be found in the instinctive pleasure in the game, or in the pleasure of the society, or in the excuse derived from experience that the fatigued condition would make study at that time prejudicial to good work on the morrow. The first two occasions for the decision lead back to heredity, to instinct, while the latter is an expression of experience. Suppose that the game had been given up and one had turned to work, the explanation would be found in social pressure, in the dominance of ideal or remote pleasures over the instinctive and experiential. One would have considered the unpleasantness of confessing ignorance before fellow-students, or one would have had in mind the desire to stand well at the end of the college course, or would have considered the importance of that lesson for success in the chosen profession, or, still more remotely, one may have developed an ideal of doing well everything that is required. Even this last ideal probably has a social origin, although, after social approval has rewarded action in harmony with that ideal or punished departures from the ideal sufficiently often, action in accordance with it becomes a habit, and there is ordinarily no thought at the moment of the decision, either of the ideal or the consequences of the action. One turns to work because one feels that one must, because one feels uncomfortable if the game is not given up. To perform the accepted and acknowledged duty is essential to immediate comfort. The factors, then, that determine choice are, on the one hand, the instincts of the individual, corrected by his experience, immediate and remote ; and, on the other, ideals derived from society. Ultimately the social factors go back to experience, so that one may assert that choice is the outcome of instinct and experience. Conflict of desires is merely conflict between motives developed in experience or heredity, each of which tends to make a corresponding course of action desirable.

The conflicts most important and most emphasised are those between instincts and instinctively pleasant habits on the one hand, and ideals on the other. On the whole, it seems at first that the acts favoured by instinct are low and unworthy, while the acts imposed by society and ideals are high and moral. The opposition is only apparent. Some of the acts in themselves noblest, such as certain forms of self-sacrifice, are instinctive, while society has endeavoured at times to enforce altogether unworthy ideals. The apparent conflict arises because society emphasises acts in themselves unpleasant which need all of the social enforcement possible, while the instincts, good and bad alike, are strong enough to take care of themselves. Society imposes rules where instincts are insufficient, or have in practice proved undesirable, or less desirable than a method of conduct that has grown up through trial and error and been transmitted from generation to generation by tradition and social institutions. Where instinct and tradition and social institutions come into conflict, all the strength of public sentiment is needed to enforce traditional and conventional acts against instinct. In consequence, a premium is put upon them by calling them high and noble, while the instincts are either considered unworthy or are taken for granted. As a matter of fact, instincts mark out only the rough outlines of conduct. The limits to instinct, or the demarkation of one necessary instinct from another, is not given in the instinct, but must be learned by the individual or society. We have egoistic and altruistic instincts, but there is nothing in instinct to show how far one should be selfish, and how far sympathetic on particular occasions. These checks and balances must arise through social intercourse. When they have developed, they are just as important for the survival of the social group as are the instincts themselves. These acts enforced by social pressure are said to constitute duties, as opposed to desires which are largely instinctive. Choice, then, is always choice of a result. Often one finds that choice is the outcome of a conflict of desires with duties, of instincts against ideals. At other times, choice is nothing more than a. weighing of the alternative methods of attaining an end that is approved both by desire and duty. Decision is in terms of past experience. The end that has proved most successful in the past or that promises best in the light of the knowledge of the agent will be chosen and will result in action.

Will Identical with Conditions of Choice. So far we have not made use of the word ' will,' although, in popular and much scientific discussion, will is the word used most frequently to explain action. Will, as Angell says, is merely a word to designate the whole mind active. Will may be defined as the sum of the conditions of choice. It is the term used to designate the entire original disposition of the individual, together with its modification by experience, when applied to action. It is no new force or thing; it is the application to the control of action of all the influences that control attention, perception, and the course of ideas. Even here, these forces control attention and ideas first, and control action only as they control attention and thought; but since action is practically the most important or at least the most striking psychological phenomenon, the term ' will ' is usually reserved for action. Ordinarily will is not applied to all of these forces, but is reserved for the ideals that enforce social traditions and laws. When one acts under the control of an ideal or for the accomplishment of a remote end, one is ordinarily said to have performed a voluntary act ; when one gives way to a desire of an instinctive nature, one is said to have acted on impulse. On the other hand, one is said to have acted voluntarily, if the act that corresponds to the ideal has been deliberately weighed against the desire, and the ideal has won. In general, voluntary acts are those which grow out of a conflict between instincts and ideals, in which ideals prevail.

Will as Control by Ideals. Again, one may see in the application of the terms strong and weak will the tendency to identify will with control by ideals. A strong-willed individual is one who works tenaciously for a remote good, while the weak-willed individual is one who is constantly turned aside by some momentary desire. Tenacity in holding to a purpose is probably inherited ; the character of the purpose is the outcome of training. The strong-willed individual may be good or bad, but he always has an ideal or set of ideals, and bends all of his acts to their attainment; while the weak-willed individual is controlled, not by his ideals, but by instincts and impulses excited by the changing factors in the environment. The ideals that control in the strong-willed man are developed by living in society ; they are very largely the ideals of the particular community or family in which the individual has grown up, modified and enlarged by the wider knowledge of the individual obtained hi any way whatever. You can see in the talk of the young boy the ideals of his parents. Later these ideals are modified by the school influences ; still later by his reading ; and then by the chosen .profession. Now and again, as the result of thinking, an individual decides that the ideals of the community are wrong, and sets up for himself some modification of them ; but important variations of this sort are relatively rare, and, before they become of value, must be tested and accepted by the wider social group. In general, the ideals of the individual are the ideals of his community.

Training of Will. Training will is, in the last analysis, training the man. Any sort of learning will have its influence upon action. The more one knows, the better one can act, and training for action cannot be separated from training of any other kind. Three topics may be discussed in this connection as having particular bearing upon the problem. First, we may say that choice is very frequently a matter of habit. If one of two alternative lines of conduct has been chosen once, that decision, if the outcome be satisfactory, will make the same choice probable under the same circumstances in the future. In the adult most choices are of this habitual kind One no longer hesitates between work and exercise. During the period habitually devoted to work, one ordinarily declines invitations to a game; when invited to walk at the hour for exercise one accepts just as immediately. One declines to consider investments suggested by the canvasser at the door, or coming from certain firms which have been sending questionable circulars. In short, most of the decisions of to-day were settled by decisions of the same kind made years ago. One moral decision strengthens a man to resist similar temptations in the future, and a large number of decisions of the sort makes it practically impossible for him to decide in the wrong way. On the other hand, when a man decides to do wrong, he makes future right conduct in that respect more difficult, and each immoral act makes the reformation more unlikely.

A second important phase of training will is in developing a system of ideals. This can be done only indirectly. Ideals come unconsciously from the society in which the child is brought up. If the boy finds that his father and older brothers constantly disapprove of certain acts and approve of others, he takes their approval for law; their ideals become his ideals. The effective moral ideals come from the approval of groups and classes. As may be seen in any community, right and wrong are made by public sentiment, not by law. A law is respected only so far as it is backed by public sentiment. This holds for moral laws as well as for statutory enactments. Development of ideals is largely through social approval and disapproval of the acts and expressions of the child. Proper ideals can be developed by placing the child in the proper social atmosphere, and in no other way. This atmosphere is most effective when it comes from actual contact with people. Books and reading and direct exhortation may gradually have an effect; but unless you can make the child feel that the class to whom the ideals belong is actually his class, reading and precept are of little value.

A third difficulty is to make the individual act up to the knowledge and ideals that he possesses. Every once in a while one observes an individual who knows the right and approves, but does wrong. The only cure for this condition is to develop a habit of action. This can be done most certainly by making the child appreciate the advantages of action and the disadvantages of inaction. An individual left to take the natural consequences of his acts will soon develop a habit of doing the thing that he sees should be done, at the time that it should be done. It is only the individuals who are protected from the consequences of inaction and indecision who continue inactive in the face of acknowledged duties. If a habit becomes established, there is no longer question whether a thing shall be done or not; the situation at once evokes a decision, and the decision evokes the act. Training will consists in establishing habits and in developing ideals. All training of whatever sort is bound to develop both habits and ideals; training of will cannot be distinguished from training the man as a whole.

This discussion of action adds but one essential fact to the list developed in the earlier chapters. This is that a movement is associated with some sensory process and is made whenever that process dominates consciousness. The movement either is associated with the idea or sensation at birth as in instinct, or becomes associated with it through the process of chance trial. The control of action is primarily control of ideas or of sensations. Except in this fact, that movement follows upon idea, the laws of action are the laws of attention, of perception, and of reasoning.

QUESTIONS

1. Describe the characteristics common to all actions. What are the forms of action ? What serves to distinguish them ?

2. Enumerate the antecedents of a voluntary act. Which can be regarded as the real cause of the act ? Is it a cause or an accompaniment of the cause?

3. Do you ever think of a movement without making it? What prevents the act ?

4. Can you control a reflex act ? How?

5. How do you choose? What do you choose ? What makes you desire to do what you choose to do ?

6. What is 'will'?

7. Trace out the instinctive, experiential, and ideal elements in some real decision you have made during the day.

EXERCISES

1. Try to develop some movement that is latent. Try, for example, to wink your right eye without closing the left. Keep a record of the number of trials, and watch the spread of the contraction from a neighbouring muscle. First try keeping attention fixed upon the eye to be kept open, then upon the eye to be closed while the other is neglected. Which is the more effective? If the movements of the eyelids have already been dissociated, try patting your chest with one hand while you rub the top of the head with the other. Keep the same records.

2. Trace the process of acquiring skill with the cup and ball. Keep a record of the proportion of successes over a period of several days. Trace plateaus and the occasions for the sudden rises. If more convenient, any other simple game of skill may be substituted for the cup and ball.

3. Procure two objects of the same weight but of unequal size, and try to train yourself to lift them at the same rate. Can you avoid the illusion of weight or rid yourself of it by practice?

4. Try writing, while with hand hidden from direct observation you watch the writing in a mirror. What is the effect ? _ Which of the three contrpls mentioned in the text is disturbed in the experiment ? Can you overcome the difficulty with practice ?

5. Study yourself while making a high dive. If several attempts are necessary before you start, try to trace the immediate antecedent of the action. If diving be impracticable, observe getting up on a cold morning, or getting into a cold bath.

CHAPTER XIV

WORK, FATIGUE, AND SLEEP

FATIGUE has a very general influence upon mental and physical efficiency. It modifies behaviour in many ways and a knowledge of its laws is highly important for mental hygiene. Appreciation of the great value of an accurate knowledge of the most profitable periods of work, the relation of the quantity and quality of work to its duration, and the general effects of work and rest upon health and well-being have furnished the incentive for numerous investigations of fatigue, particularly in the last two decades. While it cannot be asserted that agreement has been reached upon all points, it seems worth while to summarise the results so far obtained, because of their wide application to the activities of everyday life. It is desirable to know what the maximum efficiency of the individual is in each respect. It is desirable to work up to the limit of capacity, in emergencies at least, and even more important to be sure that the limit is not overpassed.

The Nature and Signs of Fatigue. The first question is, what is fatigue and what its nervous and mental manifestations? In general, fatigue may be defined as the decreased capacity for work that comes as a result of work. Mentally it is usually accompanied by sensations that are in some measure an index of the degree of fatigue. Physiologically it has been demonstrated that fatigue is accompanied by three sorts of changes. First, poisons accumulate in the blood and affect the action of the nervous system, as may be shown by direct chemical analysis. Mosso obtained striking results by an indirect method that is not altogether free from criticism. He selected two dogs as nearly alike as possible.

One he kept tied all day, the other he exercised until by night it was thoroughly tired. Then he transfused the blood of the tired animal into the veins of the rested one and produced in him all the signs of fatigue that were shown by the other. There can be no doubt that the waste products of the body accumulate in the blood and interfere with the action of the nervecells and the muscles. It is probable that these accuinitiations come as a result of mental as well as of physical work.

A second change in fatigue has been found in the cell body of the neurone. Hodge showed that the size of the nucleus of the cell in the spinal cord of a bee diminished nearly 75 per cent as a result of the day's activity, and that the nucleus became much less solid. A third change that results from muscular work is the accumulation of waste products in the muscle tissue. Fatigued muscles contain considerable percentages of these products. That they are important factors is shown by the fact that if they are washed out of the fatigued muscle it regains its capacity to contract. The experiments are performed on the muscles of a frog that have been cut from the body and fatigued by electrical stimulation. When they will no longer respond, their sensitivity may be renewed by washing them in a weak salt solution to dissolve the products of fatigue. It is probable that these products stimulate the sense-organs in the muscles and thus give some of the sensations of fatigue. Of these physical effects of fatigue, the accumulation of the waste products in the blood and the effects upon the nerve-cells are probably common both to mental and physical fatigue. The effect upon the muscles plays a part in mental fatigue only so far as all mental work involves some musculai activity.

The Analysis of Mental Fatigue. More practical are the results of the experiments accumulating in recent years upon the actual course of the work. The change in capacity in the course of work has been shown to be dependent upon a number of factors that may be isolated.

First we have fatigue, the decreased capacity for work, which may be assumed to increase regularly with the amount of work accomplished. But this decrease in capacity is partly obscured by another effect of work just as well established, the resulting practice. Every bit of work not only diminishes capacity but also gives increased efficiency for the same sort of work. These two factors, practice and fatigue, may be regarded as always present and always opposed. The result is that each obscures the effects of the other. When work first starts, practice increases more rapidly than fatigue and in consequence one can do more after working for a little time than was possible at first. The course of recovery from the two effects is very different. Recovery from fatigue is rapid. It is ordinarily entirely complete after a night's rest and begins to be appreciable as soon as a task is finished. On the other hand the effects of practice persist over long periods of time. Days and years after, some of its influence may be noticed. Two other factors are important in determining the course of the practice curve, one may be called mental inertia, the other the incentive. When one first starts a task, work is difficult and slow ; as time goes on, work gradually increases in amount and accuracy. When once started, work proceeds at the regular rate and stopping may be difficult ; or more truly, it is easier to continue work than it is to stop and begin again. Then one may distinguish the initial and final incentive. One works very much harder when first beginning a task than later. Toward the end there is nearly always a final spurt that again increases considerably the rate of work and the amount accomplished. Finally, as one becomes accustomed to the conditions, one works to better advantage than when first beginning.

The Economical Periods of Work. The most economical period of work is that in which one gets all the advantages of continued work without going on to the point of fatigue. It is of course impossible to give any general rules that will apply to all kinds of work and to all people. How much work may be done depends upon the nature of the work and upon the strength of the individual. The fact that one does more after working for a little time than when one first begins holds universally. How long one should continue after the effects of fatigue are greater than the benefits of practice depends upon the kind of work and the practical necessities for its completion. Fatigue itself is not to be avoided, for the lesser degrees wear off in a short time and are entirely overcome by a night's sleep. The poor work that results when fatigue is too great makes effort unprofitable, and the after effects in the form of overwork may have such serious results as to put a premium upon avoiding them at all reasonable cost.

The Evidence of Fatigue. It is not at all easy to know when one is in danger of permanent injury from work. Fatigue shows itself by sensations of different sorts, some from tired muscles, some of a more indefinite character from the inner organs. These sensations, however, are not always associated with fatigue itself. Often one feels tired when actual trial shows no marked incapacity for work. Rather it is usual for the best work to be done when the sensations indicate a state of bodily inefficiency before work is begun. Even the capacity for doing work is not an invariable sign, because it is not unusual to be able to do good work when the organism is fatigued to the point where continued work will do injury of a permanent character. One must be guided by taking into consideration three factors, the sensations of fatigue, the quality of the work, and what previous experience has shown to be the probable after effects. It is usually Inadvisable to persist to the point where a night's rest will not remove fatigue and restore the original capacity. Certainly long-continued work beyond this stage is bound to have serious consequences.

The Best Period for Rest. To know how long to rest between periods of work is as important as to know when to stop. Results of experiments indicate that the length of the rest that should be introduced between the periods of work depends upon the length of the previous work and upon the character of the work. The rest should be long enough to permit recovery from fatigue but not to lose the mental momentum. After long periods of work, two hours or more, the most advantageous intermission is approximately fifteen minutes; for relatively short periods five minutes has proved itself most satisfactory. Longer periods waste too much time and cause a loss of inertia and of practice that is not compensated for by recovery from fatigue. Shorter rests merely cause loss of inertia without any compensating rest.

Change of Work No Rest. Several facts that have been suggested by experiments are contrary to the common assumptions of many people. For example, it is believed usually that one may rest through change of work, that if one has been tired by mental work of one sort it is not necessary to rest altogether, but by changing to something else one may become rested through the change. The one important investigation on this point indicates that the everyday assumption is not in harmony with the facts. An hour's work learning nonsense syllables followed by a half hour's practice on mental arithmetic, with a return to the nonsense syllables, rests one no more than a continued period of nonsense syllables. This is on the assumption that learning nonsense syllables is no more difficult than mental arithmetic. If one turns from a more difficult to an easier task, one will of course not be so tired as if one had continued with the more difficult. So far as these results can be accepted, it seems that all sorts of mental fatigue are of the same kind, and that it is not possible to rest one function while exercising another. There is so. much in common between the different mental operations that all become tired together. It is possible that the commonly accepted opinion to the contrary is due to the greater interest one may have in a new task. One ordinarily turns from a task only when obstacles have presented themselves or when for some reason the work has become uninteresting. It is possible that the greater interest in the new work and consequent greater effectiveness are mistaken for recovery from fatigue.

Mental and Physical Fatigue One. Very similar is the attitude toward the problem of the relation between mental and physical fatigue. It is generally believed that one may rest from mental work while exercising, but experiments indicate that capacity for mental work is decreased by physical work if it is too difficult. If one takes a vigorous run or other severe exercise between two periods of the same sort of work, as in the experiments mentioned above, the capacity for mental work is diminished rather than increased. Here as before the effect will depend upon the severity of the task. If the exercise be mild, one will rest relatively just as one does during less difficult mental work. In fact, the whole question of work and fatigue is relative, as one never rests absolutely except during sleep, and even then there is merely gain of repair over waste, not absolute quiescence of all functions. The identity of mental and physical fatigue has been demonstrated many times, both that mental work induces physical fatigue and that physical work induces mental fatigue. One cannot do severe mental work effectively after a hard day of physical labour, and experiments show that one is less capable of physical after hard mental work. This general identity of mental and physical work and fatigue is being recognised by the physician. A patient suffering from overwork as a result of too much study or worry is no longer advised to take much exercise, but is put to bed or given very little easy exercise. Of course this does not imply that exercise is not beneficial in health. Exercise is essential to the development and health of the body, and needs no justification. One should not expect to be able to work immediately after exercise, but in the long run its effects are beneficial.

Morning and Evening Workers. Another interesting result of recent investigations is that there are daily rhythms of capacity for work, that every one has a certain part of the day during which he has greater capacity. According to one authority, men divide naturally into morning and evening workers. The one group is at its best early in the morning ; the other group does not reach its full capacity until toward evening, the amount and accuracy of the work increases steadily through the day. It has not been determined whether the difference is innate or the result of habit, but in an adult accustomed to mental work one habit or the other is always readily demonstrated, even if the individual himself is unaware of it. Evidently one should take advantage of the daily rhythm by devoting the best part of the day to the more difficult tasks.

Interest Reduces Fatigue. It should be added that the measurements of fatigue upon which these statements rest are derived from ordinary routine work under no particular incentive other than to do one's best. It is certain that a sufficiently strong desire would at any stage have brought the rate of work back to the maximum, at least for a little time. Even in muscular work fatigue comes more slowly if the worker has an incentive and the work is interesting. Phenomena of this kind have led some writers to argue that fatigue is an illusion. That what is called fatigue is really ennui or boredom. This conclusion overlooks the very evident after effects of severe prolonged work in decreased efficiency over considerable periods and even in diseased nervous conditions. While the amount of work that will be accomplished depends very largely upon the incentive, it does not follow that fatigue is not real and a factor to be considered in the arrangement of the day's routine. The statements made hold for the course of ordinary work where the incentive is constant and not particularly strong. If the incentive is increased, the absolute times given are all increased, but the relative values remain approximately the same. There still comes a time when the amount and accuracy of the work is reduced to a point where work does not pay. In some degree, too, the after effects of the work increase with the amount of work, although probably not in the exact ratio of accomplishment. Work done willingly and cheerfully under suitable incentives is apparently less fatiguing in the long run than a smaller amount accomplished under unfavourable conditions. One may even agree with James that in moments of exaltation one may perform at a rate far above the ordinary level without permanent injury, and at the same time accept the results of experiments under ordinary conditions as a guide for daily life.

Fatigue Inevitable and in Moderation, Desirable. The discussion of fatigue and the methods of obviating it is likely to leave the impression that fatigue is something to be avoided at all hazard. This is far from being the case. Fatigue is unavoidable if one works, and work is essential to all development. As was said in the beginning, work has two effects, fatigue and practice. Practice remains and furnishes the endowment of the individual for all later work ; fatigue disappears after a night. The ordinary net effect of work the day after is an increase in capacity. The general effects of work are altogether desirable. Fatigue is not something to be avoided. The most that is desirable is to consider the laws of fatigue and learn to work to the best advantage. The aim of life is not to avoid fatigue but to accomplish as much as possible with the minimum of fatigue. Fatigue is undesirable only when it threatens permanent injury, rather than when it temporarily reduces capacity. Sleep. Very closely connected with fatigue in practice and theory is sleep. While sleep is one of the most common phenomena of life, it is also one of the least understood. What sleep is or why it comes on is as yet not a matter of agreement. Something more is known of the course of sleep and we may begin our discussion with that. Several experimenters have measured the depth of sleep at different times during its course by determining the intensity of stimulus required to waken an individual. They all agree that sleep increases in depth rapidly during the first three-quarters of an hour and then decreases gradually during the remainder of the night. It has been suggested that the recuperative processes predominate in the latter part of the period, when sleep has passed its climax. Why one goes to sleep is not so easily answered. Obviously sleep has some relation to fatigue, but over-fatigue is inimical to sleep. One ordinarily goes to sleep most readily under monotonous stimulation ; but a persistent idea, if more exciting, makes sleep impossible, when all else is favourable. Opinion at present inclines to the view that sleep is an instinct, a form of reaction of the nervous system induced by certain definite stimuli, and that it tends also to recur somewhat rhythmically. This response is favoured by withdrawal of external stimuli, by quiet and darkness, by a moderate degree of fatigue, by relaxed or dispersed attention, and ordinarily through habit is more easily induced at a particular hour. No one of these conditions alone will induce the condition or response, but all together usually suffice. Like many another reaction it is favoured by suggestion or expectation. If one fears one is to have a bad night, sleep is usually slow in coming; while if one expects restful sleep, it comes promptly.

The Physiology of Sleep. What the reaction is that causes sleep is also much in dispute. Changes have been demonstrated in the circulation. Blood pressure is low in sleep and varies inversely with the depth of sleep, is lowest when the depth of sleep is greatest. The blood-vessels in the brain are relaxed, although filled with blood, and constrict when sleep is disturbed or during dreams. Respiration is changed in characteristic ways, and all of the vital processes have their activity reduced. Some change certainly occurs in the nervous system, also, but what its exact character is, has not been decided. Evidence is tending toward the assumption that there is some loosening of the connections between the different elements, such as increased resistance at the synapses to the passage of excitations, but how it is brought about is still entirely conjectural. Certain it is that the nervous system is less easily aroused during sleep and that the course of action is less controlled. Nervous action is not abolished, however, as is proved by the presence of reflexes and by dreams. Whether this reduced activity is due to the changes in circulation, or the changes in circulation are due to the reduced nervous activity, or each is a result of some common cause, cannot be decided from the facts at hand. Whatever sleep may be, it is obvious that it is a state which conduces to the restoration of the tissues that have been subjected to the wear and tear of the day. The effects of fatigue are nullified ; the cell bodies are restored to their normal condition ; the waste products are eliminated from muscle and blood. On the whole, sleep seems to be an instinctive or habitual response that comes at a more or less regular time, that is favoured by a mild fatigue, and by the absence of external disturbance. During the period of sleep the vital processes are reduced, the higher nerve-centres are only slightly active, and the processes of repair exceed those of wear.

Dreams. Dreams were among the first phenomena to direct attention to the mental life and have always been an object of interest to the popular mind. For psychology they emphasise the erratic course of mental states when little controlled. Fundamentally they are an expression of the same laws as the processes of waking life. At times, they are initiated by external stimulation ; at other times one can trace the influence of striking events of the preceding day. Thus, cold feet may induce a dream of walking barefoot through snow ; a dog shaking the bed may start a dream of a storm at sea. The images which persist from the preceding day are said by Freud to be the point of origin for all dreams. Both sensory stimuli and these persisting impressions are ordinarily much transformed. ' A woman who has been carving a duck at dinner dreams of cutting off a duck's leg, but seems to realise that it is her husband's head she is hacking at.' These transformations are usually brought about by associations, sometimes verbal, more frequently through events that have been connected in time or place. Thus a lady who had admired a baby and bought a big fish for dinner dreams at night of finding a fully developed baby sewed up in a large codfish. 1 More frequently the elements added by association are derived from earlier years, sometimes they can be traced to definite early experiences.

The constructions are usually bizarre, since the associations follow lines of least resistance with little of the restraint from context and wider experiences so prominent in the waking life. The recognition and belief processes are also impaired and one recognises objects entirely unfamiliar and accepts as true statements and constructions manifestly absurd when tested by the usual standards. This lack of control and uncritical attitude may both be explained from the fact that large portions of the cortex are asleep and the small remainder must both control and censor the mental constructions. One's emotions and moral standards too are often completely transformed, probably also an expression of the reduction in the number of experiences that pass upon the processes. The peculiarities of dreams may be in part due to the great condensation frequently present. The events are merely referred to, and then when the dream is recalled the references are expanded. It is this that makes possible dreaming of a number of occurrences in a very short interval. Lack of space makes it necessary to omit any elaborate discussion of recently developed theories of dreams which expand these points. We must content ourselves with the statement that they are expressions of the ordinary laws of mental processes, often much exaggerated owing to the weakening of the directing agencies.

QUESTIONS

1. Define fatigue.

2. How can you tell when you are tired mentally?

3. Describe the ordinary course of work. How would rate and accuracy vary if you worked hard for a two-hour period ?

4. Can you rest by changing work?

5. Is physical exercise rest for the mental worker? Is it desirable?

6. Formulate for yourself a program of work for a typical day based on the statements of the chapter.

7. What is sleep ? Is going to sleep a passive or active process ?

8. What physiological changes occur in sleep?

9. Recall a recent vivid dream. Trace the different incidents of the dream to physical stimuli and to memories, if you can.

CHAPTER XV

THE INTERRELATIONS OF MENTAL FUNCTION

Criticism of Faculty Psychology. For the sake of convenience we have been treating the mental operations separately and may have left the impression that each of the names used stands for a separate function or thing. This was in some degree the assumption of the older psychologies and still is the prevailing popular belief. One speaks of attention and of memory and of other processes because they represent mental capacities which it is desirable to discuss together. The popular mind always finds it easy to make a substance of the function and to speak of the memory, the will, and so on, as if they were separate entities or forces. In the very early psychologies, these functions were personified and the older men were inclined to speak as if mind were a partnership in which each partner had separate abilities and capacities, and as if these capacities were practically independent one of the other. In the discussions of modern psychology there is no such implication. The words stand for nothing but observed facts, the fact that one remembers, that one acts and makes decisions, or that one attends. What may be behind the activity we do not pretend to know, but we certainly do not care to assert that any ' thing ' is behind any act or activity.

The Transfer of Training. One problem of considerable practical importance is the degree of relation and the mutual dependence of the different capacities. In connection with training it is interesting to know if one may train a capacity by training some other capacity, or how far training in one field may be helpful in some other. The theoretical considerations may give any conclusion indifferently, and popular opinion seems to be much divided as to how far the effects of training may spread from the function actually exercised to other related functions. There is also equal difference of opinion as to what are related functions and how they may be trained. Two opposing general principles are currently accepted and serve as a basis for popular opinion. On the one hand, the separate functions have been regarded as absolutely distinct ; on the other, any training is assumed to be effective for all mental capacities. Obviously with such wide diversity in general theory, there is a necessity for appeal to closer analysis and, if possible, to actual trial.

The Primary Functions of Mind. Our earlier analysis has shown that the different functions have much in common. The fact that impressions are retained is fundamental, not for an explanation of memory only, but for the control of attention and action and almost everything else. It must give the materials of reasoning as well as much of the control of the reasoning operations. A complete analysis shows that we have three simple processes which are fundamental for all the cognitive operations, and for many of the feeling and active processes. These are the facts of sensation, of retention and recall, and of selection and control. These, together with the complementary processes of recognition, belief, instinct, and feeling, suffice to explain all the functions of consciousness. Perception depends upon the control of the entering sensation plus the recall of related and interpreting elements which, in their turn, are selected to harmonise with the general setting, objective and subjective. For example, one comes into a furnished room tired and accordingly a chair catches the attention. This perception involves a rhomboid of colour upon the retina; earlier experiences replace the rhomboid with a square surface, acute and obtuse angles by right angles, and so on. We have a combination of sensations and memories, controlled by the needs of the moment, a process we call perception. Similarly one comes into a bare room, feels tired, and the sensations with the general setting call out the memory of a chair, perhaps of the same chair. We call this process memory or imagination according as the recalled chair is familiar or unfamiliar. The only appreciable difference in the two processes is the presence in perception of the rhomboid of colour upon the retina. Again the memory of the chair may start a tram of movements that sends one into the next room for a chair or to the telephone to order one seen in a shop window an hour before. We call this will, but it is different from memory only in that the associated movements are permitted to run thencourse, again under the control of the purpose and knowledge of one's credit at the shop and the permanence of the need. This difference is even less when one considers that every memory and every perception tends to call out movements of some sort, and that what really distinguishes them from will is the degree or amount of the movement, not its presence or absence. In memory or perception the motor discharge ends in slight movements, while in will the movements are an important part. Any of the other functions ordinarily given distinct names may be regarded as differently compounded out of the same elements. The combinations alone are different; the elements and the conditions that control the selection are largely the same in each. It is to be expected that any change in any function will affect in some degree each of the other functions. Either it will supply new materials that may enter into other functions, or will change the conditions that control the selection and arrangement of the materials.

Names of Processes Are of Functions not Entities. Not alone are the different functions interrelated as different expressions or combinations of the same mental materials and laws, but in any single act each is likely to be involved in some degree. One turns in quick succession from memory to action, from reasoning to imagination, and then to perception, and each is distinguishable from the others only by abstract analysis. The separate functions are really not more separated than are different applications or uses of the same function. The memory employed in learning nonsense syllables is more different from that used in learning historical events in their logical succession than is the latter from the reasoning employed in reconstructing some partly forgotten event on the basis of its remembered antecedents. The first two are certainly memory, the latter is just as certainly reason. What is different and what marks the lines of division in consciousness are the uses to which certain processes are put. These processes receive names that correspond to the uses, even when the elements or conditions are essentially the same. The problem of how far training may spread must be attacked by experiment and observation. Nothing in the nature of mental capacities gives certainty that training may not spread from one function to another, and nothing indicates that training in one field has any particular amount of influence in any other. All that can be said on general principles is that where two functions have something in common, training in one will probably have an effect upon the other ; where there is nothing in common, training in one capacity will be without influence upon the other. On purely theoretical grounds one would expect that use anywhere either would provide new materials or would add new elements of control that might be used in any other field. It is altogether probable that the effect of many activities upon other capacities may be negligible in amount, and so of no practical importance. All that can be said with any certainty is that one may expect any training whatever to spread beyond the particular function exercised to any other function that has anything in common with it. The problem is to determine what functions have enough in common to make the spread from one to the other appreciable, and to discover means of measuring the practice and its effects on the other functions. Not only is it true that two functions of different names have much in common, but also activities that ordinarily are grouped under the same name need not be sufficiently alike to make training in one have any influence upon the other. For example, in memory it has long been a question whether training in learning things of one sort increases the capacity for learning things of another. The practical problems involved are twofold, first, how far is practice in a function effective in increasing the capacity for exercising the same function on other material ; and second, how far will training in one have an effect upon other functions and capacities.

Can Memory Be Trained ? For an answer to our question we must turn to an examination of the results of experiments, first of the effects of training one function upon other expressions of the same function, and second upon the transfer of training from one function to another. The field that has been best developed is memory. It has long been a question whether it is possible to train one's capacity to remember facts of one sort by practice in learning some other set of facts. The first answer to this question in more recent times was a decided negative. James argued that in learning one statement a different tract in the cortex must be involved from that involved in learning any other and consequently training one nerve tract would have no more effect upon another tract than would practice in bending a finger upon the ability to walk. James also put the opinion to practical proof by learning a bit of verse, then spending a month in practice on other poetry, and testing the efficiency acquired by learning other stanzas of the test material. He found, on the average, that there was little if any gain after the long training and concluded that memory cannot be trained.

More recent tests by Ebert and Meumann came to the opposite conclusion. They worked with various sorts of sense and nonsense material. First, the untrained capacity was tested for one sort of material; then, a long period was devoted to learning materials of another kind. Then the first sort of material was learned again and the ease of learning after practice was compared with the original. Other practice series were made and again tested. The results showed that practice with nonsense syllables would increase the ease of learning philosophical prose or arbitrary visual signs by from 50 to 70 per cent. They conclude that learning anywhere will increase the efficiency of memory everywhere, that practice in learning material of any one kind will have a marked effect on learning any other. The conclusion has been criticised on the ground that the test series for each sort of material were so long that there was considerable opportunity for training in them and that a large part of the training must have come from practice in the tests, not through transfer from practice on other sorts of material. The experiments have been repeated by Dearborn, with the precaution of taking a test series without any training, and comparing the results with those after an intervening period of training. The results indicate that the training has some effect but not nearly so much as Ebert and Meumann thought. Probably the effect of training in one field upon learning in another will amount to from 10 to 20 per cent as compared with the 50 or more that Ebert and Meumann's experiments indicated. Training Memory, Training Attention. If one asks how learning one thing can have an effect upon learning something else in spite of the fact that the nervous structures involved must be different in each, the answer undoubtedly is to be found in the fact that learning of any kind involves many common factors. One must always attend to the material learned, and in the experiments in question, one must learn to attend under new and unusual conditions and to materials that one usually has tried to neglect. The formation of habits of attending in general and of attending to unusual materials and under unusual conditions is the element that serves to facilitate learning under the different circumstances and that may be transferred to learning different material under the same circumstances. In the learning of everyday life still other common factors must be recognised. There are many structural elements in common between things and even between sciences called by different names. The same fact is used in different connections, and the resulting compound is given a different name in each connection. For example, the principles of history are frequently similar to the laws of biology, and the spirit and attitude are very similar in all sciences. All these facts and principles learned in one field save time and work in other fields. The improvement in one sort of memory acquired by training some other does not depend upon the training of some single function or thing, but is due to the fact that learning anything develops habits of attending and accustoms one to learn new materials and under new conditions. What is trained is some common function, not memory in general.

Transfer of Training in Discrimination. Very much the same result has been obtained in experiments for training discrimination. It has been shown by Coover and Angell that discrimination for visual stimuli is improved by training in the discrimination of sounds, and the quickness of response in one way to one sort of stimulus is increased by training in another form of response to another stimulus. The effects of the training again may be traced to the improvement in some capacity common to the two activities. Wang recently found that practice in discriminating the length of lines increased the ability to discriminate colours and tones. Measurements of the time required to make the comparisons showed that the child learned in the first tests to delay his judgment until sure, an acquisition that proved valuable in the later tests. Training in the control of movement shows the same transfer from one field to another as is demonstrated for these more intellectual capacities and activities. One may conclude in general that exercise of one sort tends ordinarily to improvement of related capacities. This rule is not without exceptions, for training may make learning more difficult under other circumstances and for certain sorts of activities, even if they bear the same name. An instance of this was cited in the chapter on memory. Common observation indicates that training in rote memory is likely to interfere with skill in remembering ideas, in logical memory; and vice versa, skill in remembering ideas may make one neglect the words and so make one learn them less easily than would the untrained individual. The explanation reduces to the same law as before. What is trained is a habit of attending, and attending in one way tends to prevent attending in opposed ways. Whether training is harmful or beneficial depends upon whether some habit is common to the two processes under discussion, or whether a habit established in one operation will be injurious in the other. One can assert at present only that whether training in one act or in one field will be beneficial to other different acts or in other fields depends upon whether the two functions have anything in common, and whether the common factor works in the same way in each of the activities in question.

Training of General Intelligence. Still more complicated is the problem and less definite the result, when one turns to the question whether there is anything in common between functions or capacities not of the same general kind. One of the best-known theories asserts that a definite relation does exist between skill in any field and the general intelligence of the subject. It is insisted that all capacities are sufficiently interrelated to have skill in one involve skill in any other. The facts upon which this theory suggested by Spearman rests are now generally accepted as a result of agreement in the outcome of numerous investigations. However, many, if not most, question the theory, which smacks of faculty psychology. Instead it is suggested that common capacities are involved in many seemingly different operalions. The improvement in one as a consequence of training in another rests upon use in both of a single capacity. At least fact and theory agree that it is possible that training will have some effect upon capacities that have something in common, but whether much or little can be determined only by experiment, and satisfactory experiments are as yet lacking.

Training from Subjects of School Curriculum. Still farther are We from being able to assert that certain subjects in the school curriculum will have an effect upon any particular capacity, or that one subject will have a greater effect than any other. It is frequently asserted that mathematics trains reasoning; classics, memory, and so on. These assertions are based altogether on assumption and apparently assume an out-ofdate psychology. Certainly few experiments have been performed and no tests of the effects of studying one subject apart from others have extended over a sufficiently long time to give trustworthy results. From general considerations it is evident that the results of studying any subject will depend in very large degree upon how it is studied and how it is taught. Mathematics may be made a mere exercise in memory, while history or the classics when studied by suitable methods may be primarily training in reasoning. The most that may be said with certainty is that the sort of training derived from any subject will depend more upon the way it is taught than upon the subject. Any subject may give any type of training, and probably all forms in some degree, but how much depends upon circumstances that cannot be determined from the name of the subject.

At present it is not possible to say how far any activity may be prepared for by any subject in the curriculum. Summary. The outcome of the discussion of how far doing one thing is a training for something else has been very unsatisfactory. Training gained by doing any one thing will be in some degree general, and will aid in doing anything else in the same field. How much it will aid, or whether it will aid at all, depends upon how much there is in common between the two operations, and this can be determined only by experiment. Very much the same answer must be given to the question how far exercise of one function has an effect upon others. There may be some effect or there may be none, according to the relation of the two functions. There is little evidence of any single function or faculty, like general intelligence, that may be developed by all sorts of training and be applicable in all fields. The most that can be said positively is that one may best prepare one's self to do anything by doing that thing. It does not follow that doing that thing will be the best preparation for life, or for success in any other capacity, but certainly skill in that function can be most surely acquired by practising it directly. A general training is indispensable, not because it gives command of a particular trade or profession, but because anything can be understood fully only in terms of other things, and because highest success is possible only when preparation has been, not for one task alone, but for many tasks of a related kind, for all in fact that have any bearing upon the chosen career. The main outcome is to enforce conservatism in asserting just how best to obtain a general training. The one assured result is that training for any particular task or operation can be acquired by doing that particular thing.

If the discussion has served to emphasise the fact that, on the one hand, mind is not a collection of unrelated faculties and, on the other, that it is not a single force or faculty, but rather that mind is merely a term applied to a number of different functions spoken of collectively, the time will have been well spent. When certain of these separate functions are grouped in one way or to the attainment of one end, the process is perception; when grouped in another way, imagination ; in a third, memory ; and in a fourth, reasoning. When other functions are introduced and practical activities are controlled, the process is will. Other modifications constitute the emotional and affective processes. In any event, what gives the name to the function in everyday life and in scientific usage is not the materials of which the mental state is composed or even the laws revealed in its operation, but the end that the function subserves. The fundamental laws of operation and the simple elements are relatively few as compared with the ends and the names for functions or ' faculties/ either popular or scientific. The division of the treatment of psychology into chapters devoted to these particular functions is for convenience. The functions themselves are not distinct.

QUESTIONS

i. What is meant by a faculty in psychology? State objections to the use of the term.

2. Define mental function. How many mental functions would you ascribe to man ? How is a function different from a faculty ?

3. Can you train will? In what sense do you use the term in your answer?

4. Would training in recognising flowers make one more accurate in recognising animals? What would you assume in your answer concerning partial identity of the functions involved?

5. What could one mean by general intelligence? Can it be trained if it exists ?

6. What training do you expect from mathematics? from history? from Latin? from physics? from psychology? Would it be more in any case than the accumulation of facts? What changes might be common to all?

CHAPTER XVI

THE TYPES OF MIND

IN practical life we are constantly making rough classifications of men. One hears frequently that A is a man of genius, B has good reasoning ability but little memory, C has exceptional intelligence but lacks push, etc. Obviously, if these types exist, psychology should be in a position to determine their presence scientifically, to measure the differences between individuals in these various respects, and group them more or less accurately. The practical advantages of knowing the capacities of individuals would be enormous. Could we tell in advance of trial that a man were to fail in one employment we might spare his employer the expense of training him and the man himself the pains of failure and the waste of time involved in preparation. Could a state know definitely or even within wide limits the capacities of its citizens, it might make sure that each entered the profession or occupation for which he was best adapted and avoid educating men for fields in which they could not succeed.

Conceivably men might be different in degree of ability, in kind of ability, and in the different degrees in which the different kinds of ability were present in each. There might be individuals who were stupid in every respect, others who were geniuses, and others of moderate ability. On the other hand one might have men who could reason without remembering much, others of constructive ability, but with little knowledge, etc. Were either of these latter groupings of abilities common, it might well be that one could discover fixed types or combinations of abilities and that it would be possible, first to determine the number of types and then to discover some means of recognising to which type any individual belonged without trying him in all of the different respects. It has been suggested by psychologists that one may distinguish a slow type with ability to concentrate closely as opposed to a quick, easily distracted type, that one would acquire slowly, forget slowly, and reason well, while the other would learn quickly, forget quickly, and reach conclusions by intuition. Other types have been assumed, all in advance of test or on inadequate test.

If we are to solve any of these problems large numbers of individuals must be thoroughly investigated with reference to many of their capacities, then the different ways in which their abilities are combined must be studied to determine what capacities are found together. The two problems as to whether there are types of individuals or whether individuals are all of one type with only differences in general ability are closely related. If there are types the problem is very complicated, if there are not types we can classify all on the basis of degree of ability and measure that ability in any way we please, on the assumption that degree of success in one test will give the relative standing in all other respects as well. This first problem may be attacked first, as upon the answer to it depends the degree of importance that may attach to the solution of the second.

Are There Different Types of Individuals? An answer to the first question has been sought in two ways : (1) by testing a number of individuals in several different capacities and determining what the chances are that an individual who stands high in one respect will stand high in others ; (2) by obtaining the opinions of different men as to the relative standing of others in a number of characteristics and then making a similar determination of the relation between standing in different qualities. In either case, special statistical methods are necessary to determine what the relation may be between the traits after we have either estimated or measured the standing of each individual in each trait. The problem would not arise were all individuals to have exactly the same relative rank in each. Were we, e.g. in comparing the relation between memory span and ability to solve problems in geometry, to find that the individual who stood first in the one was also first in the other, and that he who stood second in one was second in the other, etc., all the way through, there would be no difficulty. As it is, however, all that we can ever expect is that many of those above the average in one will also be above the average in another respect, and we need a way of measuring the probable relationship when some are above in both, while others are above in one and below in another.

The Coefficient of Correlation. Without giving the formula used, which may be found in any of the works on measurement methods, 1 we may say that by comparing the position of each individual above or below the average standing of all in each of two tests or traits, we obtain a ratio, that indicates the degree of likelihood that an individual who possesses one trait in high degree will possess others also in large amount. This ratio is called the coefficient of correlation. Were all individuals to have exactly the same standing in each trait, the coefficient of correlation would be + i ; were the individuals who stood in one order in one trait to have exactly the opposite order in the other, the coefficient would be i. Where the relation between the traits is close it approaches + i, where it is slight it approaches zero. A zero coefficient means that there is no relation between the traits and that it is not possible to infer anything from the standing of an individual in one trait as to how he would stand in another. The coefficient seldom rises above .90 even when the two capacities compared seem to be exactly the same, as when one measures the accuracy of comparing weights of different magnitudes, or the ability to discriminate horizontal lines and the ability to discriminate vertical lines. On the other hand correlations under .35 usually have little significance.

All Men Are of the Same General Type. The results of the different tests all agree in indicating that excellence in any desirable trait is closely correlated with excellence in all other desirable traits. Thus there is a positive correlation between memory and quickness in sorting the alphabet, between sorting cards and discriminating

weights, in fact between all of the desirable qualities that have been carefully measured and compared. If we translate this statement into our everyday expression, the all round man is the rule, the man of onesided development, the exception. More than this our present knowledge is not sufficient to show. The innate differences between types either are not sufficiently marked, or the combinations of traits are so numerous and so many different arrangements result that we have not yet been able to discover and formulate even the most frequently occurring among them.

Character Closely Correlated with Intelligence. The method of estimating the relative amounts of certain traits possessed by different individuals was applied extensively by Webb. 1 He asked several instructors to grade a large number of boys with reference to the more characteristic intellectual traits, and also on a series of more general traits, * tendency not to abandon tasks in the face of obstacles/ ' tendency not to abandon tasks from mere changeability/ ' kindness on principle/ ' trustworthiness/ ' conscientiousness/ ' readiness to become angry/ ' eagerness for admiration/ and ' bodily activity in the pursuit of pleasure.' When these were correlated with each other it was found that the first five showed a high correlation, an individual who was preeminent in one would be likely to be well favoured in the others also, while they showed a negative correlation with the last three. The last three also correlated closely with each other. Webb argued from

1 Edward Webb: Character and Intelligence, British Journal of Psychology, Monograph Supplements, III. these results that we must recognise two groups of traits, an intellectual and what he calls the character group, which depends upon what are popularly known as the volitional and emotional characteristics. The desirable traits in each are likely to be found together. Between the two groups the correlations are not so close as they are between traits within each group, but even here the more desirable characteristics show some correlation. On the whole the man with the better intelligence is also the better tempered and has the better qualities of leadership and persistence.

Interpretation of Results. Both methods seem to be at one in the positive statement that excellences in all desirable respects tend to be found together. How this shall be interpreted is not quite so clear. It may be due either to the presence of some common quality in all mental operations, possessed by each individual in varying degrees. As was seen in the preceding chapter, Spearman has suggested that we may say that there is what may be called general intelligence, and that an individual who has much of it will show all desirable traits in high degree. Its possession in high degree makes all accomplishment easy, its presence in slighter amount reduces capacity in any field. The other alternative explanation would assume a number of traits which are required for success in each of the tests. Thus, if we assume a native retentiveness, acuity of the different senses, quickness of reviving associates, and motor quickness as fundamental traits, such a test as marking the a's on a page of print might involve at least three, probably four, and almost any other test that might be given would employ more than one. High standing in any test might then be due to the excellence of any one of these capacities and the fact that excellence in one was likely to imply excellence in all might be due either to the fact that high development of one capacity might make up for lack in others, or that there was something that made it likely that the presence of one in high degree would also imply the presence of the others in high degree. As no one pretends to know how many fundamental capacities there are nor what the nature of their interrelations may be, speculation on the point is not very fruitful. We must for the present content ourselves with the raw results that high standing in one respect is likely to go with high standing in all others as well. Whether this is because there is some one capacity common to all activities or a number of relatively simple capacities, several or all of which combine in each of the activities to which we give special names, we do not as yet know.

As to how far we may distinguish between what are ordinarily called the intellectual and the voluntary and emotional characteristics which combine to give what we popularly call character we have less evidence. Webb's results stand alone on the scientific side. They would indicate that part of a man's success depends upon intelligence, part upon a pertinacity and tendency to be more or less guided by desire or pleasure. Popular observation indicates that part of a man's effectiveness depends upon pure intellectual capacity and part upon the use that he makes of his ability, including his willingness to exert himself to learn and to apply his knowledge and the positiveness with which he expresses his conclusions. In the estimates of an officer's ability on his personnel card, there is a place for an estimate of personality which includes leadership and tact, qualities which would come under our emotional and voluntary traits. These are accepted as quite as important for success as intelligence. One may fail for lack of either. Mrs. Woolley found that these volitional and emotional traits were almost as important as intelligence as determined by test in deciding what wages would be earned by children who leave the public schools. These qualities are fairly closely correlated with intelligence according to all tests. This is what would be expected from the fact that appreciation of the ends of life and the necessity for endeavour to attain, them is a large element in keeping a man at work.

The Distribution of Intelligence. The answer to the question how ability is distributed in the population is made easier by the facts already presented that ability is of one kind, or that men of good ability in one respect are likely to possess good capacities in all. Can we determine a man's capacity in one respect we shall have a close approximation to his capacity in all. It is not necessary to measure him in all the tasks to which he must apply himself, but we may measure him in one or a few and obtain his approximate rank for all. While most systems of measurement apply several tests that are supposed to involve different processes, probably the main value of using more than one test is to give an average of performance that shall eliminate as many as possible of the chance variations in the condition of the subject and of his environment.

The Curve of Distribution. Two fundamental assumptions that are made in all biological measurements must be accepted as a basis of psychological tests. The first is that in any chance collection of individuals of reasonable size there will be represented the range of qualities for all of the species. In our application if we select by chance a hundred or a thousand individuals, measurements made upon them will hold approximately of the entire population. The larger the number included in the sample, the more accurately will the selection approximate the result that would be obtained from measuring all. The second general assumption is that in any large group all characters, including mental capacity, are distributed as are errors in reading scales or as shots at a target. We may emphasise two important characteristics of such a grouping. One is that there are just as many above as below the average, that the distribution is symmetrical, and the other that the greater the degree of divergence from the average, the fewer individuals there will be who show this deviation. Thus according to Bertillon the stature of a thousand Frenchmen would be distributed about 164^ cm., with 236 between 163 and 166, 198 each between 159 and 162 cm. and between 167 and 170, 148 between 153 and 158 and 171 and 176, and only 36 at each extreme between 141 and 152 and between 177 and 188. There would be 10 each below 141 and above 188. The curve which would show the distribution of any physical measurement would have approximately the same form. It is shown in Figure 35. It will be noticed from the figures given that there are about eighty who are within a centimetre of each other in height within the three central centimetres and an average of three who are within a centimetre of the same height at either extreme of ten centimetres.

Methods of Grading Intelligence. We have every reason to believe that the same general rules hold for the distribution of intelligence. It has so far not been possible to use any measure of intelligence for which we can be sure that all steps are of equal difficulty. Remembering eight digits is much more than a third harder than remembering six digits, and no one can say how much more intelligent a man is who can give an associate in an average of half a second than one who can give one in an average of one second. Certainly he is much more than twice as high in the scale if either difficulty or frequency of appearance is used as a measure. Attempts have been made to measure intelligence in three ways, each of which has certain advantages and certain disadvantages. The first, most frequently used, is by comparing the individual to be measured with others in a group, on the first of our assumptions that a sample may be regarded as typical of a whole class. If one may assign a man to a certain position in a class of one hundred there is approximate certainty that he will have about the same position with reference to all individuals selected in the same general way. This is the basis of relative markings in school and college classes. If you grade a man as belonging in the upper tenth in a class of one hundred, you may feel assured that he will have a place in the upper tenth of the community as a whole. Since relative ranking among individuals known well is fairly accurate, estimates of this kind based on daily accomplishment and examination are a reliable index of the intelligence. The exception conies only when the group in which the ranking is made is not representative, which happens when some force other than chance has been operative in selecting it. Thus a man marked in the average of a college class would very probably still stand among the best tenth of the general population, because the men who go to college have been selected by success in the schools, have on the whole more successful fathers and probably more intelligent parents than the average. The chances are large that a man who stands in the upper tenth in a class of one hundred in one university will also stand among the upper tenth in another university. Relative grades are on the whole absolute grades as well. While this assumption works as a means of determining the ability of any individual it assumes rather than proves that ability is distributed in accordance with the curve of probability.

Mental Tests. The second method used, grading by accomplishment in some standard task, suffers, as was said above, from the fact that so far we have no tasks that can be adjusted to give equal steps, and no knowledge as to how different attainments in various parts of a test may be compared. One should obtain a series of tasks that depends very little upon past training, that is difficult enough to require effort from the best and not too hard for the most poorly endowed to accomplish something with it. If then we could determine what constitutes equal steps in difficulty we would have an ideal test. Groups of tests of this type were developed for testing men drafted during the last war and applied to a million and three-quarters individuals. It seems to be satisfactory in meeting the first two of our criteria; and using the assumption that intelligence is distributed as are physical characteristics, one may gauge the difficulty of the tests. The group includes tests for quickness and control of associations, for ingenuity in verbal and manual operations, and for retention.

Using the distribution curve and accomplishments in the tests and previous attainments, we find that among the men drafted four or five per cent belong in an A group, men who can do superior work in a university and make higher officers if they possess leadership and initiative ; eight or ten per cent to a ' B ' grade, men who are capable of doing average work in college and of making successful officers ; about sixty per cent to a ' C ' grade composed of men of average intelligence. This grade is divided again into ' C + ' of eighteen per cent who are good high school men, but men who would not do well in college, a ' C ' grade of twenty-five per cent, and a ' C ' grade of twenty per cent. Measured in school accomplishment the ' C ' would not do well in high school work, the ' C ' is of grade school intelligence. A ' D ' grade of fifteen per cent is of normal men of sufficient intelligence to make good privates. About one per cent was graded as ' D ' or ' E,' and was made up of men who could not rise above the third or fourth grade in school. 1 This classification, as was said, assumes rather than proves the distribution according to the law of probability, but the assumption squares well with attainments in other lines and is at least not out of harmony with what we know in this and other connections.

The Binet Scale. The first generally used system of testing intelligence was developed by Binet and Simon. The essentials of the method consist in comparing the accomplishments of the individuals in several tests with those of children of different ages. They selected a series of very simple tests and determined by trial upon a large number of children what the average child of a given age could do. The same tests are given to the individual to be tested and his results checked against those of a child of a given age. On this basis it

1 Terman: 'Use of Intelligence Tests in the Army,' Psychological Bulletin, Vol. 15, pp. 177-187.

is possible to assert of any individual that he has an intelligence equal to that of a child of eight or ten, or five. For convenience we speak of this as his ' mental age.' Thus we may say that the men who grade ' D ' in the army tests are below the mental age of ten. For the lower grades of intelligence these tests with their modifications have proved very satisfactory. The main objection to them in connection with our present problem of the distribution of intelligence is that we have no assurance that a child increases in intelligence the same amount in each year, but it probably more nearly approximates an equal step than any of the accomplishment tests that we have. Measurements by the scale indicate that distribution for the lower grades is in accordance with the probability curve, modified somewhat by the fact that physical accidents all tend to lower the intelligence of an individual, never to raise it. The Lower Grades of Intelligence. This method has been applied with success in determining the ability of children for practical school purposes, and in selecting the individuals of subnormal intelligence from the normal among the criminal and pauper classes. For convenience in nomenclature it has become customary to make a classification into three groups on the basis of these age determinations. Individuals of a mental age of two or less are called idiots, those of a mental age between two and seven are called imbeciles, and those from eight to twelve are called morons from the Greek word for fool. The idiots are incapable of living without constant attention; the imbeciles require institutional care in practically every case, but can satisfy their own physical needs, while the morons may seem normal or merely dumb witted, but cannot compete on equal terms in the struggle for existence and are in many cases a menace to society through their lack of self-restraint. They constitute a large percentage of the criminal and pauper class.

The Problem of the Feeble-minded. It is estimated that from one-half to one per cent of the population is found in the three classes of defectives. In the army tests of a little more than a million men more than 16,000 had a mental age of eight or less, and more than 7000 of less than seven. Of course the more obvious cases had been sent to institutions earlier or were rejected by the examining physicians. The mentally deficient individuals constitute a constant problem for the schools and for the courts. Many of the children who are constantly falling behind in the schools prove on test to belong to the feebly endowed. They cannot learn the ordinary materials or by the methods of the normal children. If they are to be taught they must be given special training and in many cases can learn to advantage only the more mechanical operations. Many of these children graduate from the schools to the police courts or poorhouses after a longer or shorter period of unsuccessful struggle with the world. Tests of the inmates of reform schools, work houses, jails, and penitentiaries in various parts of the United States show that from twenty to forty per cent are below the mental age of twelve. They are criminals because of a defect of intelligence which prevents them both from earning a living and from appreciating the aims and from being controlled by the motives of normal individuals. As two-thirds of the feeble-minded are descended from individuals themselves feeble-minded, it is probable that the condition is inherited in most cases and that all that can be done to improve the situation is to keep them in institutions, if possible in institutions where work may be provided that will make them self-supporting, where they may be kept from harming themselves and others, and prevented from propagating their kind. A proper solution of the problem of caring for them will have a marked beneficial influence upon the state in relieving the schools and preventing crime and pauperism.

Distribution of Higher Grades of Intelligence. Measurement of the higher grades of intelligence has received much less attention. Above twelve the age gradation no longer has significance. This is partly because age after that adds little to fundamental capacity, partly because the differences in training in the different capacities that are tested tend to obscure the effects of native endowment, partly, possibly, because talent begins to show more diversity. At least, whatever the reason, there is some evidence that the average intelligence of the mass is not much above that of the child of thirteen as measured by these Binet and other tests. One set of tests on a large number of men chosen at random showed an average age of twelve and a half, while not more than two per cent of the population is below the mental age of eleven. The army tests would indicate, as said above, that some four or five per cent of the population would belong to the highest grades, but whether this grade is as much above the average as the various types of feeble-minded are below we have no means of knowing. Whipple has recently devised a group of tests which enable him to select from the schools super-normal children. Children selected in this way can accomplish much more than the average child and can complete the work of the grades in two years or more less than the average time. What evidence we have puts about five to eight per cent in this superior group. The results taken together seem sufficient to justify the assumption that there is a distribution of the higher forms of ability symmetrical with the lower, that the greater the departure from the average, the less frequent in occurrence are the individuals who have the degree of intelligence in question. We are also assured in drawing the inference that the variations are gradual above as below, that there are no sharp lines of division. The genius is not a man who stands in a class by himself, altogether apart from others. He merely stands among a few in the highest grades of intelligence. While we see marked specialisation in capacity in everyday life, most statistical and experimental studies emphasise the unity of ability lead us to believe that a man who shows superior ability in one line will be superior in all or many others if he devotes himself to them. Differences between men who succeed in different departments may be due to the particular training and particular opportunities rather than to native endowment. It may be remarked that the term genius itself is open to abuse in so far as it implies the existence of super-men. The term may be regarded as a tribute paid to the man who is exceptionally successful in some one department. It may be added that this superior intelligence is in considerable degree hereditary. Galton and others have shown that men of the higher grades of ability appear in certain families much more frequently than in others.

Practical Success Harmonises with Experiments. These general conclusions, that ability is not specialised, that ability in one field is closely related to ability in another, and that special ability in one large group is likely to indicate high standing in others as well, hold for observations and statistics of actual accomplishment as well as for the results of tests. Comparison of grades of individuals in grammar school, high school, and university shows that students with a high standing in one have a high standing in others also. This correlation holds between school standing and accomplishment in later life. A man who stands high in his university class has a much greater chance of obtaining eminence than the man of average rank. A man who has been elected to the honorary society of Phi Beta Kappa, election given to the men among the upper fifth of the class at graduation, is four or five times as likely to appear in " Who's Who " as are his classmates of lower standing. Studies of the salaries of graduates of an engineering school some years after graduation showed that there was a close correlation between salaries received and standing while in college. The statement that ability is not specialised is strikingly confirmed by the fact that high standing in the undergraduate college in Harvard College foreshadows success in the medical or law school of the university, whether the subjects studied are or are not closely connected with the later work.

While we cannot emphasise too strongly this general statement that ability is all of one kind, it is at the same time well to admit that denial of a specialised ability rests upon negative grounds alone, that it is safer to say that we have not yet discovered different types of mind than to assert that they do not exist. Certainly in everyday life we find men who succeed in business who did not do well in the university, and men who do very well in specialised professions who were of only moderate ability in the professional school. They will not infrequently win fame where their fellow of higher standing is only moderately successful. These cases may be explained in two ways. In the first place, our general statements hold only in the long run and on the average.

Many exceptions are admitted in the averages. These are lost in the general statement, are outweighed by the great majority, while just because they are exceptions they are likely to attract the ordinary observer. In the second place, the differences may be due to training. The general belief in types may thus be due to mistaking the exception for the rule, it may be due to mistaking success due to special training or to special opportunity for success due to special aptitude, or it may be due to failure on the part of psychologists to devise tests that will discover special aptitudes, and lack of investigations of the ways in which they may be combined. It is altogether possible that the relatively few studies published have not happened to hit upon the proper methods or have not been sufficiently detailed to discover differences which may be slight and still in the main constitute types of intellect. Certain it is that popular belief in the existence of groups of traits in individuals that constitute them distinct types is strong, and one cannot be equally certain that the psychological studies are sufficiently advanced to dispute this belief. It seems, then, that we may feel fairly well assured that all forms of excellence in mental capacity are closely correlated, that a man who stands well in one capacity is likely to stand well in all. That there are numerous differences in the grades of accomplishment in different lines is equally certain. So far, however, we are not able to sort forms of capacities into distinct groups. There probably are many of these types, certainly no two men are alike in all particulars, how many we are simply not able to say. Furthermore we cannot say to what these differences are due, whether to differences in native endowment, to differences in training, or to opportunity. In this sense the psychology of mental types or of individual differences is yet to be written.

CHAPTER XVII

THE SELF

THE last problem, the nature of the self, the * I/ is fundamental. Throughout the book, we have been asking what man can do and what his mental processes are and what they mean. Now we must raise the more general question, what is it that makes the self, and how is the self known ? Much of the discussion of the nature of the self in philosophy and in popular thought and conversation has little to do with psychology. On many of these problems the opinion of the psychologist is little if any more valuable than that of the untrained layman. Certain phases of the problem of the self are of a psychological character, however, and consideration of them is not only important for itself, but serves to give a review in perspective of many of the more concrete discussions. Without prejudice to the problems that lie beyond the range of psychology, we speak from the standpoint of the psychologist.

The Content of the Idea of the Self. The self may be approached from two distinct sides. One may ask what is in mind when one thinks ' I.' This question is on the same level as any other concerning the nature of a mental state; it is a question of structure. Questions of the other type deal with the capabilities of the man ; they ask what the self does in different relations, they raise problems of function. The one problem is of what the man himself appreciates as himself ; the other asks what it is that makes an observer regard the man as continuously the same person, why he is trusted to act in a definite way, at all times. The problems are different, although closely related. What one accomplishes colours one's idea as to what one is, and, conversely, what one thinks one's self to be has a considerable effect in determining what one can accomplish. For our purposes, one is the problem of the self as viewed from within, the other the problem of the self as it presents itself to the onlooker.

The idea that is in consciousness when one thinks ' I ' varies from moment to moment and from individual to individual. It has been suggested that it is made up in part of the mirror images of one's self, in part of the framework of nose and eyebrows through which one views the world, and of the constant background of tactual and organic sensations. Probably some of these elements may be present in the idea of the self, and each has, at some time or other, helped to make the individual acquainted with himself. The most prominent group of elements in the total picture is the mass of organic sensations. They are always present, although they vary in quality, and probably always colour the mental life. When ' I ' feel ill, they are of one sort ; when ' I ' feel well, they are of another character. In either case, illbeing or well-being is appreciated through them. The importance of these organic sensations has been emphasised by the fact that in certain cases, loss of appreciation of self-identity seems to depend upon a transformation of the organic sensations. The individual whose permanent sensations have undergone a change, no longer feels himself. It seems likely when a patient in delirium seems to be watching himself from above or from somewhere else outside of his body, that the disease processes have changed these sensations, and the man no longer recognises himself. These sensations constitute only a part of the idea of the self regarded as content. One must add the social elements in the idea that are probably even more important. It is not so much how one actually does appear, as how one thinks one appears to others that constitutes the notion of the self. In this idea, as James points out, a large place is taken by external belongings, clothing, automobiles, bank account, and possessions of all sorts. One grows with one's goods, and even with one's friends and the circle of acquaintances. But while all of these elements serve to give tone to the idea of the self, that idea itself is a concept developed through the experience of 'the individual to represent and, in part, to account for himself. Like all concepts, the content may vary greatly; but the thing represented is more fixed, although that, too, is subject to constant change with growth and with the phases of experience that it represents.

The Active Self. The treatment of the active self offers more difficulties. The idea of the self as an agent has developed to explain the unity and continuity of conscious processes in any individual, and to make the consistency of the different acts of the same man conceivable. If consciousness were merely a mass of states, an individual's experience would not be regarded as continuous, as parts of a single whole, but would be a mere jumble of separate events or things. Even the mental states of any moment would be only separate states, it has been asserted, unless they were held together in some way. The concept of the self has been developed popularly and philosophically to make conceivable the fact that mental states do constitute a unity and that all states of whatever period are regarded as my states. The facts implied by the term self are that the different experiences are parts of a single whole which persists from life to death, and that the thoughts of any moment constitute a unity. More practical is the problem as it presents itself to the friend or business associate. This is, why does the same man act in approximately the same way toward the same situations, and why are his methods of action peculiar to himself? When a man makes a sudden change in his course of action, it is at once said that he is no longer himself. The facts to be explained in connection with the self are first, the continuity of conscious states ; second, the unity of consciousness at any moment ; and third, the self-consistency of action.

The Self as Accumulated Habits. One of the most superficial explanations of the consistency of action from moment to moment is to be found in the persistence of habitual responses. In considerable degree, it is possible to read character from the face. So far as this is possible at all, it is, as was said in an earlier chapter, because the face retains the imprint of the earlier expressions of emotions and of feelings. Every thought and feeling induces some contraction of the facial muscles, and each of these contractions leaves its impress on the face by enlarging the muscle or by wrinkling the skin. Thus old expressions and indirectly old experiences write their record on the face for him who runs to read. But these same experiences induce habits, not merely in the facial muscles, but in all parts of the psycho-physical organism ; in consequence, even the most general mental and physical responses and attitudes correspond to the configuration of the face. Both have been developed in the same way. In truth, very many of the subtle peculiarities, which together constitute character, are traceable to habits. Much of good temper or bad temper is dependent upon the habit of smiling or of scowling, upon the habit of sharp speech or of mild speech. Whether the first and natural attitude toward a situation is of pleased acquiescence or of fault-finding is very largely a matter of habit. Even the moral elements of character have their habitual constituents. One has habits of honesty and punctuality in meeting obligations, just as one has habits of rising or of eating. It is as difficult to break a habit of paying bills at the end of the month as a habit of late rising. Bad habits in morals may reach the point where they are as difficult to break as a drug habit, where all the consequences of the acts are neglected. At this stage, the man has become an habitual criminal, and self-restraint must give way to restraint by others. A self of one sort may become altogether changed in the course of a few years, merely through the development of a new set of habits. The self from this simple point of view is in great part merely the accumulation of habits, the outcome of the earlier actions of the individual.

The Self as an Expression of Organised Experience. Still more intimately connected with the development of the self and self-control is the effect of earlier experiences as they are expressed in present experience. Throughout our treatment of the earlier topics, particularly in connection with reasoning and action, we have had occasion to emphasise the importance of the system of knowledge and the system of purposes. It has been pointed out that attention, perception, memory, and action in all of its higher forms are controlled by earlier experiences, not as single and sporadic elements, but as organised systems. Practically all of the important functions ascribed to the self are, when examined critically, seen to be due to the action of earlier experience. What makes one man different from any other is that he sees differently, thinks differently, and acts differently. These depend upon the actual knowledge that he has accumulated, upon the associations and habits that he has developed, but, above and beyond that, upon the control of organised knowledge and upon developed purposes. The individual starts life with certain instincts that are a part of the common racial inheritance. The early self, so far as one may speak of the infant as having a self, is dependent upon these instincts for its character. As he grows, these are first modified by experience, then experiences become the dominating factors hi determining the nature of the responses, mental and physical. There is seldom a complete and sudden change in the character. It is only gradually that the original instinctive character is modified by experience; the single experiences in the later stages work but a comparatively slight change. The original kernel of the self constantly grows and expands by taking up into itself new bits of knowledge. As Tennyson sings in his ' Ulysses/ ' I am a part of all that I have seen.' Ordinarily it takes years to make a marked difference. The self of to-day is not noticeably different from the self of yesterday, although it is markedly different from the self of twenty years ago. Occasionally one will see a sudden ' about-face ' in a character. Instances of sudden conversion may be cited. Some striking event seems to throw new light on the relation of the individual to the world and his fellows, and his entire attitude changes, and with that his actions. Sometimes a sudden misfortune will destroy the confidence built up through a lifetime of successful activity. The resolute, self reliant man of affairs becomes hesitant, dependent, and all initiative is lost ; he becomes a human derelict who cannot be relied upon for even the simplest tasks. Such sudden changes are the exception; usually character is of slow growth and the changes can be detected only after the lapse of years. The individual peculiarities and the consistency of action that mark the self depend in part upon the habits, and in part upon the control exerted by the accumulated experiences and purposes upon thought and action.

The Self as a Continuous Existence. The second function or characteristic of the self is to explain the fact that all mental states are regarded as belonging together. This depends in part at least upon the continuity of memory. Professor James has asserted that what makes the self continuous is that one mental state always laps over upon the next. There are no blank spaces that separate one process from another. At any moment, several ideas are represented at different stages of development or disappearance. Other factors are found in the persistence of memories, and in recognition. The self probably is recognised in very much the same way as any object. The older experiences interpret the new. Recognition of objects, as well as the recognition of the self, serves to prove the continuous identity of the train of experiences. To these must be added the fact of the return of old memories, and the anticipation of future events in the light of the past. When these anticipations are confirmed by actual experiences, the new is more firmly bound to the old and the old to the new. That one is constantly looking forward and backward from the present and, particularly, that the past anticipations are confirmed by the events of the present, serve to bind past, present, and future into a single whole. The continuity of reference, the development of types and meanings, and the confirmation or partial modification of the meaning of one time by the meaning of the next, all contribute their share to establishing the belief that the self persists.

' The Self as the Unity of Experience. To say that the self of any moment is a unit means merely that the component elements, in addition to being controlled and subordinated to the whole, must all be connected, and each must add its share to the whole. As was said in the second chapter, the consciousness of any moment corresponds to the action of many different nerve units in many different parts of the cortex, but to be conscious, any one of these elements must be connected with all of the others active at the time. To be conscious and to belong to the unity of the self are synonymous. This mass of mental states not only belongs together, but acts as a unit in the control of all subordinate mental activities. No experience is ever of discrete units, nor is any single process alone effective in determining the course of mental or physical activity. This interconnection, at once passive and active, is the basis of the unity of the self at any moment. One often speaks of the unconscious or the subconscious, as if there were a consciousness detached from the main or dominant consciousness, separated from the unity that has just been mentioned. It is true that movements are often made without consciousness, and still seem to be controlled by purposes. There are other instances in which all or part of a course of thought shows characteristics of purpose that might have been developed by conscious states, but in which there is no evidence of consciousness. In all of these cases it is probably safer to assume that the determinants are physiological or nervous, rather than conscious. Surely the only safe evidence of consciousness is consciousness itself. An unconscious conscious state is a contradiction in terms.

Dissociated Selves. The consistency of thought and act that marks the man as peculiarly himself, the persistence of self-appreciation from day to day, and the momentary unity of experience, each goes back for its explanation to the fact that all the accumulated experiences of the individual are combined into a single whole through the manifold interconnections of the parts. These interconnections give meaning to the different parts, and serve to direct and coordinate the various activities. That these relations and factors are actual, not hypothetical, is demonstrated by the numerous cases of dissociation of the self, in which the continuity of thought and action is broken. An individual who is dominated at certain times by one set of purposes and ideals will, at other times, be dominated by other purposes and ideals. At the instant of change, there will also be a break in the continuity of memory, and a transformation in the attitude toward conventional and moral restraints. The individual will carry on the ordinary routine life until some emotional shock or injury is suffered. Then all memory of the past will be lost ; he will start up with no remembrance of his surroundings; in some cases, with no appreciation of any of the things about, and none of his accumulated knowledge. In many cases, the selves alternate. One self with its peculiar memories and characteristic actions and feelings will be dominant for a time, and the individual will have one set of memories, one emotional attitude toward the world ; then suddenly the other will get the upper hand, all memories acquired by the earlier self will be forgotten, and the entire character of the individual will change. One of the earlier cases reported was of a woman, Felida X, who in the one self vas moody and bad tempered ; when the other self came, she would be cheerful, a more capable worker, and different in every respect from the first. These states alternated for a period of thirty years or more. They would be separated by a period of unconsciousness at times, and at times the change from one to the other would be sudden and with but slight warning. After the change, the immediately preceding events would not be remembered. Later, when Felida had come to know the symptoms of the change, she would write down the things she would need to know in the approaching state. She was a small shopkeeper, and if she felt the change coming in the midst of a sale, she would record the amount of the purchase or of the money that she had received that she might continue the transaction without mistake when the new self appeared.

The Nature of Dissociation. So far as present knowledge extends, it seems that the cause of the dissociation of the self is to be found in a disturbance of the connections between the experiences. An emotional shock breaks the associations between groups of cells, or cells that correspond to groups of memories. After the shock, an event in one group will recall other members of that group alone ; the recall will not extend to the memories dependent upon the other group. Also and more important for the explanation of the active self, the acts and thoughts and emotions will be controlled at any moment by the experiences that belong to one group ; elements from the other group will have no effect upon action at the times the other group is dominant. The acts of the one self, or group of experiences, will be consistent, but the acts of one self will not be consistent with the acts of the other self, or group of experiences. When the connections between different experiences are broken, the disappearance or the modification of qualities ordinarily attributed to the self is strong proof that the self hi the normal individual is largely determined in its character by the way the different experiences interact. This series of connections gives continuous memory, makes the experiences of any moment a unit, and through directing thought and act keeps the self of one moment consistent with the self of other moments.

Minor Forms of Dissociation. Slighter signs of alternating selves may be found in normal individuals. The hypnotic condition differs from the -normal very much as one of the dissociated selves differs from another ; and selves may be induced in the hypnotic state that are related in every practical respect, as are the dissociated or alternating selves. In the normal state one seldom has memories of the hypnotic state, and by suggestion during hypnotism it is easy to change the character of the self, practically at will. Similar normal divisions in the self may be seen in the life of any individual. The ordinary business man is one man at home, and another in his place of business. He thinks differently, and acts differently. Of course here the dissociation is restricted to the control of action ; memory is continuous, and the actions are not sufficiently different to prevent the man from being recognised as himself. It is very interesting to note that various groups of responses are aroused on relatively slight suggestions. Frequently men undergo el'" ages as they change their surroundings. A man mav be perfectly at his ease in his own home, and very much embarrassed or very diffident when in a strange place. Clothing frequently plays a considerable part in suggesting selves or groups of responses. All one's self-possession may be destroyed if one finds one's self in company without some usual article of apparel, a cravat, for example. Manners frequently are put on with the garments. It is said of Stanley, the African explorer, that his ability to make a speech depended upon his wearing a small cap that had been given him by Livingstone. When called upon to reply to a toast, or when lecturing, he invariably donned this cap. Without it, he seemed tongue-tied. Many lecturers feel lost without a reading desk even if they never use notes, and the absence of some familiar article of furniture may destroy their composure. In each of these cases, the familiar situation or the familiar article arouses a group of experiences that will not be present without it. The actions grow out of the experiences. When all of the usual accompaniments are present, the course of thought and speech or act runs smoothly ; without some apparently insignificant element, the whole complex is disturbed.

The Self a Social Product. One is aware of the character of the effective self altogether through the social relations. Were it possible for a child to grow up alone, he would have no appreciation of his character. He would not know whether he were quick-tempered or slow to anger, whether he were honest or dishonest, strong or weak. The questions that grow out of the self problem would not occur to him. All of these characteristics of the self are appreciated only when there is a chance to compare himself with others. He knows himself only as he sees himself reflected in the opinions of others. This statement is the converse of the other statement, that man knows others or at least the mental processes of others only in so far as he can interpret their acts in terms of his own conscious states. The processes of knowing one's self and of knowing others are correlative. Each can be known and appreciated only in the light of the other. One passes judgment on the acts of others and then compares his own acts with them, to obtain the judgment of himself and others upon himself. What is constantly dominant in the idea of the self is the impression that others have. One holds one's self at the estimate others have or are imagined to have. The Self a Concept. For psychology, the notion of the self is a concept similar in origin and development to any other. The elements about which the concept centres are the organic and other persistent sensations. These elements are closely connected with the original egoistic instincts and receive constant additions by the development of new ideas and new habits. The concept probably always represents activities rather than mental states. In its developed form it is the representative in thought of the continuity of consciousness, of the fact that the different experiences all belong to the same individual, and that the acts of the individual are consistent at all times. The occasion for the development of the concept is largely social, as the need for the idea is social. Society must know to what extent an individual is to be relied upon and how he will act in all respects in any set of circumstances. The self is society's way of formulating this knowledge. It is important, too, that the individual should know how he is regarded, and for his own benefit should know what he is likely to do in any situation. These needs have led to the development of the notion of the self with all that it implies.

Thus for psychology the self is a concept to be traced to its sources, is one phenomenon among others to be explained as best we may, but such a treatment will never be satisfactory for any one else. What for the psychologist is just one problem on the same level as any other, is for the layman or for any one in a non-psychological attitude the very core of his being. From it irradiate all desires, its advancement is the goal of all egoistic instincts, it is the centre of nearly all our joys and sorrows. To it are referred all of our purposes in life, its exaltation is the object of most of our activity. All social and physical events are measured by their effects on our personal ambition and personal welfare. As the occasion of solicitude in all of our social and religious aspirations, the self takes on a value that makes any scientific analysis seem entirely inadequate and even presumptuous. The treatment of the psychologist grows out of his peculiar methods and needs, and much still remains to be done even to attain his end in his own way. The answers it gives must be unsatisfactory to the popular mind, for the problems that most interest it lie far afield for the psychologist. They can be approached to advantage only by the methods and on the assumptions of ethics, metaphysics, and religion. On these problems psychology has nothing to say, since the limitations of its methods and its knowledge give it no right to an opinion.

QUESTIONS

1. Under what circumstances and for what end does the idea of self develop?

2. Would you have your present idea of self if you had chanced to survive alone on a desert island?

3. What do you have in mind as you think 'I' (a) when striving to win in a wrestling match? (b) when you think of a rival for a class honor? (c) when conversing in a congenial group?

4. What is the relation of the 'self to the other psychological processes? to will? to emotion? to attention? Are they whole and part or independent partners?

5. What gives consistency to the actions? What do you mean when you say you were not yourself in a certain emergency?

6. What do you mean by continuous self-identity? What makes it possible?

7. How are these last two functions disturbed in a dissociated personality?

8. Is it more nearly true to say that for modern psychology there is no self or that man is all self?